A MUSICIAN BEFORE HIS TIME

A MUSICIAN BEFORE HIS TIME

Constantin Silvestri

CONDUCTOR, COMPOSER, PIANIST

John Gritten

Warwick Editions

1998

First published 1998

Copyright © John Gritten 1998

ISBN 1 900496 12 7

Designed, produced and published for Warwick Editions by
Kitzinger, 17 Willow Street, London EC2A 4QH

Printed and bound by
Biddles Ltd, Guildford

FOREWORD

BY LORD MENUHIN OF STOKE D'ABERNON

I have often played with Constantin Silvestri in his adopted English town of Bournemouth, and I recorded the Beethoven Concerto with him in Vienna. What distinguishes him very particularly is that East European grasp of and grip on music, for those people are born with music in their soul; and what endeared him to me especially was his knowledge of and close association with the music of Enescu. He knew Enescu's great opera 'Oedipe' and conducted it many times. This is the greatest tribute I can pay him.

Yehudi Menuhin

To my wife,

pianist

Anda Anastasescu,

who inspired the genesis of this biography

after founding the

Constantin Silvestri International Festival

and Concerto Competition

CONTENTS

ILLUSTRATIONS

So much wisdom, so much talent. And they're forgotten as soon as they die. We must do everything possible to keep their memories alive. . .

Dmitri Shostakovich

PREFACE

A meteor flashed through the mid-20th century musical firmament and burned out on February 23 1969. Though at the time the premature death in London of Constantin Silvestri was acknowledged as a tragedy for the world of music, subsequently little was done in Britain to keep his memory alive. Not, that is, until his name and reputation were revived during the centenary celebrations in 1993 of the Bournemouth Symphony Orchestra.

Had he lived, the celebration of his own 80th birthday would have coincided (within nine days) with the founding date 100 years before of the UK's oldest full-time symphony orchestra. It was with the BSO's rapid rise to national status and international fame during the nearly eight years he was its principal conductor that Silvestri's name will always be associated, especially in Britain, the country of his adoption. In the words of one artist who played many times with him: 'The BSO, as reconstructed by Silvestri, came to be known as the third greatest international British orchestra.'

But the brief entries dealing with Silvestri in various compendia of musicians are often conflicting and, in places, misleading. Even in Romania, where he lived his first 45 years, there was no official posthumous recognition of the pianist, composer, teacher and conductor on whom the state had bestowed its highest honours. Official obliteration of his memory was the penalty of his 'defection' to the West.

Only after the toppling of the Ceauşescus was the annual Silvestri International Festival founded, in 1991, with Yehudi Menuhin as its patron, and the following year the first Silvestri International Concerto Competition was held as part of the Festival. Both of these were joint British/Romanian initiatives. This was consistent with Romanian-born Silvestri's enjoyment of his too brief domicile in England; with him and his wife becoming British citizens; and with his promotion of British and Romanian music here and overseas. In 1995, a Silvestri String Quartet became the quartet-in-residence of the University of Valencia, Spain, and a Silvestri Quartet was formed in the UK. In Romania, the official orchestra of the International Festival and Concerto Competition which bear his name became the Constantin Silvestri Philharmonic; it made a successful initial concert tour of Britain and Eire in 1994.

In the opinion of the Bournemouth Symphony Orchestra's general manager, Anthony Woodcock: 'A detailed study of Silvestri's life and work would be most appropriate and provide the music world with an invaluable reference source.'

What follows is an attempt to fill the vacuum.

'Attempt' is used advisedly: disinterring details about someone who lived half a century ago and about whom there has been only one other biography, published in Romania in 1975, has meant reliance on the memories of some 40 composers, conductors, soloists, orchestral players and other of his contemporaries now living in Romania, Britain, France, the USA and Australia; and on material containing many conflicting details. It has meant an attempt to separate fact from fantasy; to obtain corroborative evidence; to check one account of an event or given date against another.

It is a tribute to Silvestri's personality that so many retained vivid memories of him. One interview, during a train journey in Romania, was curtailed when an orchestral player, who had rehearsed many times and performed with him on a memorable operatic occasion, was so overcome with emotion that he excused himself from going on with his recollections of 33 years before; he explained how he felt it was a tragedy for Romanian musicians like himself that they never again had the opportunity of repeating the experience of working with Silvestri because he left the country soon afterwards, never to return. And after a quarter of a century, a member of the Bournemouth Municipal Choir paid this tribute:

> The tragedy of Silvestri's death still haunts us. Yes, we remember him for his magic, but mostly for his wonderful insight, energy and powers of communication. Uncompromising in his demands for the highest standards, he transformed the orchestra.

Such was the respect and affection the Bournemouth players had for him that several have been eager to take part in the festivals in Târgu Mureş and Bucharest honouring his memory. For them the experience was of particular interest since it was the first contact they had had with Silvestri's erstwhile compatriots. New Anglo-Romanian friendships were formed as a result and in 1997 Bournemouth was twinned with Târgu Mureş.

When he first came to Bournemouth, Silvestri was only known to the players by reputation and from his fine recordings with the Philharmonia and the Paris orchestras. Though they instantly decided that this was the resident conductor they wanted because of his, for those days, unorthodox methods and revelatory (if controversial) interpretations, they never got to know more than fragments of his previous history. It has been fascinating to find that views of him and accounts of his methods in his earlier career with Romanian orchestras were often echoed by his British colleagues.

The Dutch conductor, the late Edouard van Beinum, has been quoted as saying that anecdotes are all that is left 25 years after a conductor dies. There are plenty of these in the following pages, but it would be depressing to take such a pessimistic view of Silvestri's legacy. Not only do those who played with him and are still active in the profession maintain that the style of playing he initiated has influenced directly or by hearsay subsequent generations of players and conductors, but the creations of Silvestri the composer live on.

Although conducting, teaching and artistic direction progressively encroached upon his time for composition – which ceased altogether in the early Fifties – he was nevertheless the composer of over 40 works: for full orchestra; chamber music, such as sonatas for a diversity of instruments; works for the piano and songs. Trace has been lost of some of these manuscripts, despite the efforts of his former archivist in Bournemouth, Raymond Carpenter, who over the years persisted, practically singlehanded, in keeping Silvestri's name alive. Carpenter sifted through and catalogued 400 reel-to-reel tapes of radio broadcasts Silvestri bequeathed to the orchestra and which are available for reproduction today. He also collected from many quarters other memorabilia concerning Silvestri and the orchestra, which will be on public view in the Russell Cotes Museum in Bournemouth. Moreover, he listened to the BBC recordings Silvestri made which had been taped by the British Library's National Sound Archives in South Kensington and found them 'in pristine condition.'

The Wessex Film and Sound Archives in Winchester hold a unique collection of hundreds of reel-to-reel tapes of BBC recordings of Bournemouth Symphony Orchestra concerts conducted by Silvestri – invaluable since most of the master tapes were destroyed by the BBC. Moreover, the Winchester collection also houses the hundreds of recordings Silvestri made himself of other conductors and orchestras both in the UK and all over the world. These include the recordings he made in Romania and Eastern Europe as well as those made in the three years he was based in Paris before his Bournemouth appointment.

In Appendix 4 will be found a comprehensive list of over 100 of Silvestri's recordings with British, French, Czech, Romanian, Hungarian, Austrian, Russian and American record companies. Several artists told me they still treasure some of his LPs and were emphatic that, at a time when many vintage records are being granted a new lease of life as compact disks, an invaluable

service would be rendered to musicians and music lovers if serious consideration were given to reissuing more of Silvestri's superb recordings. Since 1990,
about half a dozen have indeed been released; and Testament Records are
reissuing an EMI recording of him conducting the Tchaikovsky *Manfred
Symphony* coupled with Liszt's symphonic poem *Tasso: lamento e trionfo* and
intend producing further Silvestri re-issues. In October 1994, *Daily Telegraph*
reviewer Brian Hunt had this to say about an EMI 'Profiles' CD with Silvestri
conducting five orchestras in seven works:

> I cannot recommend the Silvestri set too highly. In the Vienna Phil-
> harmonic's account of Ravel's *Rapsodie espagnole*, the intricacy of balance,
> phrasing, judgement of pitch and instrumental colour is breathtaking . . .
> In all these performances there is excitement, subtlety of articulation and
> limitless fantasy and imagination.

I would like to think that this biography may contribute to persuading
recording companies to produce not only more of the same but also to record
some of the works of Silvestri the composer. The initiative has been taken by
Cressidia Classics who have issued his *Three Pieces for Strings* on CD performed by the London Schubert Players.

BBC Radio Three presenter David Mellor and producer Nick Morgan are
to be congratulated for their two-hour *Vintage Years* programme in September 1997 devoted to Silvestri's recordings, which included an example of one
of his own works, and interviews with members of the Bournemouth
Symphony Orchestra who played under him.

CHAPTER I

DESPAIR TO TRIUMPH

A young man is sitting at a window writing a letter. Rather squat, with a head big in proportion to his body, he lifts what an admirer would one day describe as his 'huge eyes set in a face of an angel of stone on a monument,' and gazes ruminatively at the wintry landscape.

When the snow melts, revealed in spring and summer will be a vista of stepped ornamental gardens with a profusion of flowers and rich in foliage of chestnut and maple, willows and silver birches. Columns of cypresses march to the margins where conifers stretch to the distant wooded foothills of the Făgăraş Mountains. Not visible from where the young man sits, the Făgăraş are dominated by Romania's highest peak, the 2,500m Mt Moldoveanu.

But now the granite-chip quadrangle and gardens beneath him are clothed in the white anonymity of February snows that also hide the terracotta roof tiles of this extensive two-storeyed building; the only contrast is the ochre of its colourwashed walls between the white pilasters and windows and a strip of the umber base that can be seen above snow level.

The colouring and ornamentation of this handsome building would seem designed to alleviate some of the distress of those within. For this is the Baron Bruckenthal Sanatorium in the village of Avrig in the tranquillity and pure mountain air of this part of Transylvania, where people with nervous complaints are given special treatment and those with congested lungs, like this young man, Constantin Silvestri, come to recuperate.

He has had another attack of pleurisy but for two months has had to forego treatment because there were concerts to conduct at the Opera. Nor could he afford it, even though he is already the composer of over 20 works and a virtuoso concert pianist.

The uniformly white landscape beyond the window offers no relief to his anxieties and his eyes drop back to the letter he is writing to the artistic director of the Romanian State Opera. He has already recalled that after months of intense depression he had set fire to some of his own compositions. Now, following months in the sanatorium and 'overwhelmed by debts,' he has come to the conclusion: 'I can no longer foresee a future for myself as a conductor. No more have I any confidence in what I can do from now on.'

A few weeks before, he had written to a friend he has known since he was a boy of 12: 'I have had such a series of setbacks over so many years,' – he is now just short of his 27th birthday – 'that I am exhausted physically, morally and financially.' Symptomatic of his mood, the lines of his rather crabbed but legible hand undulate unsteadily.

Eight years before this, his renowned compatriot, composer, violinist and conductor George Enescu, speaking about this same Constantin Silvestri, had expressed the hope that 'in the years to come, he achieves everything we expect of him – and we expect great things.'

The distinguished musicologist, Mihail Jora, less than a year before, had declared:

> Not one of us at his age could have produced such beautiful things as he has. His is an exceptional talent, whether as conductor, composer or pianist.

In less than seven years after the despair, doom and gloom manifested in these letters, Silvestri – who at the age of 32 had been appointed principal conductor of the Bucharest Philharmonic Orchestra – was being carried shoulder-high from halls in Budapest by ecstatic admirers of concerts he had conducted in the Hungarian capital, where critics gave him rave reviews.

Another decade passes; and on January 25 1957 he makes his London début in the Royal Albert Hall conducting the London Philharmonic Orchestra in a programme that opens with George Enescu's *Romanian Rhapsody No. 1* and ends with Ravel's *Bolero*. *The Times* the next day described him as 'short, stocky and dapper,' a conductor

> who sets about his business vigorously but without fuss, using sparse gestures for the most part, but lunging at strong beats or marcato entries. He has evidently a keen sense of rhythm which he deployed to good purpose not only in Falla's *El amor brujo* and Enescu's *Romanian Rhapsody* but even in Britten's *Young Person's Guide* which is less obviously lilting music. He has a turn for speed, too, and loves to whip up a climax.

The reviewer added that perhaps his most valuable attribute was his ear for timbre and balanced sonority. The programme was repeated in the Albert Hall a week later and again in Brighton's Dome.

The story will unfold in the following chapters of just how the wheel turned in the fortunes of Constantin Silvestri – so desperate he had even written a memorandum to his king about the plight of young musicians like himself.

We will explore the ambiguities of his origins; his boyhood in the heart of Transylvania, a fertile soil for myth and legend; his rise from dependence on a friend's metaphorical begging bowl to fame, honours and wealth, in the days when Nicolae Ceaușescu was still a singularly incompetent novice in the shoemaker's craft; the sequel to his impressive London début; how and why he acquired a reputation as an *avant-garde* composer and conductor, vestiges of whose revolutionary methods still survive in the music-making of some players and conductors today.

That he was recognised by his contemporaries as one of the world's most remarkable conductors must first be established, particularly for the benefit of those generations who may not have even heard of him; for his career was tragically curtailed before his reputation could reach its zenith and was put in the shade by some who survived or some who succeeded him.

Initially, this will be attempted mainly by recourse to the critics' appraisals of his concert performances since coming to the West.

Three days after the first Albert Hall concert, he was making his Royal Festival Hall début and in a letter he wrote at the time to a friend in Romania he revealed he had qualms about it:

> On Monday I will conduct the first concert in a series of nine in the Royal Festival Hall on the occasion of the London Philharmonic Orchestra's centenary. The orchestra is good but, with only two rehearsals, the outcome won't be up to much. As I expected, the orchestra and choir were from the beginning full of enthusiasm, though I believe it will be one of the worst concerts of my life as there is only enough time to explain a quarter of what I want to.

Only a week before, someone describing himself as one of the 'younger British conductors,' whom *The Times* had recently lamented were very few, wrote a letter complaining bitterly about lack of adequate rehearsal time:

> Conductors of my standing are allowed one three-hour rehearsal for a two-hour concert. . . This means that most of the subtleties of phrasing and style, which as part of ourselves we burn to express, must be communicated on the spur of the moment at the concert. . . Our distinguished foreign colleagues . . . regard anything less than two rehearsals as a joke in questionable taste. . .

But evidently two rehearsals – if, indeed, that is what Silvestri was allowed – were not enough in his opinion. When he returned home he told his countrymen in March:

The orchestras in London and Brussels could have achieved better interpretations with me and corresponding more to their actual artistic potential, which is truly remarkable. Unfortunately, the time factor was our sovereign enemy, with the English saying: 'Time is money. . . every penny counts'.

Apart from the paucity of rehearsals, the Musicians' Union rules protecting its orchestral members' rights to tea or smoking breaks and to the stipulated duration of rehearsals must have come as an eye-opener to Silvestri. Tacitly, he must have contrasted this situation with an incident during his Russian tour which immediately preceded this first visit to London.

It was in Kiev where he had wanted to rehearse his own *Three Pieces for Strings* as a possible encore after a programme that included Britten's *Young Person's Guide*. But by 2.30 p.m., when the rehearsal was due to end, the *Three Pieces* (which he had brought as a gift for the Kiev Philharmonic's repertoire) had not been touched. Nevertheless, Silvestri told the orchestra they were free to leave; at which the leader insisted: 'But at least, since you have offered it as a gift, we must give the *Three Pieces* a sight-reading. We want to know what it is like.' So, it was not only sight-read, but the orchestra actually asked the maestro to go through it twice more with them. 'When we looked at our watches,' Silvestri would recall, 'it was four o'clock!' This episode was repeated in Moscow.

For all his qualms concerning the Festival Hall concert, however, the *Daily Telegraph* recorded: 'Mr Constantin Silvestri proved himself a musician of exceptional gifts, especially in a spectacular performance of Scriabin's *Poème de l'Extase*,' while the *Glasgow Herald* critic (himself a composer) noted that

> the orchestra showed their appreciation by also applauding, which is perhaps without precedent, for British orchestras reserve their applause (if any) for a conductor until the end of the programme. . . This concert must rank as one of the most memorable heard in London since the war.

This particular critic, as will be seen later, had a personal interest in Silvestri, but that his enthusiasm was not unwarranted can be attested by the view of the late Sir Neville Cardus writing in the *Manchester Guardian*:

> The evening introduced London to a very commanding conductor, Constantin Silvestri, from Bucharest. . . He asserted his mastery in Debussy's *Three Nocturnes*; and it was a quiet, firm, authoritative and sensitive mastery. The wonderfully evocative instrumentation and rhythms were controlled with complete knowledge and aim; seldom has the LPO achieved so much imaginatively nuanced tone and shading.

Present at this first of the Music of the Century series in the RFH was the LPO's assistant conductor, George Hurst, who had studied under Pierre Monteux. 'I never thought Scriabin's *Poème de l'Extase* was worth doing,' he recalls,

> but when Silvestri did it, it was beyond belief, absolutely extraordinary. As I would discover later, he could make pieces that were clearly not beautiful – in fact in some respects quite inferior – sound like masterpieces.

I was also at this concert and noted how skilled Silvestri was in controlling 'vast waves of sound' from the orchestra, choir and organ in Stravinsky's *Symphony of Psalms* and 'the great ovation this newcomer to London got which he demonstrably shared with the performers.'

The Times went as far as declaring: 'It is some time since the LPO played with such polish.' Silvestri had obtained 'a glowing, tingling and formally coherent reading of the *Poem of Ecstasy*' and the striking feature of the *Symphony of Psalms* was that

> Mr Silvestri achieved an effect of nobility and intense emotional effect without apparently sacrificing the strict tempos or hard, bright tone colours which Stravinsky sought.

After these four concerts he evidently created a sufficiently good impression for the LPO to have invited him back in June 1957 to conduct Beethoven's *Mass in D* in the Albert Hall in which, according to *The Times* 'there were beauties and stretches of nobility in his conception' and the LPO

> responded to the conductor with some fine execution in the *Benedictus* and the martial section of the *Dona nobis Pacem*, but elsewhere it could have done with extra rehearsal,

to which we can imagine Silvestri giving a hearty 'Amen.' Incidentally, only two months before, he had conducted and recorded the *Missa Solemnis* in Bucharest. He had also directed it in 1952 for the 125th anniversary of Beethoven's death.

In January and February 1958 – that is before returning to Romania for the last time prior to his 'defection' to the West – he conducted seven more concerts with the LPO, including one in a 'historical series of all-Russian music' which was broadcast on Radio 3. In 1959 he did nine more concerts with the LPO and in 1966–67 he would do four more. In 1959 he also conducted the Hallé four times, in Manchester and Sheffield.

It was in the LPO's 'Music of the 20th Century' concert in March 1959 that the *Observer*'s music critic Edmund Tracey thought that 'none of the three works' Silvestri conducted – Bartók's *Concerto for Orchestra*, Britten's *Serenade* and Stravinsky's *Symphony in Three Movements* – 'wholly came off' and in effect took the audience to task for its 'frenzied approval' and 'tumultuous applause.' Furthermore, he criticised the orchestra for showing respect for Silvestri by not responding to his gestures for them to rise and share the applause with him. This earned the critic a rejoinder from one of the LPO players in the *Observer's* letter column the following Sunday.

Tracey had written:

Mr Silvestri was holla'd to the unreverberate roof [of the Festival Hall] not only by the audience but by the orchestra too – which is even more remarkable. Why should the LPO resolutely refuse to take a bow, insisting that their part in the triumph was small and that all the glory should be the conductor's?. . .

To which the player, John Montgomery, replied:

Perhaps as an orchestral player I can amplify his comments a little. Most orchestral musicians feel that of all instruments, the conductor's baton is the easiest 'to get away with.' Given a good orchestra and a straightforward programme, the notes look after themselves and the only useful function of the conductor is to contribute something more subtle – to mould phrases, relate speeds delicately, adjust balance. Many conductors just fail to do this, and nobody can spot this quicker than the players. The smooth clichés of the critical fraternity . . . 'the strings seemed tired, the ensemble slack. . .' are a euphemism for the sombre truth: 'Mr X bored the players so much that they played worse than usual.'

Some conductors make themselves objectionable to the orchestra, whether by mild sarcasm – 'Are you satisfied with that?'; direct abuse – 'A bunch of cretins'; rhetorical question – 'Why did you take up music?'; plain invective – 'Watch the beat, damn you!'; or sheer slander – 'Let's face it, gentlemen, this must be the world's worst orchestra.' (All real instances – no prizes offered.)

So when a conductor appears who treats the musicians civilly, uses a stick with certainty and effect, knowing what to rehearse and what to leave to the inspiration of the concert, the players' tribute is to give him an extra bow.

During these early visits to Britain, Silvestri also had concerts in Watford, Bristol, Folkestone, Hastings, Eastbourne and Southampton. In addition he made a recording of Dvorak's *Symphony No 8* and the *Carneval Overture* with the LPO and 10 records with the Philharmonia, with whom he would make another three in 1959. (*See* Appendix 4.)

With Romanian pianist Valentin Gheorghiu in Paris in front of a placard advertising his concerts and HMV records with Gheorghiu and Christian Ferras

Silvestri also made his concert début in Paris at this time and, allowing for the euphuistic style of some of the reviews, his impact on most French critics and audiences certainly seems to have been a *coup de foudre*. Not untypical is *l'Express*'s:

Unknown in Paris until yesterday, Silvestri has established himself as one of the star conductors. This Romanian is a mixture of Toscanini and Furtwängler. It may be banal, but we have to resort to the only fitting description of him – sensational.

Silvestri almost certainly read this and it could not have pleased him more if he had himself written the allusion to Furtwängler and Toscanini. For, 12 years before, he had told the Romanian composer Anatol Vieru that ideally he would like to model his own style on a synthesis of the styles of these two conductors; that while Toscanini, he maintained, always tried to keep strictly to the score, Furtwängler's approach was that of a poet: seeking its emotional undertones by studying its every minute detail and then recreating it. He repeated this view throughout his career.

Hélène Jourdan-Morhange in *Les Lettres Françaises* for March 1958 eulogised:

Seldom have I seen musicians of the Société du Conservatoire applaud a conductor with such enthusiasm. The concert began with Brahms' *First Symphony*. Straight away one could sense the strength, the sensitivity and warmth which Silvestri imparted to the varying moods of the music. He is particularly adroit in the building up of crescendos: from plunging into terrestrial depths, to the final launching into celestial flight. He makes the strings sing and his rhythms are strict. It is a pleasure to watch such zest for the work, tempered by economy of gesture. It was also a revelation to discover how close he got to the spirit of Debussy. . .

Silvestri was particularly pleased with how his records, made with the French National Radio Orchestra (ORTF) and the Orchestra of the Paris Conservatoire, were received in France. There is a hint of Mozart's gratification at the reception of *Le Nozze di Figaro* in 1787 in Prague when he wrote to a friend: 'Here, they talk about nothing but Figaro. Nothing is played, sung or whistled . . . nothing, nothing but Figaro,' when Silvestri, interviewed in Bucharest in April 1957, claimed:

> In all the music shops I visited in France and Switzerland I found that, of all the 11 versions of the *New World Symphony* conducted by great conductors, people are choosing mine.

In fact, his *From the New World* with the ORTF was awarded the Charles Cross Academy first prize. Because it was a stereo prototype a copy has been carefully preserved in Paris as an historical artefact. He also won the *Grand Prix du Disque* for his recording of Enescu's *Dixtuor for Winds in D major* Op.14.

Rehearsing the Vienna Philharmonic in 1959 prior to the Australian tour

Dutch audiences and critics were no less enthusiastic in December 1957 about his conducting of six concerts with the Concertgebouw. In Hilversum 'with the *New World* he threw down his trump card,' wrote one.

> From beginning to end audience and orchestra were under the spell of a conductor in a class of his own . . . a born musician. The ovation for Silvestri and the orchestra lasted many minutes;

and another, in Amsterdam:

> We have made the acquaintance of a conductor of the old school, in the sense that he is not afraid to give us a romanticism which gladdens the heart, yet at the same time he is a man of our time.

In Belgium, Italy, Greece and Switzerland during these last years of the Fifties there were similar expressions of admiration for the man who, less than 20 years before, had written he was giving up conducting and had lost confidence in the future.

Though it was by no means unanimous, he won Australian acclaim right across the continent during his tour in May/June 1959. In Sydney, Dr R. Dalley-Scarlett considered Silvestri 'one of those rare conductors who can persuade an orchestra to play above the top of its form by his own personal magnetism.' Another critic said his musical approach justified his 'super-personal interpretations' of Brahms' *First Symphony*; and the Queensland Symphony Orchestra 'responded by producing a piece of playing more taut and telling than ever before.'

July found him the other side of the Pacific for a six-week tour of Mexico where he received 'frenzied ovations,' according to the press, which spoke of his 'exceptional virtuosity' and of 'transforming' the orchestras he conducted.

When he directed the Berlin Philharmonic in a series of concerts in March 1960, the reviews spoke of him as 'a musician of great calibre,' one of the few international conductors at that time who promoted contemporary music – the programme included Kurt Weill's *Violin Concerto*, Stravinsky's *Chant du Rossignol* (which he had already recorded with the Philharmonia) and his own *Prelude and Fugue for Orchestra* which *Der Tagesspiegel* described as 'an artistic contrapuntal study pulsating with temperament' – and were full of praise for his interpretation of Mahler's monumental *Third Symphony*. It was its first performance in Berlin – the works of this Catholic convert from Judaism had been banned by the Nazis. Silvestri was invited back to Berlin in December for a programme which included a performance of Bartók's *Violin Concerto No. 1* with Max Rostal.

In fact, in 1960–61 Silvestri's 'West' European fame spread from Lisbon to Stockholm.

In July 1960, after his first concert with the Chicago Symphony Orchestra, reviewer Roger Dettmer concluded it was the best summer concert since Georg Solti's 'electric performance' six years before and that Silvestri was

> one of the precious few conductors anywhere in the world who is 100 per cent professional with the baton. . . He is wonderfully sensitive to the difference in musical styles and periods. In other words he does not conduct Schubert as he conducts Ravel.

After his last concert in Chicago, there were 'waves of applause and volleys of cheers' after a bravura reading of Tchaikovsky's *Fifth Symphony*, but Dettmer by this time felt able to make a more balanced appraisal.

Mr Silvestri's music-making is not to everyone's taste. He inclines to overinterpret in a romantic fashion, in the manner of Stokowski and the late Mengelberg – a fashion that has gone quite out of style in recent years. . . He is a seeker of the music's spirit, if need be at the expense of the letter. . . However, to impugn his professionalism and his extraordinarily developed musicianship is simply and merely ignorant.

The following month, August 1960, there were more 'tumultuous receptions' and 'brilliant performances,' this time in South Africa where the *Cape Times* said the three concerts he had conducted there would be remembered as 'the greatest highlights of the year.'

Back in the USA in November 1961, according to one reviewer, he 'scored one of the biggest successes within memory' when he conducted the Philadelphia Symphony Orchestra in the absence on vacation of Eugene Ormandy.

But to return to Silvestri's reception in Britain, where he was to settle in 1961 and which eventually became the country of his adoption:

On March 15 1961 the Festival Hall audience and the Royal Philharmonic paid silent tribute to Sir Thomas Beecham before Silvestri 'paraded the orchestra in a stunning performance of the Tchaikovsky *Fourth Symphony*,' as the *Daily Telegraph* put it. (Six years later there was another short silence, in the Manchester Free Trade Hall, before Silvestri conducted the Royal Liverpool Philharmonic, after it was announced that Sir Malcolm Sargent had just died. On that occasion the programme included another Tchaikovsky symphony, the *Manfred*.)

Yet another orchestra would respond to Silvestri's baton, the BBC Northern Symphony Orchestra, in the Chester Festival of the Arts in July 1967, with Paul Tortelier playing the cello in Richard Strauss' tone poem *Don Quixote*.

That made the sixth British orchestra that invited him as guest conductor or with whom he recorded and by February 1965, the *Daily Telegraph's* Colin Mason, reviewing a RFH concert, was writing:

Silvestri's control of the London Philharmonic Orchestra gave strength to the belief that we have no finer conductor in England today. . . The orchestra was magnificently responsive to him, at his subtlest no less than at his most urgent.

Silvestri conducting the Bournemouth Symphony Orchestra. His appointment, which would last over seven years, at first provoked both criticism and enthusiasm

The name Constantin Silvestri, however, will inevitably always be associated in this country first and foremost with the Bournemouth Symphony Orchestra whose principal conductor he was from September 1961 until his death at the age of 55 in February 1969.

In due course we will see how this association came about and why the BSO admitted in its programmes in the early days after his appointment that it had 'caused considerable interest and *diversity of comment*' [my italics J.G.] – to be changed within a short time to the more positive 'provoked considerable attention and enthusiasm.'

But first we will note the BSO's progress under his tutelage as it was recorded by some of the critics.

Six months before his appointment – certainly before Silvestri himself or the players had any inkling he would become a resident of this Dorset (or Hampshire as it then was) seaside resort – he was invited to conduct the BSO on March 8 1961 in Portsmouth and the following night in Bournemouth itself – concerts at which his own *Prelude and Fugue* were performed. The most prolific and well–informed of the local critics, the Bournemouth *Evening Echo*'s Kenneth Williams, expressed a view which, with hindsight, sounds almost prophetic or, at least by implication, made him a keen advocate of Silvestri's candidacy for the post:

It is safe to say that Bournemouth will not hear another performance of Tchaikovsky's *Fourth Symphony* like that in last night's Winter Gardens concert for many a long year – *unless, of course, Constantin Silvestri, who was guest conductor of the BSO, returns in the meanwhile.* [My italics J.G.] If he does come back he will be certain of a big audience. Most will be there to sample again the tremendous excitement generated by this little man with the tiny baton. Others, the more scholarly section of the audience, will go to hear what audacious tricks of interpretation Mr Silvestri will try next.

The following October the *Sunday Telegraph* had this to say about his first concert in the Bournemouth Winter Gardens after his appointment (his very first concert had been in Southampton on September 26):

Mr Silvestri is a virtuoso and a musician. He can make the orchestral tone glow and sparkle over a wide range of colour. His phrasing has distinction (if sometimes at the expense of formal cohesion), his rhythm, urgency and bite as well as weight. He is, moreover, brilliant at conveying to players the sound image in his own mind – a conductor's first gift, often withheld. Orchestra and audience were obviously delighted to welcome him, and well they might be.

Again, the programme included his own *Prelude and Fugue* (which he had also conducted the year before with the Royal Philharmonic in the Albert Hall). *The Times* said it was 'brilliantly and imaginatively scored for a large orchestra' and 'showed a conductor's understanding of orchestral technique and effect.' (Actually, he had not done much conducting when it was composed, 1937–38, though he did revise it in 1956.)

A week later, as we have seen, he was standing-in with the RPO in the Royal Festival Hall for Sir Thomas Beecham who had died suddenly. He would return almost exactly a year later with his own orchestra 'to score the greatest public success it has ever achieved in London,' as Kenneth Williams would record with civic pride. He added:

Each of the three works in the programme [which was broadcast] was greeted with cheers and prolonged applause. When the concert ended, Silvestri was recalled to the platform half a dozen times. . . He was congratulated backstage by many leading musicians who were attracted to the concert by the intriguing combination of a world-famous conductor with what was once regarded as one of the lesser provincial orchestras.

Silvestri opened the programme with Berlioz's *Symphonie Fantastique* which received such an ovation – which he shared with the orchestra, singling out the woodwind principals – that he had to return four times to the rostrum. French pianist Samson François was the soloist in Prokofiev's *Piano Concerto No. 5* and the concert ended with Silvestri's lollipop: Enescu's *Romanian Rhapsody No. 1* (which would have been encored, as the Bristol audience had insisted two nights before, had not the concert already been running late.)

Silvestri would conduct six out of the eight concerts in the following month's Bournemouth Easter Festival and Desmond Shawe-Taylor in the *Sunday Times* was full of praise for 'the orchestra's new director' in his review of the festival's first concert.

> I had not heard the Bournemouth players for some time, and was struck by the standards of discipline and tonal beauty they have now attained. . . The string choir plays with a fullness and warmth which are rare in England; the woodwind is clear, firm and accurate; and the brass superb.

In March 1963 *The Times* came to the conclusion after a concert in Bournemouth:

> It is no secret that, since Mr Constantin Silvestri became principal conductor some two and a half years ago, the BSO have both raised their standard of playing and grown more adventurous in their programmes. . . These players can now tackle almost any work of the current modern repertory since under Mr Silvestri's careful training they have been transformed into a reliable and very competent all-purpose orchestra. . . Mr Silvestri did in most respects full justice to Bruckner's *Third Symphony*. The performance was spacious and imbued with the grandeur and simple nobility which are part and parcel of Bruckner's style. . . All in all, it was a performance reflecting great credit on conductor and orchestra.

The following October, R.L. Henderson in the *Sunday Telegraph* had 'only the highest praise' for the orchestra's playing, this time of Bruckner's *Second Symphony*, which Silvestri 'had the curious effect of making sound less typically English,' and he added: 'The wind is not soloistic; the strings he has trained into a splendid ensemble; at least as good as anything in the country.'

In this concert in Bournemouth the Lebanese-born violinist Yfrah Neaman gave a first performance of Liverpool composer Malcolm Lipkin's *Violin Concerto No. 2*. It was during a rehearsal of this work that a player recalls Silvestri, with his composer's ear for colour in orchestration, remarking with pleasure in his quaint English: 'Here is a new convention!' and ringing with his pencil a happy juxtaposition in the score. Ever ready to promote young composers, Silvestri had included one of the 31-year-old Lipkin's shorter works in a previous programme.

The critics seem unanimous in their plaudits for the Festival Hall concert on October 26 in which Gary Graffman played the *Emperor* and the only other work was the Shostakovich *Tenth Symphony*. The *Daily Telegraph* said it represented 'a great tribute to the prowess of Constantin Silvestri both as trainer and interpreter'; David Cairns in the *Financial Times* said the BSO had been 'making a reputation as one of the liveliest in or out of London' and that it played the Shostakovich 'with splendid fire and dash'; while *The Times*' view of the symphony was:

> It is a real joy to hear something that can be called, in the fullest sense, an interpretation. This is precisely what Mr Constantin Silvestri seems able to achieve with the BSO. . . By temperament he inclines to cherish details rather than to clarify a grand design . . . both the fast movements were thrown off with breathtaking brilliance and unanimity. . . Whatever reservations one may have about Mr Silvestri's feeling for large-scale musical architecture, there can be no doubt at all that he has an exceptional ear for sonority. . . Selfishly, one wishes that Mr Silvestri and his players could appear in London more often.

But it would be naive and quite misleading to pretend that all the critics praised Silvestri after every concert or that even favourable reviews were never unqualified. Some of the BSO players had the impression that he got upset with bad reviews, especially with those in the national press. He was once heard to mutter a deprecating 'critics and other cabbages' and would sometimes show a temporary bias towards or against a player or a section of the orchestra if attention had been drawn to them in a review, depending on whether it had been favourable or adverse.

So, to balance a little the appreciative comments that have been quoted so far about his pre-Bournemouth concerts, here are two reviewers who were evidently less impressed: first, Romanian–born Antoine Goléa who was the doyen of France's music critics up to his death in 1983. In February 1959, he attended a concert in Paris in which the principals were also Romanian: Silvestri conducting l'Orchestre National and Clara Haskil playing the Mozart *Piano Concerto in F major K459*. In Goléa's view

> Clara Haskil found it a little difficult to project her ethereal poetry; Silvestri was accompanying her rather indifferently: all the nuances of the orchestra were too thick, the tone too bright and too aggressive.

(The following year the world would lose a very sensitive pianist: Clara had a fatal fall down some steps in a Brussels station after a concert.)

Goléa was no more enthusiastic over Silvestri's interpretation of *Prélude à l'après-midi d'un faune*: 'He never knew how to make us feel the overwhelming Pan-like sensuality which lifts the work and without which it is nothing.' And as for *Bolero*, Silvestri's interpretation shocked Goléa: 'There are certain things which one should not allow oneself to do,' he chided.

> For instance, one should not do rubato all the time; or overdo the changes in tempo in a work which must flow with the inexorability of a metronome; otherwise it is not what Ravel meant it to be. . .

In March 1959, Silvestri was conducting an International Celebrity Concert in the Festival Hall and *The Times*, under the heading: 'Mr Constantin Silvestri in wilful mood,' took him to task for 'imposing his own views on the music [Dvorak *Symphony No 4*] throughout all four movements.' Silvestri had whipped the last movement

> into a fever of excitement towards the end. All this was very stimulating for a change, though we would not want to hear the symphony in this way every time. But the enchanting, wistful Scherzo really would not do as Mr Silvestri played it. . .

Jumping four years to after the Bournemouth appointment, although Clive Barnes in the *Daily Express* reviewing a Festival Hall concert in March 1963 thought the BSO 'under its new conductor' (that is after only 18 months) had 'developed into one of the finest instruments in the country and certainly the best orchestra outside London,' he tempered this with

> Mr Silvestri's merits as an orchestra trainer – and clearly he is among the world's best – are not matched by his skill as an interpreter. . . Even while I disagree with his unduly personal interpretations I enormously admire his orchestra.

The same month, when the BSO played in Manchester's Free Trade Hall, the *Daily Telegraph* was critical of Silvestri's 'meticulous attention to detail' which 'paid modest dividends in enjoyment but robbed symphonies by Dvorak and Brahms of much spontaneity.'

In November 1963 Deryck Cooke in *The Listener* condemned a broadcast of the Bruckner *Third Symphony*, though when it was performed the previous March *The Times* had given it lavish praise. Now, Silvestri 'vulgarised this noble work by injecting a theatrical emotionalism into every note and continually holding up the argument by exaggerated rubato.'

Even the laudatory review of his first London concert, quoted earlier, had mentioned that the 'helter-skelter pace' at which he drove the LPO 'had the major drawback that the orchestra simply could not articulate rapid phrases, least of all in the woolly acoustics' of the Royal Albert Hall.

There was an echo of this in John Emery's stricture on Silvestri's *Overture to Die Meistersinger* in October 1964's *Musical Times*: 'He seemed determined to break all speed records and succeeded easily.' But this was a model of restraint compared with some of the uninhibited but irresistibly amusing diatribes he had to endure during his Australian tour, like:

> Last night Constantin Silvestri drove the Sydney Symphony Orchestra through Tchaikovsky like a square-wheeled locomotive through lilac. . . The *String Serenade* and *Fifth Symphony* . . . were given no chance by the restless, thumping, clock-racing approach that Silvestri made to both of them.

That was the reviewer in the *Sydney Morning Herald* and his colleague in *The Sun*, reviewing the *Eroica* in an earlier concert, said it was the fastest performance he had ever heard – 'his most astonishing burst of speed was in the Funeral March, which put the deceased away at a canter.'

Whatever 'nuggety' means Down Under, that was the description Silvestri was given by another reviewer who explained to readers of *The Daily Mirror*:

> Nuggety Silvestri works like a shadow boxer most of the time and his favourite baton stroke is a curving left which should terrorise most players into instant obedience.

These few examples give us a taste of Silvestri's interpretations and style which disturbed some while evoking in others – almost certainly the vast majority – quite different sensations. Varied individual reactions to any performance are inevitable. A concert pianist friend with a predilection for playing Schubert attended a Svyatoslav Richter Schubert recital in the Festival Hall years ago and was ostensibly in a minority of one in his, albeit tacit, disapproval of the performance. He registered this by firmly remaining seated and not applauding while the rest of the audience gave Richter a standing ovation. This stubborn non-conformity so enraged a lady standing behind him that she leaned over and demanded the reason and when he explained he did not like Richter's performance she slapped him – chastisement sometimes reserved for sedentary objectors to the playing of the National Anthem.

The 1963 Edinburgh Festival was a highwater mark in the rising tide of Silvestri's triumphs with the BSO. An eyewitness account of what happened in the Usher Hall on the night of August 31 will appear later; suffice it here to give a sample of the critics' reactions, of which surprise seems to have been a common factor – at the apparently unexpected quality of the performance and at the audience response, which one Scottish critic, with perhaps a wee dram of Calvinist disapproval, compared to what 'one would expect at an exciting Cup Final rather than in a normally sedate concert hall.' In recompense, he did concede that it was 'a remarkable début.'

A compatriot in the Edinburgh *Evening News* ventured:

> The Bournemouth players gave a performance that equalled – dare one say surpassed? – anything purveyed at this year's Festival.

The transformation of the BSO 'under the inspiring leadership of Constantin Silvestri' was noted by Christopher Grier of *The Scotsman*:

> The days when its predecessors wore dark-blue uniforms and gold-laced pillbox hats are long past and what was once a municipal band has, after various vicissitudes, turned into the highly respected Orchestra of the West with a farflung parish.

In similar vein, *The Times* after registering surprise at the 'firework display' from the BSO under Silvestri, said those that stayed at home

> in the belief that a provincial orchestra would not aspire to the standards of a great international festival, in fact robbed themselves of a remarkable display of orchestral clarity, suppleness and discipline of every kind. Thanks to Mr Silvestri's training the word 'provincial' no longer applies: the Bournemouth players have now acquired the status of a national orchestra.

From March to May 1964, Silvestri conducted a series of concerts in Tokyo with the NHK Symphony Orchestra for the 35th anniversary of the inauguration of the Japan Broadcasting Corporation. At one press conference, here, he was asked whether Mr Bournemouth was a millionaire after whom his orchestra had been named; at another, whether it was a district of London.

But any lacunae in Japanese knowledge of England's geography was more than compensated by traditional hospitality which provided VIP treatment for Silvestri and his wife – a flat with chambermaid in attendance and a chauffeur-driven car at their disposal – terrific audience reception (he is said to have played his own *Prelude* three times on demand at one concert) and there were rumoured offers of a contract with the NHK orchestra.

At the end of the year, he did a three-months series of guest concerts: with the Suisse Romande in Geneva; the Orquesta Nacional in Madrid; with the Radio Orchestra in Turin; and a return to Scandinavia. Here he had conducted every year since 1960 – Stockholm, Malmö, Göteborg, Copenhagen –

Consulting his desk diary. Silvestri worked from 16 to 18 weeks a year with the BSO and avoided, if possible, working with it for more than four weeks at a stretch. It relieved tensions and gave him the opportunity to guest-conduct other orchestras at home and worldwide

and would do so again in 1967 and 1968. In 1967 he also conducted in Helsinki.

It was when this Swedish tour of 1964 had finished that he took a trip to the far north and from there sent a postcard postmarked 'North Pole Express' to Romeo Drăghici, lifelong friend and biographer of George Enescu. The postcard was in answer to a registered letter Drăghici had sent Silvestri and which had caught up with him in Lapland after being forwarded from Bournemouth to Spain, to France, Denmark, Sweden and Norway. Silvestri wrote to his friend on January 10, 1965:

> I cannot describe to you how moved I was to receive your letter only 12 days after it was sent from Bucharest, at this place in Lapland which is so far even from the fjords, among the eternal snows. . . It followed me everywhere I have been and reached me in a hut, which doesn't even have an address, in the middle of the ice, reindeer and Eskimos [*sic*]. As to a post office, there isn't one, and there are only 12 dwellings. In spite of this it reached me by dog sleigh. But the sleigh has left already, so you will probably get my answer in a few days from another area which does have a post office.

*Checking with EMI staff the Bournemouth Symphony Orchestra's
recording of* Sheherazade *in December 1966*

Other concerts abroad since his Bournemouth appointment included: in
Lisbon (1961); San Remo (1963); four in Argentina (1965) and six in Holland
(1966 and 1967).

Nicholas Braithwaite, who was the BSO's assistant conductor from 1967
to 1970, says Silvestri worked from 16 to 18 weeks a year with the orchestra and
avoided if possible working with it for more than four weeks at a stretch.

> I think he felt the tensions built up too much after three or four weeks of
> most intensive work and it was very important for the orchestra to see
> someone else and for himself to work with others. After all, the conductor
> has absolute authority over 80-odd musicians, all of whom have an equal
> right to believe how music should go, yet most of the time are being told to
> do something in a different way from that which they would choose them-
> selves. Consequently, there is a lot of tension in the relationship between a
> conductor and an orchestra. From experience with my own orchestra
> [Braithwaite subsequently became conductor of the Glyndebourne
> Touring Opera] I really tried to follow Silvestri's principle – and it worked
> absolutely. It's good for the audience, good for the orchestra, and good for
> the conductor's home life! The only time it didn't work has been on the few
> occasions I have had to work eight weeks continuously with an orchestra.
> At the end of that time, we couldn't wait to see the back of each other.

However, the year following his own overseas concert peregrinations, Silvestri went with the BSO – with its 100 players and 2¹/₂ tons of instruments – on its first European tour (October 1965) which would involve 13 concerts in five countries. The first was in Amsterdam (where Silvestri had conducted the Concertgebouw in December 1957–January 1958).

Raymond Carpenter, the BSO's principal clarinetist for 38 years, recalls:

Our concerts were billed:

SILVESTRI

in big letters in comparison with a minuscule

Bournemouth Symphony Orchestra

underneath.

Whether or not it was because news of the salubrious amenities of Bournemouth had not reached the ken of the burghers of Amsterdam, the Concertgebouw hall was only half full. 'On the other hand, the critics turned up in force,' says Carpenter,

to see what Silvestri had made of this unknown orchestra. We did Stravinsky's *Nightingale* and in the second half the *Manfred* – quite ambitious for a first trip abroad. But when we had finished this performance everybody in the hall stood up, including the critics. They wouldn't let us go until we'd done an encore, so the Maestro plunged into Enescu's *Romanian Rhapsody No. 1*. That really brought the house down and they actually had to fetch the orchestra off because we were on our feet up and down, up and down. Otherwise we would have been doing that all night. The papers the next day were full of notices praising Silvestri and his orchestra. One critic raved: 'Was it Mahler who said that possessing an orchestra makes a town habitable? Bournemouth can consider itself lucky to own such a precious possession.'

(Left to right) Silvestri, the Czech conductor of the Leipzig Gewandhaus, Vaclav Neumann, and his wife, and 'Pupa' Silvestri socialise during the Bournemouth Symphony Orchestra's European tour in October 1965

After Belgium and West Germany, the BSO went on to play in Poland and Czechoslovakia. But Silvestri, who at that time did not have either French or British citizenship, was unable to go to the other side of the Iron Curtain. Instead, this part of the European tour was conducted by Austrian-born Rudolf Schwarz, one-time inmate of Belsen, the notorious Nazi concentration camp. He had settled in Britain and been principal conductor (from 1946 to 1951) of what was then called the Bournemouth Municipal Orchestra.

In April 1966 the BSO gave the London première – the first performance was in Bournemouth in October 1964 – of a work dedicated to both the orchestra and to Silvestri: the *Sinfonia Concertante (Symphony No. 1)* of Malcolm Rayment, the *Glasgow Herald* critic quoted earlier and whose chance meeting with Silvestri in Bucharest had led to Constantin's own London début nine years before. One-time jazz trumpeter, Rayment had written music for documentary films, television, drama and ballet. He went to school in Bournemouth and in due course we will see how he met Silvestri – hence the double dedication of the symphony, which contains a motto theme introduced by a trumpet fanfare derived from the musical letters in Bournemouth Symphony Orchestra.

The Guardian called it 'a striking and successful work, challenging the players and using the orchestra with great skill. The BSO played the work splendidly'; Christopher Grier in *The Scotsman* (who had reviewed it after its Bournemouth first performance) spoke of 'its assured craftsmanship, idiomatic writing, fluency and felicities of scoring.' Rather condescendingly, *The Times* wrote: 'There is much in the work that is agreeable and attractive' but it 'inevitably calls to mind the kind of symphonies we hear from the people's republics of Eastern Europe.' A more sympathetic colleague from the same stable who had attended the first of its two Bournemouth performances had found it 'constructionally full of ingenuity'; it 'offered a refreshingly different interpretation of symphonic form' and 'the instrumentation is constantly skilful.'

What neither the critics nor the public knew was that Rayment was still doing alterations and correcting parts for the orchestra the day before its first performance.

But it was not only the works of composers establishing their reputations which Silvestri introduced to British audiences.

In January 1968 he conducted the first performance in Britain of a work by the Czech composer Bohuslav Martinu, who had died nine years before in

Switzerland: his *Concertino for Piano and Orchestra*, composed over 30 years earlier. The soloist in Bournemouth was Martinů's compatriot Eva Bernathova. Malcolm Rayment in his role of critic called it 'a most attractive and unproblematical work with brilliantly written parts for both soloist and orchestra – it could easily become very popular.'

Two months later Silvestri conducted, seated in the midst of his players, a work of Enescu composed and first performed in Paris in 1906 (and for which Silvestri had won the Grand Prix du Disque) but never before in England. This was his *Dixtuor for Winds*.

In the same Bournemouth concert Silvestri also conducted the British première of a work by Leonard Bernstein written 14 years earlier: his *Serenade for Solo Violin, Strings, Harp and Percussion*, with the Hungarian violinist Thomas Magyar as soloist. Joan Chissell in *The Times* found the

> beautifully mellow string tone from soloist and orchestra alike made the performance enjoyable; though what the score really needs is choreography: with the eye to help out the ear, all would be well.

At the risk of labouring the point, further evidence of the critics' recognition of the BSO's development under Silvestri mounted in the following years. Hence *The Times* in February 1967:

> The Bournemouth players' tremendous playing in the Franck symphony would have held its own with any British orchestra. The unanimity of musicianship in every instrumental department, and the superbly blended corporate sonority each displayed, proclaimed a completely disciplined body which seemed to listen to itself and continually adjust tone with the response of a chamber group, though no doubt Mr Silvestri was more than a little responsible for such sensitivity. . . In Dvorak's *Cello Concerto* they continued to perform with complete sensitivity of response in accompanying Paul Tortelier, who was playing at the very height of his powers.

Alan Blyth in the *Daily Express* in May 1968:

> Last night's concert proved just why the BSO is now one of the best orchestras in the country – London included. . . Silvestri is obviously a superb trainer of players.

And finally *The Guardian*, reviewing the last concert Silvestri conducted in the Royal Festival Hall on November 23 1968:

> Thanks to the musical inspiration, the energy and – in the best sense – showmanship of the conductor, Constantin Silvestri, the BSO has now

become an orchestra to stand comparison with any in the country. Even London has to look to its laurels. . .

The first performance of Andrzej Panufnik's *Sinfonia Sacra*

> proved a splendid Saturday-evening piece (and potentially a good Proms one too), which had a riotous reception. Silvestri is a real magician when it comes to putting modern music over to a wide audience. . . Confident attack, refusal to flinch from the weightiest fortissimo but also subtler, more tender qualities lie behind Silvestri's success.

The concert included German soprano Irmgard Seefried singing three excerpts from Berg's opera, *Wozzeck*, and Hindemith's *Marienleben Songs*.

Enough has surely been adduced so far to establish for those of a later generation that 'the little man with the tiny baton' won a worldwide reputation as one of the foremost conductors of the Fifties and Sixties. There were and still are controversies over his interpretations, but nobody could deny his dramatic impact on an audience whether it was in Chicago or Chichester, Besançon or Bournemouth.

The man who was probably closer to Silvestri than any other in this country was Kenneth Matchett, the BSO's general manager and secretary, who had had considerable experience having been concert manager of the Royal Liverpool Philharmonic, general manager of the Birmingham Symphony Orchestra and business manager of the D'Oyly Carte Opera before choosing Bournemouth.

'Many critics regarded Silvestri, if not *schmaltzy* at any rate bizarre, eccentric,' Matchett maintains.

> His readings were eccentric to some extent, but what I feel about him is that, while he may not have made the grade with the musical Establishment in London, audiences absolutely adored him. Up and down the country, wherever we played with him, there were rave ovations. Compared with other conductors I have known, foreign as well as British, few could produce the audience reaction to the extent Silvestri did. It was on a par with the fanatics of Beecham (with whom I worked a lot) or Malcolm Sargent who would produce a tremendous audience reaction, too, but it was not as deeply felt as Silvestri would produce. I've seen people walking out of the Winter Gardens crying their eyes out, tremendously moved.

But for all his audience popularity, his love for his orchestra, for the seaside town of his adoption and its people, Kenneth Matchett sensed a sub-surface insecurity in Silvestri which another musician had noticed in him even as a young man – and which the post-war xenophobia of the 'London musical Establishment' did nothing to allay. Matchett claims that Rudolph Schwarz had also been a victim in the immediate post-war years of this alleged anti-foreigner prejudice on the part of the BBC (he would nevertheless become chief conductor of the BBC Symphony Orchestra) and of some of the critics in the metropolis who held on for too long to their condescending attitude to this 'end-of-the-pier band.'

And not altogether confined to the critics: Matchett relates how when Silvestri's predecessor, Charles Groves, conducted the orchestra in the 1955 Proms, as soon as the players began filing on to the platform, the Promenaders started singing: 'Oh, I do like to be beside the sea. . .' – more a typical manifestation of Promenaders' good-humoured high spirits, one would have thought, than of big-city chauvinism, though perhaps there was an unconscious element of that too.

Twelve years elapsed before the BSO would play in the Proms again – under Silvestri in 1967 – and by then its reputation seems to have been sufficiently well-established for the Promenaders to have forgotten their little bit of seaside nonsense and for Silvestri to remark: 'The atmosphere is wonderful – how you say? – no snobbism.' He was also gratified by the backstage visit of Edward Heath (Sir Edward was then Leader of HM's Opposition) who congratulated him on the performance (which included two of Silvestri's favourites: the Shostakovich *First Symphony* and the *Manfred*).

If, indeed, insecurity was a component of Silvestri's makeup, when, where and how did it originate?

CHAPTER 2

HOW NOT TO BE AN ALIEN

The Southern Television announcer, introducing an interview with the newly appointed principal conductor of the Bournemouth Symphony Orchestra in 1961, explained to viewers that Mr Constantin Silvestri had 'very limited English.' That also seems to have applied to his understanding of the language, for he gave a very oblique answer to the first question put to him: 'Mr Silvestri, you have had a very distinguished career in your country. When did you leave?' Came the reply: 'Now I live in Paris. I was born in Bucharest, but my origin is Austrian and my ancestors were Italian.'

Already in 1959, on arriving in Australia for his antipodal tour, he had told journalists, tongue in cheek, that his English was limited to five words. One of them reported that though this was obviously not so, nevertheless he was not fluent and it was 'plain he was not thinking in the language.'

Former Bournemouth Symphony Orchestra manager Kenneth Matchett confirms

> his English was terrible, though it improved over the years. He had the laughable habit, if he didn't quite know the English word for what he wanted to say, of making up his own, insisting that that was the correct English and we were wrong. He would say some word shouldn't be pronounced or spelled like that, but like this – and would start quoting Latin. It was great fun.

One can see Silvestri's point; after all, Romanian is a predominantly Latin language and his pronunciation of English would therefore be akin to that of other Latin-based Continental vernaculars rather than to our idiosyncratic Anglo-Saxon vowel pronunciations and first-syllable accenting.

Aware that he had a mischievous sense of humour, one can never be sure whether his malapropisms were deliberately disingenuous or due to actual ignorance of the language. Clarinettist Raymond Carpenter holds to the latter view:

> He was severely limited in the number of words he could use. He wasn't like Rudolph Schwarz who learned a number of words every day. So he had to mimic or describe shapes in the air with his hands.

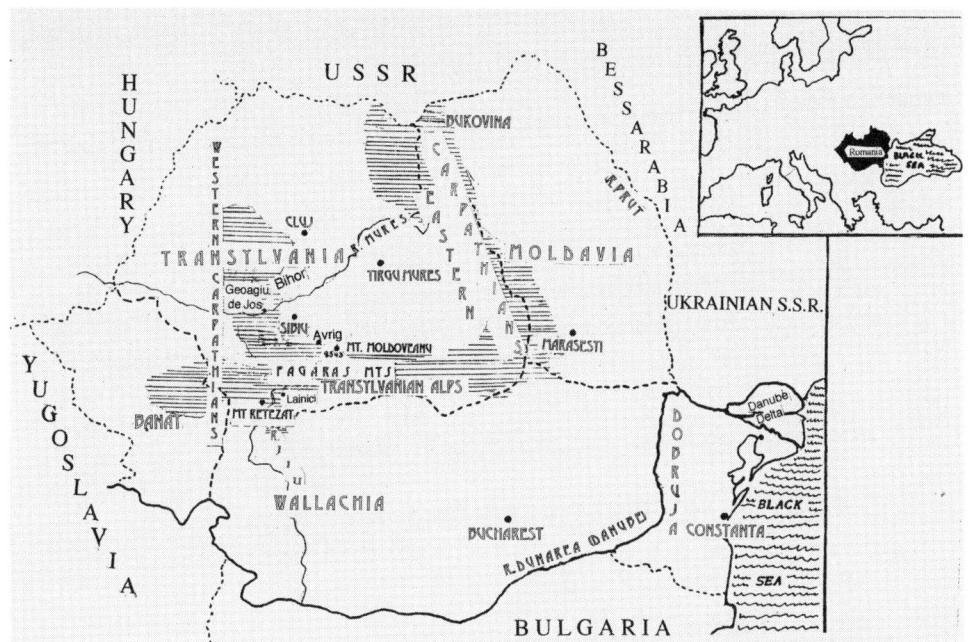

Romania in the 1940s and 50s

Double Bass Lyndon Thomas, straight out of college in 1965, remembers his first rehearsal with Silvestri:

> It was Strauss's *Don Quixote* – I had never encountered anything like it. I had no idea what was going on. I couldn't follow his beat or understand what he said – yet the orchestra was producing this amazing, co-ordinated sound from a few of his twitches and gestures. I was told to follow his left eyebrow, but that didn't help either. . .

Carpenter again:

> On one occasion when we were rehearsing, he got fed up with the First Violins and exclaimed: 'The Cellos, they play sexy. The Violas, they play sexy too. Even the Second Violins, they play sexy. But you', nodding towards the apparently impotent First Violins and registering his disgust: 'Och! I must bring you some pictures, yes?'

Brian Johnstone, one of the First Violins in the Silvestri era, speaks of Costi's 'international vocabulary' which led to the players extending their own knowledge of foreign tongues.

> We learned, for example, that *Fata Morgana* meant a mirage (in the *Manfred Symphony*) and *gran cassa* was a bass drum and *cinelli* meant cymbals in Respighi's *Feste Romane* and *Pines of Rome*.

The few words he did use were often misused and his expectations of British players' acquaintance with foreign literature was, at least on one occasion, too ambitious. In a rehearsal with the Royal Liverpool Philharmonic, when he had finished an explanation of how he wanted a certain passage to be played, he indicated in the usual way where to recommence: 'Now, we'll take it from K – K for Kant,' he said, an innocent allusion to the 18th century author of *Critique of Pure Reason.* Unfortunately, Silvestri's pronunciation of the vowel 'a' resulted in the German philosopher's name sounding uncommonly like that 'short and unattractive little word,' so described in the scatalogical jingle attributed to A.P. Herbert, and of course Silvestri could not understand why he had caused such hilarity among the (predominantly male) players.

On another occasion, very early in his Bournemouth career when he had difficulty in stringing together a sentence in English, he fumbled for the formula to silence a rather persistent member of the orchestra who kept raising technical points. A colleague remembers:

> Silvestri got out his phrase book, muttering: *'Qu'est-ce que c'est le mot? Je voudrais expliquer à mon ami. . .* Ah!
>
> I . . . DO . . . NOT . . . HAVE . . . TIME . . . FOR . . . YOUR . . . PROBLEMS,'
>
> he read out slowly, causing much mirth. It had a nominative, a verb and an accusative and it was all in the right order. Marvellous! The player concerned had to put up with a lot of 'I-don't-have-time-for-your-problems' leg-pulling after that and it passed into BSO mythology.

Two incidents in connection with the St Cecilia Festival concert for the benefit of musical charities in the Royal Albert Hall in November 1966 could be attributed to misunderstandings, unrelated and quite different from each other, except that Silvestri was the common denominator.

This was a royal occasion: both the Queen and the Duke of Edinburgh were attending and their arrival was to be announced by *A Royal Fanfare* composed by Sir Ernest Bullock and played by trumpeters from the Royal Military School of Music at Kneller Hall conducted by a lieutenant-colonel. A bouquet would then be presented to the Queen and as the royal pair entered their box there would be another fanfare and the National Anthem played by the trumpeters together with the BSO, both conducted by Silvestri. To do honour to such an auspicious occasion he was determined to rehearse more diligently than ever.

But when in the rehearsal he raised his baton to start the National Anthem the only response came from his own orchestra – not a sound from the 24 soldier trumpeters. Their colonel, standing to one side, had a faintly sardonic smile at Silvestri's evident mystification. The maestro had not bargained for the colonel's *amour propre*, seismically shaken by the realisation that it was not intended he should conduct his trumpeters in front of *his* Queen. And since the squaddies had not been given any order to obey the command of this foreign conductor, their burnished brass remained muted. Although it struck at least one member of the BSO as 'a farcical situation,' nevertheless by the time of the actual royal entry that evening, Silvestri and the colonel had reached a compromise so that the honour of the British Army remained untarnished: both conducted the National Anthem simultaneously.

The concert proceeded with Vaughan Williams' overture *The Wasps*; the Treorchy Male Voice Choir singing Bruckner's *The Consolation of Music* and Welsh airs; and John Ogdon was the soloist in Rachmaninov's *Rhapsody on a Theme of Paganini*.

Silvestri had long become a confirmed Anglophile and had actually applied for naturalisation a month before. For him, as for many expatriates who admired the 'British way of life' – whichever way they interpreted that omnibus term – the monarch was a symbol of it. He was therefore very eager to be included among those to be presented in the interval to the Queen and the Duke.

To reach the ante-room adjacent to the Royal Box from the Conductor's Room in the Albert's labyrinthine lower depths (where he would have to return for the second half of the concert) was an exercise in itself and this, added to the excitement of the occasion, probably led to stimulation of Silvestri's adrenalin by the time he joined his wife and reached the gaggle of notabilities to be presented. (These included the aviator Sir Alan Cobham, chairman of the Western Orchestral Society, the Mayor and Mayoress of Bournemouth and the Principal of the Royal Academy of Music. Kenneth Matchett and the leader of the BSO, Gerald Jarvis, were also awaiting their turn.)

After Silvestri was presented to Her Majesty, pleasantries were then exchanged with Prince Philip who asked about Silvestri's background in Romania. 'I believe, Your Highness, we have something in common,' the maestro is alleged to have replied. 'We are both mongrels.'

Schooled in diplomacy at least since his marriage, the Duke probably only allowed himself a slight quizzical uplifting of an eyebrow before Silvestri went on to explain: 'I am Italian-Austrian-Romanian.'

The Duke is supposed to have deftly changed the subject of their respective ancestries to something approximating to: 'How do you get on with these beastly tails? Don't you find it a bit stuffy conducting in this outfit?' To which the maestro apparently replied: 'Unlike yours, Your Highness, these are my working clothes.'

After a decent interval, Silvestri hurried below and, following another fanfare, the concert resumed with Britten's *Four Sea Interludes* from *Peter Grimes*; Elizabeth Harwood singing Glière's *Concerto for Soprano and Orchestra*; and ending with the *Romanian Rhapsody* which, as usual, roused the audience to cheers.

In due course, the BSO and its conductor would receive a telegram from the Queen's private secretary expressing her and Prince Philip's pleasure at the concert; also a message of appreciation from the organisers; and Silvestri would relate with pride how 'the Duke and I had a long talk.'

It was one evening in April 1967, that is less than five months after the royal concert, that Silvestri's wife Regina – he and their friends called her Pupa – came home after a tiring day and called in on their neighbours on the ground floor before going upstairs to their own first-floor flat in Bournemouth. This was in a pleasant double-fronted house with blue window frames and its name, 'Addiscombe', in blue wrought-iron letters above the entry, which was within a stone's throw of the Winter Gardens concert hall.

By now, Pupa was speaking English quite fluently but occasionally a colloquialism would get inverted. 'I am beat dead,' she announced and agreed to join Jane Judd and her mother for a drink. 'But first,' she said, 'I will fetch Costi,' (as she and close friends always called him.) In a few moments she returned with a blissfully happy-looking Costi holding a bottle of champagne in one hand and brandishing a British passport in the other.

Harking back to that moment, Jane reflected nearly 30 years later:

> I suppose we don't realise what it's like to be stateless. They were both overjoyed. He insisted I should get out my passport and we went through it page by page, cover to cover, comparing it with his. He could hardly believe his luck. So we celebrated with champagne.

Within a few days he was presented with a parchment scroll from the Western Orchestral Society on which was inscribed not only its 'admiration and respect for his musical achievements' since being appointed the BSO's principal conductor but also 'pleasure that he has become a British subject.'

Yvonne Loriod, wife of Olivier Messiaen, visiting Bournemouth to play the Mozart *Piano Concerto in F major K413* and her husband's *Le Réveil des*

Oiseaux for piano and orchestra, was invited as a special guest to the private dinner where this scroll was presented to Silvestri. It is tempting to speculate whether Costi mentioned to his French dinner companion that, not so many years before, he had made an application for the *droit de séjour en France* with a view to ultimate naturalisation as a French subject.

At least it could be said for the 'British way of life' one could call the Queen's husband a mongrel to his face without fear of the consequences.

Indeed, Costi had known for long periods in his life 'what it is to be stateless' and from remarks he made in letters written in Romania during the war and from the observations of those who knew him before that time or in the immediate postwar years, it is clear the ambiguity concerning his nationality affected him deeply.

To some of his Bournemouth acquaintances, Silvestri used to make the somewhat cryptic claim that his origins were 'Etruscan.' No one seems to have asked him what he meant by this and, again, one can imagine it was accompanied with a mischievous twinkle, since the mysterious Etruscans – themselves of much disputed and unauthenticated origin and with a language that was not Latin – ruled Rome briefly in the sixth century BC. (The last Etruscan king of Rome was expelled in 510 BC.)

Costi's recent paternal forbears came from somewhere along the River Piave to the east of Venice. His grandfather, a stucco moulder, seems to have left the Piave district to earn a living in Bucharest, where some of the monuments he helped to decorate grace Romania's capital to this day.

With every justification one could say that granddad Silvestri – also a Constantin – was of Italian stock. But Etruscan? Apparently, the Etruscans did for a short time spread as far north as the Po Valley (which is still a fair distance south-west of the Piave); but it is overstretching credulity to claim ancestry from a race that may have briefly inhabited, no less than 2,400 years ago, an area where one's grandfather was born.

Grandfather Constantin must have moved to Vienna for a time because that is where our Costi's father, Aloysius Silvestri, and his three brothers were born. Aloysius – or as the Romanians called him, Alois – was therefore Austrian by birth and citizenship. But the family must have moved back to Bucharest because Aloysius was brought up there and he must have been bilingual: German and Romanian.

The grandparents of Costi's mother, *née* Ana Havlíček, were Czechs. The Havlíčeks apparently fled their home in Bohemia in 1848 and sought refuge in Bucharest when the autocratic Habsburg monarchy was clamping down on the liberal revolutionary movements sweeping across Europe from Paris. Ana was born in Bucharest in 1891.

Alois, who worked in Bucharest colouring and touching-up photographs, had what Costi would one day describe as 'a beautiful tenor voice which was greatly appreciated by the public.' He joined a *liedertafel* – our nearest equivalent would have been a glee club – where he met Ana. They married when he was 38 and she was 21 and on May 31 1913 their only child was born. Their home was in a street named V.A. Urechia, after the founder of the Athenaeum, Bucharest's principal concert hall where Costi would conduct many times and in the vicinity of the Opera House where he would become artistic director.

The boy was christened Constantin, presumably after his grandfather, into the Catholic Church (though he would be non-practising throughout his life).

At a rehearsal of the first performance in Bournemouth of the overture to the opera *Donna Diana* in July 1962, Silvestri explained to the players that it was composed by his uncle, Emil Nikolaus von Reznicek, born in Vienna in 1860 and who died in Berlin in 1945. Though Costi had three uncles on his father's side, they were all presumably Silvestris; so the connection must have been through his mother with her Czech lineage. We know that Ana Havlicek had one sister who married a double-bass player called Josef Prunner; she may also have had another, probably older, sister who could have married Reznicek, in which case he would have been Costi's uncle-by-marriage.

Within 13 months of Costi's birth, Europe's armies were mobilising for the massive slaughter which would be World War One. Alois, who had given up his photo-tinting for running a restaurant on Victory Street, one of Bucharest's main thoroughfares, got his call-up papers into the Austrian army.

But Alois was both tubercular and a heavy drinker and after two years, now aged 42, he was invalided out of the army. He tried to return to his family from Vienna but as soon as he crossed into Romania in August 1916 he was interned.

After the Russian army under General Aleksei Brusilov had broken through the Austrian front in June 1916, Romania at last declared war on Austria-Hungary at the end of August*. Alois, an Austrian national, was therefore

---

* Romania's Prussian King Carol I signed a secret treaty with Bismarck's Germany and the Austro-Hungarian Habsburgs in 1883. When World War I started in 1914, Carol for the first time in over 30 years revealed the existence of this treaty (which he had, again clandestinely, renewed the year before) to his astonished ministers and claimed it was a matter of honour for Romania to declare war on the side of the Central Powers. Instead, Prime Minister Ion Brătianu, aware that this would be against majority Romanian

The Athenaeum, Bucharest's most prestigious concert hall where Silvestri performed, first as a pianist, then as principal conductor of the Bucharest Philharmonic

considered an enemy alien. He was not released until 1918, the end of the war, when the five-year-old Costi virtually saw his father for the first time.

That is the story that lay behind Silvestri's remarks about his origins, on Southern Television and to Prince Philip, and in the *curriculum vitae* he prepared for the French authorities in 1958 in order to obtain a *carte d'identité* in which he described himself 'of Italian origin, an Austrian citizen by birth.' Although he had been born in Bucharest and brought up in Romania, he was automatically given at birth his father's registered (though not lineal) nationality: Austrian. From childhood he must have heard his parents speaking German to each other as well as Romanian, probably with a German accent.

Costi would not obtain Romanian citizenship until January 1935, when he was a 22-year-old student.

Towards the end of a long discussion in his Bucharest home about Silvestri, the composer Anatol Vieru made some perceptive observations concerning

public opinion, insisted on neutrality and on waiting for an opportunity to join the Allies. This came when Brusilov's Russian offensive was planned to coincide with that of the French and British on the Somme, and the Allies informed Brătianu that this was the moment for Romania to join them. A reluctant King Carol declared: 'I have to do what my subjects wish me to do.'

Costi's feeling of insecurity – at least in that period when he knew him – and the reasons for it.

Vieru had already explained how he had been a pupil of Silvestri, who was the principal teacher of conducting at the Bucharest Conservatoire (some say from 1944, but at least from 1948, until he finally left the country). Vieru also studied in Moscow where his first important work, *Concerto for Orchestra*, dedicated to his teacher Aram Khachaturian, was given its first public performance there with Gennady Rozhdestvensky conducting. But it was Silvestri who conducted its first performance in Bucharest, in a concert in 1956 in which three other Romanian works were premièred: Mihail Jora's *Cantata*, Paul Constantinescu's *Concerto for String Orchestra* and George Enescu's *Third Orchestral Suite* which he had composed in 1938 and which was his last large-scale work for full orchestra.

'I was a young man of 30 and this was very important for me. I was very happy,' Vieru recalled.

> After all, Silvestri didn't conduct every new work of his young students, but because he took the trouble to criticise my work I felt – and this he actually told me – he expected more and better work from me.
>
> After he conducted my concerto, I wanted to dedicate some songs to him which I had composed to the words of our poet George Topârceanu. He expressed his appreciation of them, but advised against it because of the fate of his own attempt at dedication. He explained he had dedicated his *Suite No. 1 for Piano, Jeux d'enfants*, composed in 1931, to the boy-Prince Michael who was then heir to the throne. He did become King Michael but, of course, was forced to leave the country after the war and no work dedicated to him would have been allowed to be played.

Vieru explained that, though Silvestri's culture was very Romanian, he was not an ethnic Romanian and in East European countries ethnic legitimacy ranked high in people's priorities; the current ethnic explosions were a manifestation of this.

> He felt himself nobody's son because of this lack of Romanian ethnicity and it caused problems within himself. He was not a happy creature, except in his music. His was a restless soul; he was attracted to different things: archaeology, parapsychology and philately; he was an aesthete who collected paintings and oriental carpets. His soul was not here in this country; he was listening in the middle of the night to foreign broadcasts. He was everywhere and nowhere. . .

In a letter to an old friend in March 1940, the 26-year-old Costi, referring to his attempts to compose in Romanian folk idiom, wrote:

> I am not 100 per cent Romanian and I'm only used to living in the city. I'm not very close to the Romanians in the countryside. I only know from books and things written by others about their musical talent. As you know, I tried to get close to this culture and, somehow, to get it into my blood, so to speak. Maybe the first attempts to do this were good, but when the aim of those around me was to discourage me and also when it meant I could not be true to my own nature – which made it all the worse considering that Nature has been quite generous to me – then, all too easily I dropped my arms and gave up fighting for a cause which has been denied me. . .

When in the last decade of his abbreviated life, having attained a greater measure of success and far more approbation than is the lot of most people, were there ever moments when these submerged anxieties – about not belonging and of being 'discouraged by those around me' – were involuntarily dredged up from the years when he found them disturbing enough to express himself in these rather desperate phrases?

One can only conjecture that, unless Kenneth Matchett and those who thought like him were being oversensitive, Silvestri himself must also have been aware of the coolness of what Matchett likes to call 'the very strong musical Establishment in London.' He explains:

> If you didn't fit, it didn't matter how good you were, you would get nowhere – and Silvestri was not a part of the Establishment. He gave wonderful performances, included a lot of British music in his repertoire, would cheerfully play with British artists and enjoy it, yet he was never quite accepted in certain circles.

Fourteen months after his appointment, the London-published magazine *Musical Opinion* was referring to Silvestri as being an 'unknown' conductor and, in answer to a stiff rejoinder from Matchett, the editor replied:

> The question I ask (and shall go on asking) is: 'Why was it necessary to go abroad for this appointment instead of giving it to an English musician?' . . . We had precisely the same business with [Karl] Rankl at Covent Garden, [Andrzej] Panufnik at Birmingham. . . And how does Mr Matchett know that a British conductor (had he been appointed) would not have achieved even better results than Mr Silvestri?. . .

He was still an alien and at least in some quarters remained the butt of British xenophobia.

The genesis of this prejudice, Matchett maintains, began even before Silvestri was appointed.

> The BSO had a very long history of supporting British artists and composers, going back to its foundation in 1893 by Sir Dan Godfrey. So there was great pressure to make it a British appointment. Sir Adrian Boult was very angry indeed with me for appointing Silvestri and sent me three letters, each one more irate than the one before. Who was I to judge the merits of conductors? Who did I think I was?

But at least these differences had their humourous side and Ken Matchett appreciated the irony of a sequel, some five years later, to the Boult *contretemps* over Silvestri's apppointment:

> I had persuaded the Gulbenkian Foundation to provide some money for a scholarship for young British conductors. I invited both Boult and Silvestri to be on the panel of this Gulbenkian Conductors Competition in which six young conductors had been shortlisted from the original total of 60 applicants. The purpose was to give an opportunity to a young conductor to work with the BSO for three years. Both Boult and Silvestri bent over backwards to be polite. It was all very comical because they obviously took totally different views of whoever was being discussed. I was sitting with them, thoroughly enjoying this ridiculous situation.

(But though Boult's and Silvestri's musical perceptions differed – inevitably given their totally dissimilar backgrounds – nevertheless there was mutual respect: Boult once remarked to a Bournemouth Symphony Orchestra player, on listening to Silvestri recording *In The South*, how Elgar would have approved; while, as we shall see, Silvestri in an interview in Romania, would make a complimentary reference to his English fellow conductor.)

In the event, no appointment at all was made. The following year, the same panel sat again and, this time, agreed to appoint the 27-year-old Nicholas Braithwaite to be the BSO's assistant conductor.

As a Romanian Neville Chamberlain might have put it in the 1950s, as far as his compatriots were concerned 'Britain is a faraway country about whose people we know nothing' and Silvestri, prior to his early visits, must have had the usual stereotypical preconceptions about them, including their alleged frigidity. In March 1958, that is over a year after his first UK tours, he was telling Radio Bucharest listeners that at the start of a concert with the LPO in Brighton he had had the impression that the audience was 'aristocratic and glacial,' yet the warmth of the demonstration at the end was 'almost Southern in its effervescence.'

At this same concert an even more surprising thing happened, according to Costi himself: in the interval after the playing of the Dvorak *Ninth Symphony*, a message 'from the audience' was brought to him saying they had been so impressed with *From The New World*, please, could they have a repeat instead of the rest of the programme as scheduled? He left his Romanian listeners (and us) in suspense as to what actually happened in the second half.

But at least this radio interview gives us a hint that Silvestri anticipated some glacial draughts in Britain and was all the more delighted when he was greeted with 'Southern' warmth.

Twice Anatol Vieru described him as 'a complex figure' and it would be brash to conclude that earlier uncertainties – about his career prospects and statehood – were altogether eliminated by recognition of his achievements with the BSO, the belated security provided by a British passport and the convivial atmosphere he found in Bournemouth. But undoubtedly all three made their respective contributions to his peace of mind.

At four he had still not seen his father

Costi with his mother Ana

Aloysius (Alois) Silvestri, Costi's father.

At 14, the boy had already been at the Târgu Mureș Conservatoire for five years and, in another two, he would be studying at the Bucharest Conservatoire

CHAPTER 3

BEATING TIME

When Alois (or Aloysius) Silvestri eventually came home from internment to his wife and five-year-old son, it was not to domestic bliss. Probably neither army life nor his short stay in Vienna had done anything to curb, far less cure, his predilection for the bottle – rather the opposite. We know nothing about the conditions in the internment camp in Romania, but if they were harsh or monotonous, Aloysius evidently meant to compensate for them when he came out. Whatever was the particular form of what has euphemistically been described as 'his gay life,' Ana decided not to put up with it.

After all, the time they had spent together as a married couple was at most one year; what opportunities, if any, they had had to meet even briefly between 1914 and 1918 must be conjectural but that they were scarce is certain and during that time Ana had the responsibility of bringing up the child.

Within four months of Romania having declared war in August 1916 on the side of the Triple Entente (France, Britain and Tsarist Russia), the combined German and Austro-Hungarian army, as well as Bulgars and Turks, had entered Bucharest and, in December, a German military administration was set up in the capital. Although the French-trained Romanian army carried on fighting, mainly in Moldavia, and even inflicted defeat on the combined German and Austro-Hungarian army at the week-long battle of Mără-şeşti in August 1917, the Russian collapse that year made it a forlorn fight: the Central Powers (Germany and Austria) forced the Romanians to capitulate in December 1917 and sign the Peace Treaty of Bucharest in May 1918.

However, six days after the final collapse of the Central Powers and the surrender of Austro-Hungary on November 3 1918, the Romanian army was mobilised again, the Germans given 24 hours to leave the country, and the army pursued the retreating enemy as far as the River Mureş in Transylvania. Even after the armistice was signed in Compiègne Forest and the First World War was over, demobilisation for the Romanians came much later than for soldiers of the other ex-belligerents.

That is the historical setting in which Costi lived the first years of his life. As for so many relationships, Alois's and Ana's marriage was doomed by the forced separation of military service and war. For the virtually single-parent Ana and her son, life – as for all Romanians save a few privileged, pro-German aristocrats – was exceptionally harsh. The Germans occupied three-quarters of the country and, in Bucharest, they requisitioned two-thirds of all stores; much of what was left had to be given up to the soldiers of occupation who could send home up to five kilos in food parcels. In the words of the American ambassador: 'One can imagine how the people live and suffer as they have no fuel to prepare their meals.' By the end of the war – and for some time afterwards – Romania was in a state of famine. Even ships bringing Australian wheat to Britain were diverted to Constanţa. Ana sought and obtained a divorce. She remarried in 1922. (Aloysius died in 1933 aged 59.)

For Costi to have recalled when he grew up that his father 'had a beautiful tenor' it is possible he had heard him sing, but more likely that he learned about it from his mother. Although Ana had also been an amateur singer, it was in those early years in Bucharest that his uncle-by-marriage, Joseph Prunner, seems to have had the most influence on the boy's musical education. He was the Austrian double-bass player who had married a sister of Ana. He had come to Bucharest from Vienna at the invitation of George Enescu and the cellist Dimitrie Dinicu in 1909 and for 60 years he was either playing in the Bucharest Philharmonic or teaching at the Conservatoire. (Prunner would die in the same year as Costi, 1969.)

Josef befriended the virtually fatherless boy, took him to concerts and to listen to the organ in church. It was in Prunner's house that the little boy first met Enescu and one would like to imagine that Costi's uncle took him to at least one of the nine concerts Romania's most celebrated musician conducted in Bucharest in 1921 – that is just before the boy left Bucharest – or even to the Opera as a New Year's Eve treat, to see Enescu conduct the newly-formed opera company in its first performance of *Lohengrin*.

After that, Enescu resumed his heavy schedule of concerts and recitals abroad as violinist, pianist and conductor. But Enescu, the composer, had already been working for some years on his *magnum opus*, the opera *Oedipe*, and this year, 1922, he would complete the final draft. Events 36 years later connected with *Oedipus* would either be the last straw which made Silvestri make the momentous decision to leave his country for good or, more likely, confirmed him in the wisdom of a decision he had already made.

In a letter to the musicologist George Breazul in 1932, Costi recalled:

I began [my music-making] by playing by ear on the piano the famous aria *La donna è mobile* from *Rigoletto* and then started to improvise on it. When I was five, I had my own first Euterpean notions. My lady teacher did not excel in erudition and I'm afraid the pupil himself was not over-diligent.

At first, little Costi had private lessons at home before he went, for two years, to a primary school in Bucharest. Then his life changed radically. In 1922 his newly-acquired stepfather, Thomas Cariade, was appointed Prefect of Târgu Mureş, a city in the heart of Transylvania in central Romania, and that is where Mrs Ana Cariade and her nine-year-old son, Costi Silvestri, found themselves for the next seven years.

Since at least the beginning of the 17th century when Michael the Brave proclaimed himself 'Prince of Wallachia [the province in which Bucharest is situated] Transylvania and all Moldavia,' the mixture of races in Transylvania – of Romanians, Hungarians, Saxons and others – had led to claims and counterclaims from Bucharest, Budapest and Vienna on this mountainous region lying inside the inverted 'L' of the Carpathians. At the end of the 17th century the Ottoman Empire, which continued its dominion over the Romanian principalities of Moldavia and Wallachia, was forced to give up Transylvania to the Austro-Hungarians under whose rule it remained, even after the rest of Romania succeeded in breaking away from the Turks and declaring its independence in 1877. But by siding with the ultimately 'victorious' Triple Entente in the First World War, Bucharest reclaimed Transylvania, which it always maintained had a majority Romanian population, and this was endorsed by the Allied powers under the Treaty of Trianon in 1920.

Cariade, the new prefect of Târgu Mureş in 1922, was presumably taking over from an administration which, since the suppression of the Hungarian revolution in 1849, had received its orders from the Governor whose residence was in Sibiu, an ancient town 40 miles to the south-west and he, in turn, had been appointed by and was directly subordinate to the Habsburg court in Vienna. Cariade, in contrast, would have been responsible to the Ministry of the Interior in Bucharest for the keeping of the peace by the, at that time, 36,000 population of Târgu Mureş, which was fairly equally divided ethnically between Romanians and Hungarians. It seems Tom Cariade was a kindly man who took his parental role seriously, was tolerant of the boy's piano playing although he had little taste himself for classical music, and introduced Costi to what would become one of his life-long interests, stamp collecting.

Standing today in the centre of Târgu Mureş (meaning market on the River Mureş) is the Palace of Culture, a many-storeyed building with a steep roof with multi-coloured tiles and an *art nouveau* interior, every square inch of surface area ornamented in some way: gilt scrolling and piping, murals and stained glass depicting Transylvanian history and mythology, and a

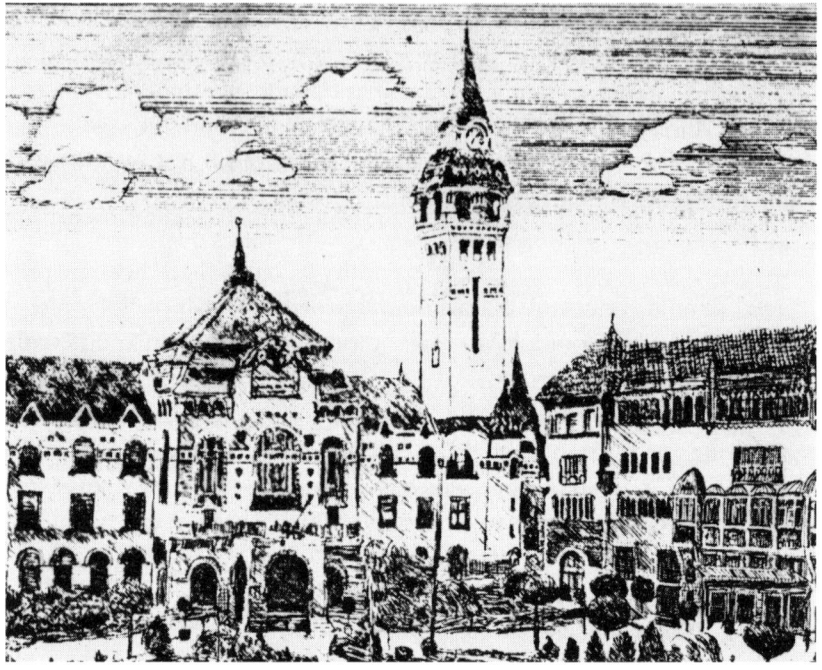

The Palace of Culture, Târgu Mureş, Transylvania. Built in 1913, the year Silvestri was born, it housed the Conservatoire where he gave his first public performance aged 11, and studied from 1922 to 1929

handsome marble staircase dominated by a window portraying Franz (or Ferencz in Hungarian) Liszt who stayed and played here. It has two smaller halls for *soirées* or recitals and a fine large hall housing an organ, claimed by the Târgu Mureş State Symphony Orchestra to be the finest in Romania.

The Palace was finished in 1913, the year Costi was born. It became the new home of the Târgu Mureş Conservatoire, founded in 1907. It was here, in rooms which today display an archaeological collection, that the boy continued his music studies; here, in the Great Hall, that he is said to have given his first public piano recital aged 11 and his first public improvisations; where he did his fourth-year piano exams and was declared top student; and where he learned to play the organ.

None of those who knew Silvestri in Romania have referred to his organ playing, but that a recording by the BBC was made in Bournemouth of him doing just that and is in the archives, we have the evidence of James Loughran, associate conductor of the BSO at the time (and subsequently principal conductor, first with the BBC Scottish Orchestra then with the Hallé). But because of the curious circumstances in which it was made, there will never be acknowledgement or proof that it is Silvestri playing the end of the Tchaikovsky *Manfred Symphony* in which either an organ or a harmonium can be used to suggest the benediction of the Church on the dying Manfred. Loughran tells the story:

> We did a BBC transcription of *Manfred* in the early days. I went to the recording performance in the Winter Gardens. When it was finished, Silvestri said to me: 'What did you think of the organ?' and I answered: 'Not very good, really.' So he said: 'Stay behind. Let's do it ourselves.' He waited until everybody had left except the BBC technicians and then, while he played the manuals, I got on my hands and knees and played the pedals – with my hands. That recording is at the BBC Transcription Services, but no one knows how the organ was played. Rather than embarrass the man who played it originally, Silvestri first sent everyone away. If you haven't played the organ for some time, you lose co-ordination of feet and hands. It had to be done for a broadcast and there was no time to practise, so he did the right thing – and it worked!

In Bucharest, I visited Judith, widow of the composer and musicologist Zeno Vancea who died in 1990 in his 90th year. Mme Vancea was a delicate-featured lady with silver hair drawn back in a pony tail. She entered her book-lined drawing room, with its pictures of Romanian Impressionists and a large bust of Beethoven on the baby grand, slowly on two sticks. For all her 81 years, she proved a lively, lucid *raconteuse* of the friendship between her husband and young Silvestri, punctuated with spontaneous laughter and stopping now and again to focus on lighting a cigarette. This is her account of the beginning of the friendship between Zeno and Costi.

Zeno's brother-in-law, Maximilian Costin, was the director of the Târgu Mureş Conservatoire (and would subsequently become administrative director of the Opera in Bucharest) and his wife, Olga, also taught there. They became friendly with the Cariades and it was through his sister, Olga, that Zeno met Costi, then 12 years old. Zeno himself was 24, professor of harmony and theory, and he noticed the boy had a perfect ear for music and was keen to learn. Zeno started to teach him composition and general musicianship and found him very talented. Max Costin initiated him into music theory and the organist Zsizsmann in harmony.

At first Ana and her husband were apparently not too keen on the idea that Costi should pursue his musical studies with the aim of making music his career; they wanted him to become a lawyer. Through Olga's persuasion, a compromise seems to have been reached: he would continue to study music but also have a general education. As Judith Vancea put it: 'He was captivated by music,' got his distinction in harmony and composition, including a choral piece, and when he was 15 passed with honours one of the advanced courses at the Conservatoire.

Perhaps the Cariades were also influenced by praise from the esteemed professor of music at the Conservatoire, Arpad Laszlo, who, though he did not actually teach Costi, followed his career closely and was very happy with his playing. 'This boy will really become somebody one day,' he told Costi's stepfather.

For seven years Laszlo had been a pupil of Anton Dvorak, when he was director of the New York Conservatoire. The Czech composer had been so impressed with Laszlo that he paid his Conservatoire tuition fees which were quite high and beyond the young man's means. It was because of this relationship with Dvorak that Laszlo used to expatiate to Costi on the *New World Symphony*. Perhaps when Silvestri was rehearsing with the French National Radio Orchestra for the recording which would win the Charles Cross Prize in 1957 he passed on to them some novel aspect of *From The New World* which had been revealed to him in these talks with the erstwhile student of Dvorak.

Laszlo had also at some period in his career been a student of Liszt. He became Professor of Piano at the Budapest Conservatoire. His fame as a teacher at Târgu Mureş was recognised by Enescu himself who, when Laszlo reached the stipulated age of retirement and was forced to do so, would protest that young people would be deprived of a superb teacher.

When Enescu came to Târgu Mureş for a concert, he was invited to the Conservatoire where eight boy pianist students had been selected to play to him. (Perhaps it was thought there were no young fiddlers good enough to perform before such a celebrated violinist.) Costi, in his shorts, big white starched collar and navy blue cravat, played a Chopin mazurka and waltz which earned from Enescu a prediction similar to the one Laszlo had made: that the boy Silvestri had a brilliant future ahead of him.

Musicologist Teodor Bălan, who would describe Costi as 'my oldest friend,' first met him in Târgu Mureş when he was about 12 years old and, five years after Silvestri died, he recalled some of the characteristics of the boy who was indeed to have a brilliant future.

'Even at that age,' Bălan remembered,

*Statue of George Enescu
in the Museum of Art,
Bucharest.*

*In a testimonial preserved in the Târgu Mureş Palace of Culture, Enescu wrote: 'I
always feel a special pleasure in citing the Târgu Mureş Conservatoire as the one
which has so many eminent teachers – each of them really distinguished. For this
country it is unique.'*

Costi's knowledge of music revealed precocious maturity and his sound was crystal clear and transparent. Every term there was a competition in the Conservatoire for the students of that particular year. The jury would listen to them from behind a screen, but they always recognised Costi's tone immediately – and he was always the winner.

Bălan, too, is dead and there is no telling how much of his appraisal of the boy Costi is a hostage to hindsight; or he may even have felt under constraint to qualify his otherwise laudatory appreciation of the man who, in the regime's eyes, had defected from his country. It is with that caution in mind that we should assess Bălan's opinion of his fellow student of over 40 years earlier:

> Costi's character was quite bizarre and so it is not surprising he had so few friends. . . He was suspicious of anybody who would praise him, especially if it were exaggerated, though he confessed to me more than once that he liked it and was flattered by it.

The process of estrangement between his parents; adjusting to his mother's new man-friend and, subsequently, husband; the news of his father's death; the move to an entirely strange environment where, even after three years at the Conservatoire he still only knew three other boys from his own province of Wallachia and where communications with his mainly Hungarian-speaking teachers was through German – all these had been trying experiences for a sensitive lad.

Although to his friend Bălan, Silvestri, now in his early teens, generally had a meditative air which made him seem withdrawn, even aloof, and more mature than his years, he enjoyed some sports including gymnastics. Self-conscious about his below-average height, he hoped these would help him grow and he evinced a strong competitive instinct. He had always been particularly fond of swimming, though it is odd that no one has made any mention of Silvestri's claim (made to Australian journalists in 1959) that he was 'breaststroke champion of Romania' in 1927 (when he was only 14). Nor is there any evidence that he was president of a sports association, as he is supposed to have told journalists in Bournemouth.

After he died, a former pupil wrote an unsigned memoir entitled 'Silvestri Conductor and Teacher,' in which he claimed he once made Costi a present of a fishing rod just to remind him of his predilection for telling 'fishermen's stories'. These included, the article alleged, a claim that he had conducted the whole of the Bruckner cycle in Vienna 'about 1930 or before when, if you think about it, he was probably wearing short trousers, and that he had obtained the best results in some medical exams.' The writer added he was sure Silvestri himself came to believe in the authenticity of these stories and that, at any rate, no one objected to them because they were told with such an air of 'almost baronial authority.'

Whether or not getting very cold swimming in the Mureş for too long had anything to do with it, Costi developed pleurisy and at this period began having above-normal temperatures from time to time, a phenomenon which would occur throughout his life. Sometimes when this happened in Târgu Mureş he would take his friend, Bălan's, hand and inquire with a quizzical smile: 'Reckon it's over 38?' (Normal body temperature is 36.6° Celsius.)

His Romanian biographer, the late Eugen Pricope, who had conversations with Ana Cariade before she died, says she used to reward Costi for playing the piano to the young ladies of Târgu Mureş after they had finished their ballroom and folk dancing lessons, proficiency in which was considered a social necessity; and with this and other pocket money which he had to 'earn' he bought stamps for his collection, paraphernalia for fishing – another lifelong pastime which originated in Târgu Mureş – gramophone records, and chemicals for his lab which he set up in the loft of his home.

In 1929, when Costi was 16, the Cariades returned to Bucharest. Not long afterwards his stepfather died and, with Ana, he went to live in the same area near the Opera where he was born.

The following year he passed his baccalaureat at the St Sava Lycée, but with very modest marks – for instance, he got only five out of 10 for Romanian grammar and apparently with many spelling mistakes, according to Bălan. That is hardly surprising since, as we have seen, his teaching at the Târgu Mureş lycée was a mixture of Hungarian and German. On the other hand, he does not seem to have worked very conscientiously at this Bucharest lycée, preferring to invite his musician friends home and playing on the upright piano until the small hours – a cigarette usually dangling from the corner of his mouth – instead of preparing for the next day's lessons. But he did attend lectures by such distinguished musicologists as Mihail Jora, who was then music director at the Romanian Radio, Emanoil Ciomac, artistic director of the Bucharest Philharmonic, and George Breazul, a music historian at the Bucharest Central Seminar.

It was in a letter to Breazul in October 1932, that is two years after he had entered the Bucharest Conservatoire, that Costi explained: 'For the moment I follow the necessary courses in composition and conducting (which is my principal aim). . .' He was studying composition with composer Dimitrie Cuclin; fugue-counterpoint, harmony and composition with Jora, and folklore with the composer Constantin Brăiloiu, leading exponent and author of many works on the subject. 'In parallel with music,' he told Breazul, 'I follow law in which I am in the third year' – the last we hear of that from any source.

He had passed the exams for entry into the Conservatoire (in a few years to be renamed the Royal Academy of Music and Dramatic Art) both in theory and practical (for which he played the Beethoven *Appassionata*). Aged 17, he was immediately accepted into the fourth year and became a pupil of the famed and formidable Professor Florica Musicescu who was already teaching Dinu Lipatti, four years Costi's junior. They became good friends, but while Dinu was super-conscientious and attended the Conservatoire with clockwork regularity, Costi was more laid-back, had difficulty in accepting Musicescu's iron discipline – which he styled 'military' – and attended only when he felt like it. To his friends he justified this attitude with: 'Why should I kill myself with so many exercises, scales and technique when my fingers know how to play by themselves?' For him, expression and colours had priority.

It was a long time before he could be persuaded to take the exams to obtain his diploma because, as he explained, he wanted to be a composer and did not understand why he needed a piece of paper endorsing the fact that he could compose.

Even if Costi gave the impression that he was something of a law unto himself, this did not conflict with the view that he was a hard and methodical worker, in his own way, and lived modestly. (Uncle Prunner helped with the fees, but the sole income of his mother with whom he lived was her pension.)

Bălan, who had followed him to the Conservatoire, recalls:

His room was a model of tidiness, with everything meticulously classified. We were amazed how this young man, who was just 20, could have collected such a huge library of records and scores. He had exercise books in which he noted all the different performances of works to which he listened and the exact length of time of each one. He had his own markings which no one else understood. He also had this passion for stamp collecting which I think showed his need to put things in order, classify and label.

While Costi was still formally a student he considered himself a fully formed musician. He was giving public concerts in the Dalles Hall and the Athenaeum and building his reputation for improvising for which he would soon become renowned. In Mozart's time improvising was not unusual and even in the early 20th century musicians with a high standard of composition

Nineteen, and friends with Dinu Lipatti, four years his junior. Both were being taught by the formidable Professor Florica Musicescu. Silvestri had already decided 'my ultimate aim is the baton and composition'

and organists – Debussy and Ravel for example in Notre Dame in Paris – used to improvise on themes given them, even coalescing two themes in juxtaposition. But because it was such a novelty in Romania, people flocked to these performances by Silvestri where members of the audience would hand him themes, sometimes written on blank spaces on scraps torn from newspapers. He would improvise on these in the style, for instance, of Chopin, Schumann, Reger, Wagner or Debussy and, particularly in the Dalles Hall, mostly Bach and Beethoven. His friend Dorin Speranția recalls how, at a party, he even improvised on a phone number (23411) in the style of Chopin, César Franck, Debussy and Romanian folk idiom. Judith Vancea recalls that Enescu came to one of these performances in 1941 and after Costi had as usual improvised in the style of various composers, he asked him: 'And now, what about doing something in the style of Silvestri?' And in one day he is supposed to have composed two sonatas: for *Bassoon and Piano* (Op.22) and for *Clarinet and Piano* (Op.23 No. 1).

When Costi was well into his conducting career, Anatol Vieru was at one or two of his last performances as a pianist when

he would perform his own works, then ask the audience to give him themes on which to improvise. I remember once he did this at a special concert for leading members of the new Union of Composers that replaced the old one after the war. He not only improvised in the style of composers like Beethoven or Verdi, but also imitated the styles of his contemporaries like Zeno Vancea, Alfred Mendelsohn and Hilda Jerea. Why I remember this so well is because I was 24, at the very beginning of my career, and had composed a cantata for orchestra and choir (*Mierla lui Ilie Pintilie*). Silvestri did my 'portrait' as well – and not a flattering one by any means. For me it was something of a self-revelation, as if I was looking into a mirror and seeing my music for the first time. It was frightening.

Poetess, composer, translator Nina Cassian (Anatol Vieru wrote a cantata to her verses and she translated *Twelfth Night* into Romanian) attended many of Silvestri's piano recitals in the Dalles Hall, Bucharest, and reviewed some of them. In one of these, in February 1947, she wrote:

His fantastic pianistic verve and agility, the tones and nuances he produces have won and are still winning him standing ovations, an honour which in Romania is only accorded visiting artists who bring with them their prestige and the aura of an established reputation. . . In all the improvising recitals at which I have been present, Silvestri has succeeded in producing a performance of high artistry – an artistry of only a few minutes duration but evidence of a prolonged routine or a miraculous musical sense and of the free-flowing intelligence of the artist.

Over forty years later, Nina Cassian's admiration had not waned. During a stop-over at Heathrow returning from Bucharest to her home in New York, she confirmed:

His improvisations were really incredible, not only for their virtuosity – which it was of course – but for the capacity of imagination and for building several universes. He would start with a simple, sometimes dull, theme like *Come with me, maid, to the hillside vineyard*, a quasi-folksong which had already been altered by some cheap arrangement, and then provide us with scores of variations which Beethoven himself might have envied.

The conductor Mircea Cristescu told me that one of his earliest recollections of Silvestri was turning pages for him at *soirées* in his own uncle's home where Bucharest's musical personalities, including Enescu and Lipatti, used to gather. (The uncle, although a businessman, became Enescu's private secretary and remained so when they left for Switzerland in 1948.) At one of these *soirées* Silvestri asked the visiting cellist Italian-born Antonio Janigro, who was then head of the advanced cello class at Zagreb University, if they could do the Saint-Saëns *Cello Concerto* together, to which the cellist replied that unfortunately he did not have the piano reduction with him. Silvestri said never mind, and proceeded to accompany Janigro from beginning to end of the concerto from memory.

Cristescu also remembered hearing Nicolae Kirkulescu playing one of his own works and Silvestri immediately improvising on it. Kirkulescu was 12 years older than Costi, composed for the theatre and films and put scores of lyrics to music.

Silvestri the improviser was also vividly remembered by composer Radu Paladi, now a benevolent sexagenarian with a halo of white hair and Gladstonian whiskers; but in 1943 when he first met Costi he was an impressionable 16-year-old who had come all the way to Bucharest from the little town of Storojinets in North Bukovina (since 1940 part of the Ukraine) and was already a little bemused by the big city. He had passed the entrance exam for the Conservatoire and his request to study under the famed Musicescu had, to his delight, been granted.

Within two days of arriving in Bucharest, I was invited to Madame Musicescu's home for a lesson and that, too, was a surprise. The lesson took place and I was just about to take my leave when Silvestri arrived and Musicescu told me to stay.

Silvestri had two reasons for coming, I would learn. First of all, he had come to report on his conducting the Berlin Philharmonic at a festival put on by or for the Wehrmacht magazine *Signal*. He showed us a photo of himself conducting the Brahms *First Symphony* and was obviously very proud of having conducted Furtwängler's famous orchestra.

The 'Iron Lady' was in a very good mood that day, which I would come to learn was unusual. But I think she treated Silvestri differently from other pupils; she often put Lipatti to shame in front of the others and also treated Mîndru Katz [the pianist who emigrated to Israel in 1958 and died playing on stage] harshly. But she was not so strict with Silvestri. I think she could see that he was more likely to make a career as a conductor than as a pianist.

It was rare for her to make concessions for anybody, but in fact she did give Costi 'special treatment.'

Anyhow, I was so embarrassed at being in the presence of such famous personages that I wanted to leave, but Musicescu insisted I stay and treated us as equals in the service of music. Costi was totally at ease and produced a sheaf of papers from his case, placed them on the music rest, sat down and began to play his *Piano Sonata No 3* [Op.24]. This was the second reason for his visit.

All the while, I had been sitting still and not saying a word, overawed at this marvellous event: not only had I had my first lesson with the renowned Musicescu, met the already famous Silvestri, but actually heard him play one of his own works which he had just composed and never played in public. When he'd finished, Musicescu said to him: 'Costi, look at this young man – he also has a gift for improvisation' and then she turned to me and said: 'I will give you a theme and I want you to improvise on it.' When I'd finished, she told Costi to improvise on the same theme – and the man who had just conducted the Berlin Philharmonic and played one of his own creations was asked to improvise in front of me, a young greenhorn from Bukovina. And he did, without hesitation as if it were a most natural request. It made me feel as if I were one of the family – a family of musicians.

Radu Paladi also recalled that he went to one of Costi's last recitals at which he improvised and someone in the audience, probably a 'plant,' passed him up a request to improvise on a theme in Shostakovich's *Seventh Symphony*, the 'Leningrad.' This Silvestri did in the manner of a fugue and everyone was amazed because, though first performed in Russia in 1942, it was still little known in Romania.

Whether indeed Florica Musicescu 'treated Silvestri differently,' testimony to her undoubted esteem for him is given by another of her pupils, the Romanian-born composer and orchestrator Marius Constant who lives in Paris, the collaborator with our Peter Brook in *The Tragedy of Carmen* in the Eighties and, more recently, in *Impressions de Pelléas*:

I first met Silvestri in about 1944 when I started at the Conservatoire in Bucharest. He was finishing playing a piece in a competition and Musicescu said to me: 'Listen to this man, he is great. Let him be an example for you.' For me the two greatest examples of piano players were Lipatti and Silvestri. I now realise the school of Musicescu was something fantastic. . .

In the mid-1930's Silvestri the pianist often performed with Theodor Rogalski – in 1936, for example, they played the Bach C major Concerto for Two Pianos with the Bucharest Philharmonic conducted by Ionel Perlea.

On at least one occasion, Silvestri the improviser caused problems for Silvestri the concert pianist. He was conducting from the keyboard Handel's *Concerto Grosso in B minor* Op.6 No. 12 which, at one point provided him with the opportunity to play a cadenza and indulge his talent for improvising. But he got so carried away with his modulations and harmonies that he could not get back to 'Handel.' Eventually, he decided to strike a dominant chord, stayed on it for a while and then gave a sign to the orchestra to come in.

It was not the fashion in Romania at that time to play and conduct at the same time, but Silvestri was hardly one to be inhibited by convention. Towards the end of his life he confided in pianist Peter Frankl why he had suddenly stopped doing this: he claimed he had actually played and conducted the Brahms *B flat Concerto* some 20 years before in Romania – something probably never attempted before or since – and he admitted it was a total disaster, 'the biggest in my life' (a phrase he grew rather fond of.) He vowed there and then he would never again conduct and play at the same time.

Silvestri's career as a concert pianist continued until after the end of the war, broadcasting over Radio Bucharest, sometimes playing his own works and frequently performing with Theodor Rogalski. In one of his last piano performances, in November 1945, he played the Bach *C major Concerto for Two Pianos* with Rogalski and the Radio Symphony Orchestra – a repeat of the performance they had done together nine years before with the Bucharest

Silvestri with Ionel Perlea
and Romanian pianist
Magda Nicolau

Philharmonic conducted by Ionel Perlea. (Rogalski, one-time pupil of Vincent d'Indy, also became a full-time conductor and Perlea won a reputation conducting in the USA.) That this concert, in February 1936, was the only engagement Silvestri had with the Philharmonic as a pianist is not surprising when it is realised that keyboard performers of world repute were playing with this orchestra – some of them several times during this period – such as Alfred Cortot, Rudolf Serkin, Claudio Arrau, Wilhelm Kempff, Arthur Rubinstein, Robert Casadesus, Wilhelm Backhaus, Walter Gieseking and Silvestri's compatriots, Clara Haskil and Dinu Lipatti. In fact, one writer in a musical magazine in April 1937 actually stated: 'Young Romanians are not playing in public any more because they are intimidated by the big names from the West' and in addition to some of the pianists mentioned above he added the cellist Pablo Casals and violinist Jacques Thibaud.

In the same letter he wrote to George Breazul in October 1932, Silvestri confided: 'My ultimate aim is the "baton" and composition, which so far have provided me with some welcome successes.'

He was presumably only referring to his compositions (up to this time they included his *Jeux d'enfants* suites and the *Bihor Dances*), for if he also meant conducting 'successes' what these can have been is something of a mystery. Claims made on his behalf in the West in later years that his conducting début was 'in a series of concerts with the Radio Symphony Orchestra' in 1930 with a programme that included *Le Sacre du Printemps* and a work by Bartók – that is, when he was only 17 and working for his baccalaureat – cannot be substantiated in the Radio's records. Bălan refers to a 'spectacle' concert two years later, that is in 1932, which again is supposed to have included works by Stravinsky and Bartók. 'Spectacle' presumably means that there was a visual aspect to the concert, perhaps a scene from the Stravinsky ballet. Silvestri would have been 19, but again there is no record in the Radio's archives of such a concert, even at this later date. In fact, these records show that up to 1935, Silvestri's radio performances were solely as a pianist and in March of that year what appears to be the first time he conducted the Radio Symphony Orchestra was a performance of his own *Five Capriccios* Op.10 for which he had won the Second Enescu Prize the previous year.

The next reference to him conducting the RSO is in March 1939 when he was one of three composers conducting first performances of their own works in a concert in the Athenaeum under the auspices of the Association for New Music. Silvestri conducted Filip Lazăr's *Music for Radio*, a Scarlatti *Bagatelle* orchestrated by Rogalski, one of his own *Concerti Grossi* Op.14 and *Three Grostesque Dances* from his friend Zeno Vanceas's ballet, *Priculiciul* (The Goblin). In a letter to Zeno, he said he had found many literal errors in the manuscript which he had corrected and 'you can rest assured everything is as it should be.' He added:

> I also think the parts for the orchestra are full of errors, which means it will take me a long time to correct and we only have two rehearsals for the whole concert and that gives little chance for a good result when so many works are being given their first performance – and all of them in manuscript!

It was not until the following month, April 1939, that, apparently for the first time, Silvestri was the sole conductor of a complete concert on the Radio. He was not quite 26.

Progress on the conducting front was going to prove slow and very frustrating. It was a paradox that his success as a pianist and composer militated against him getting conducting engagements because he was stereotyped as either one or the other and not thought of as a conductor.

When he was 22 he at last succeeded in getting work as a *répétiteur* at the Opera, which no doubt was a help financially and he evidently thought it would mean getting a toe in the door that might open to future conducting. In the long run he was right, but to a young man confident in his own potential it seemed a very long run indeed. In fact, it was nine years later, in October 1944, that he addressed the following complaint to the Opera managment:

> I was engaged [as *répétiteur*] after being rejected for three years, although those who were chosen instead and given conducting engagements are no longer with the Opera. After two years [i.e. 1941] and a lot of pressurising on my part, I was at last given run-of-the-mill productions and even one first performance.

In spite of this, I remained a *répétiteur* for another two years and on the same salary. Because of this injustice, I was obliged to hand in my resignation and only then did the director recognise my just deserts, but because he didn't have a conducting post to offer me, nor the resources (as is always the case), I was given the additional job of librarian.

Constantin Petrovici, today a conductor at the Opera, explained that at the time Silvestri was making his complaint there were three conductors at the Opera, all senior to him and so he was given only light opera to conduct, such as the Hungarian composer Heinrich Berte's operetta *Das Dreimäderhaus* (The House with Three Daughters) based on Schubert melodies and which was supposed to depict episodes in Schubert's life.

The conductor and composer Constantin Bugeanu also confirmed that when Silvestri was *répétiteur* at the Opera he

wasn't taken seriously and was given only insignificant operas to conduct. But I became very interested in him after we had a talk about *La Bohème*. I was impressed with how well he judged and analysed his tempi. For, in the Opera in those days, there was a very amateurish atmosphere and conductors were learning the music by ear and not looking at the score.

Bugeanu added that even George Georgescu, the most successful conductor in Romania at that time, used to come to rehearsals at the Opera and learn by ear as the *répétiteur* played operatic scores on the piano. 'Georgescu was a diletantte with no knowledge of harmony or composition and Silvestri was the only one who knew harmony and musical forms,' Bugeanu maintained. 'Like me, Silvestri believed that one couldn't become a truly professional conductor without mastering composition.'

But Costi's most bitter and explicit catalogue of reproaches was in a memorandum to the Romanian Musicians' Union in September 1945. This concluded:

Up to 1935, though I had given numerous concerts, won a George Enescu prize and many of my compositions were known throughout the world, performed by Hermann Scherchen, Lotte Lehmann and Felix Borowski, I couldn't get any position in any institution in my own country. With great difficulty I managed to get taken on at the Opera. Symphony concerts were categorically denied me; only after dozens of memoranda was I allowed to conduct a few concerts – *and that did not happen until 1941*. [My italics J.G.] Since then, both the Radio and the Philharmonic have closed their doors on me – as composer, pianist and conductor. At the Opera my salary was reduced four times. From the artistic point of view – well, that's not even worth mentioning: I was conductor of matinées and cheap productions turned down by my colleagues. In order to live, I was forced to sell my piano – yet Toscanini was conducting some of my works and, at the same time, they were being printed in America. . .

It is a pity, at least for posterity, that he was not more specific about which of his compositions had been performed, 'up to 1935,' by Hermann Scherchen, the violist and conductor who left Germany in 1933 to conduct music courses and summer classes in Switzerland; which of his *Lieder* were sung by the renowned Wagnerian soprano Lotte Lehmann; or which of his (presumably) works for strings were performed by the English-born composer and violinist Felix Borowski, who was by then in the US writing music reviews for the *Chicago Sun*. And would not the Musicians' Union have been more impressed if he had given the titles of his works Toscanini was supposed to have conducted?

In May 1939, he had written to his friend and former teacher in Târgu Mureş, Zeno Vancea:

Dear Zeno, thank you very much for inviting me to your place. However, I don't think I will be able to leave Bucharest. I have to stay here so that I can conduct and play as many times as possible at the Radio. I am in an ex-tremely difficult financial situation. I have been fighting for years the criminal irresponsibility of those leading the destinies of Romanian music, those who grab for themselves salaries of some 60,000 to 70,000 lei per month for three or four sinecure posts. Of course, they make out that others, especially the young ones, are useless and put all possible barriers in their way. Yet these last are precisely the ones who are doing the work; apart from [Mihail] Jora, [Sabin] Drăgoi and [Mihail] Andricu, all the others are utter musical nonentities.

Very recently, I wrote a memorandum to the King, but unfortunately it fell into the hands of the very people I was criticising – so you can imagine what good relations I am in now with everybody!

Yet, in another letter to Zeno little more than six months later (November 1939) he was writing:

Recently I have had a remarkable success conducting in the Opera House Puccini's *Gianni Schicchi*. This is one of the most difficult works, for ensemble and precision, with very difficult bars. It attracted to the

One of Silvestri's letters to his composer friend Zeno Vancea.
Dated November 8, 1939, this page reads:

Lately, though I promised Mr Stamatopol to send you a few lines, I didn't keep my word because of so many activities taking up my time. Apart from being a conductor and a répétiteur at the Opera, part of the time I dedicate to the piano – I had two concerts on the Radio with music by Brahms (Intermezzi and Capricci) – then there were Enescu's concerts and, of course, no musician could miss rehearsals for those. Finally, I had to correct the last suite by Enescu, a task that took me nearly one month to do. Only five minutes ago, I finished the last line of thousands of pages which I had revised and now I'm hastening to write to you.

From what I've heard, you didn't receive my three consecutive letters about the concert with the new music...

première all the musicians, including George Enescu himself, so now I am definitely known as a conductor for the future.

Then in the same letter his mood changes abruptly:

Unfortunately, my rosy future about which everyone talks is for me a chimera. I think very soon I will abandon the lyre for something more prosaic but more rewarding.

I hear you have a project for a concert in Bucharest. Write and tell me about it. But I warn you from the start not to risk your money. In Bucharest the only successful concerts are those with Enescu and everybody else's attempt [to put on a concert] results in certain fiasco.

In a postcript he wrote: 'The concert in Venice, though announced with cymbals and trumpets, fell through because of the events.' [The outbreak of the Second World War.]

There was more to Costi's jeremiads than frustration at the tardiness of effective recognition of his conducting talents. His fellow student at Târgu Mureș, Teodor Bălan, had remarked even then, as we have seen, how he had been afflicted with bouts of pleurisy; by the time he was in his early twenties, a doctor strongly advised him to get some mountain air into his lungs and to have a long stay in a sanatorium. He chose the one at Geoagiul de Jos and later confessed to Bălan: 'I went there with the thought of never coming back.'

It is a token of the esteem in which Silvestri was held by Mihail Jora that the 47-year-old professor of harmony, counterpoint, fugue and composition at the Bucharest Conservatoire and shortly to be its rector – Anatol Vieru described him as Romania's 'Pope of composers' – continued to receive by post from Geoagiul all the young man's manuscripts so as to read and where necessary correct them. Even more exceptional was his kindness and generosity in regularly sending Costi every month 5,000 lei towards the cost of his health cure. Perhaps being someone who had known physical pain himself – wounded in the First World War, his leg was amputated without an anaesthetic and he had a wooden leg – he had that little extra compassion for a fellow sufferer. Costi only agreed to accept this bounty after a great deal of persuasion.

In March 1938 Jora wrote to Costi:

At last I have received news from you. . . Your physical condition is such that it will take more than a month or two for you to recover. You have to have the willpower to get better at any price and to look on the bright side. We have shown how we are supporting you, but we also need your co-operation. 'Stand easy!' Put aside all your disappointments, mistrust and black thoughts! Stay there for at least another year, without worrying. Just look after yourself and get better – for your career's sake you will have to keep healthy. Please don't feel guilty and oppose our decisions which have been made with your best interests at heart. Put aside any childish pride and scruples. . .

From Jora more advice in similar vein came a few months later:

> I am pleased to hear your health is improving. . . In your isolation, don't work yourself up into a state, because it will only put back your recovery by several weeks.

Two years pass and, on March 5 1940, Silvestri was writing from the Baron Bruckenthal Sanatorium at Avrig near Sibiu to George Georgescu, at this time director of the Opera, pleading for an extension of his leave because

> I need many, not just one or two, months of rest: the shock I suffered some time ago (caused not through anything rash I did but because of the interruption of the treatment which I was not able to continue) brought about the state in which I am now.

He went on to explain that he needed another month to get over the influenza which he thought he had caught on the train journey on the way up to the sanatorium. He had been offered, he wrote, a job with a forestry company at Lainici on the River Jiu, with a five-year contract, a roof over his head and 11,000 lei a month; that this would be his 'only salvation' health-wise and that he had every right to accept it even if it meant tearing himself away from music, 'after 10 years' work, my health destroyed (not through work but through misfortune!) and faced with ruin – I even started to sell my library – and with very scant prospects for the future.'

He then explained to Georgescu how

> Maestro Jora came to my aid and if today I'm not yet in the 'world of absolute renunciation' I owe it entirely to him. Going around, hat in hand, he collected enough money for me to be able to stay seven or eight months in a sanatorium. The miracle of youth's resilience pulled me through; but I needed three years of total rest to recuperate fully.

But out of his salary of 7,000 lei he had had to pay doctor's fees of 3,000 lei and was obliged to return to Bucharest. 'Overwhelmed with debts,' he could not continue with the recommended treatment. 'You know the result: pleural shock, pleurisy – sputum.' He continued:

> Having gone around again with the plate, Jora insisted I should return to the sanatorium for a month or two (depending on my finances) to try and get well again. I don't know if you can understand the immeasurable gratitude I owe Mr Jora. He is more than my teacher or mentor – he is a father to me. Unfortunately, I don't owe anything to my country – one flower doesn't make a spring. . .

Costi added he only wanted to work loyally and earn enough to live on.

> I don't have sybaritic tendencies, but I cannot maintain my social situation on my current resources. . . It is not to my shame if I have to live on charity; nevertheless it is unbearable.

Then he struck his most despairing chord:

> Unfortunately, I can no longer foresee a future for myself as a conductor; I don't have faith any more in what I am capable of doing tomorrow.

If some of his expressions may sound on a par with the melodramatic libretto of one of the 'run-of-the-mill productions' about which he was so dismissive, it was not just because he wanted to impress his chief at the Opera with his feelings of frustration or to reinforce his request for a prolongation of leave. Viewed from the perspective of the letter he wrote three days later, his despair seems genuine enough. This time it was to his friend Zeno Vancea, from whom it could not be said he was seeking any favours; on the contrary, he was giving his friend information, encouraging on the whole, about the prospects of Zeno's ballet, *Priculiciul*, being staged at the Opera.

> As far as me conducting it, that is very problematical. I'm not at all well and I don't think I will be able much longer to make the effort of beating time. It's a shame, because I have prepared myself so seriously and thoroughly that I'm sure I could have had, with a lot of practice, a most successful career. It's not my fault I couldn't take care of myself when I should have done; on the contrary. . . 'But that's another story' as Kipling says. . . [Silvestri was quoting from Rudyard Kipling's story *Three and – An Extra* in his *Plain Tales From The Hills*.]

Not surprisingly, Zeno Vancea in his analysis of Silvestri's works, which he published nine years after his friend's death, wrote that some of them – specifically his *Six Concert Pieces* and his *Chants Nostalgiques* had an 'atmosphere of profound depression by which the composer was sometimes overwhelmed.'

On more than one occasion when Costi felt he was a victim of fortune's buffets, the wind suddenly changed and fortune brought him reward. Within only two months of him doubting whether he could 'beat time for much longer' – on May 2 1940 to be precise – he was conducting the Bucharest Philharmonic, his most important concert to date. This was in the Athenaeum, the capital's most prestigious concert hall, an impressive rotunda with huge murals depicting scenes from Romania's history, where he had often performed as a pianist and where he had conducted his own *Concerto Grosso* the year before. He was within a fortnight of his 27th birthday.

Eugen Pricope believed that he arranged the order of the works in the programme for this concert to create a sensation: instead of the convention of beginning with an overture followed perhaps by a new work and leaving the major item to the end, Silvestri the innovator introduced the programme with Bruckner's *Second Symphony* which took up the whole of the first half. After the interval, as if he intended it as contrasting light relief, he conducted a first performance in Bucharest of Bizet's *Jeux d'enfants*. Then, to create the maximum impression, his own *Prelude and Fugue* Op.17 No. 2 was performed where a major work is usually placed – an inspired piece of showmanship. The *Fidelio Overture*, contrary to all precedent, ended the concert almost as a lollipop.

His *Prelude and Fugue* (later renamed *Toccata*) would be played thereafter by the Bucharest Philharmonic on its foreign tours, by other Romanian orchestras, and Silvestri would introduce it to more than half a dozen countries (including, as we have seen, Japan where it seems to have had a rave reception).

It was nine months before he conducted his second concert with the Philharmonic: in a programme which included the seldom performed *Sixth Brandenburg Concerto* and a first performance in Bucharest of Mozart's *C major Symphony No. 28*. In a third concert with the Philharmonic, in June 1941, he again started the programme with the symphony (Brahms *Third*) and also directed from the keyboard Handel's *Concerto Grosso* – but this time with his cadenza under control.

In fact, between his first concert with the Philharmonic in May 1940 and 1946 he had a total of only 10 concerts and probably most of them in the 1945 season.

We can only conjecture what Silvestri's reactions were to an unusual, if not unique, programme decision George Georgescu made for a concert he conducted on February 1 1942. This consisted of Haydn's *'Surprise' Symphony*; Lalo's *Symphonie espagnole* and Respighi's *Pines of Rome*. But in addition Georgescu handed the baton to Silvestri to conduct the first performance of one of his own works: the *Concerto Grosso for Strings No. 2* – or rather, part of it, the adagio. Why only one movement? Did this imply misgivings on Georgescu's part about Silvestri's conducting expertise (although he had already conducted two concerts with the Philharmonic); or doubts about his composing ability?

And for his part, was Silvestri gratified that the public would at least hear part of a work he had composed four years before and that, hopefully, it would stimulate a desire to hear all of it? Or was there mute resentment at not being allowed to conduct the complete work? If so, it is very unlikely he would have dared express it, however mildly, to his boss at the Opera, his country's pre-eminent conductor and 26 years his senior.

What Georgescu's motives were can also only be conjectured: was the *Concerto Grosso* too long for a programme which already had two symphonies and another piece? Was there a risk of boring the audience if this unknown work of Silvestri were played in full? Was he critical of other parts of it? Or did Georgescu, at this early stage in Silvestri's conducting career already, perhaps only half-consciously, sense a potential rival who might move him from centre stage?

Today, several contemporaries testify to Georgescu's jealousy of the younger man and make comparisons between the two. If this did manifest itself later, there was at least one very cogent reason for it: a circumstance which, in 1942, neither Georgescu nor Silvestri could have foreseen. Fortune was again to smile upon Silvestri and it would be Georgescu who suffered the buffeting. But to understand the implications of this it is necessary to explain briefly Romania's position in the Second World War.

King Carol II of Romania (of Hohenzollern-Sigmaringen descent), who had set up a royal dictatorship in February 1938, visited London and Paris in November of that year in a vain attempt to obtain economic and military aid from Britain and France. Immediately afterwards, he paid an unofficial visit to Nazi Germany, met Hitler and Goering and, the following March, an economic treaty was signed which in effect was an attempt to subordinate Romania to the Third Reich. In April 1939 Britain and France gave guarantees to Romania (and Greece) to come to their defence if attacked, though with scant chance of these being effective. When Poland was invaded by the Nazis on September 1, by the Russians on the 17th, and carved up between them, Romania declared its neutrality. Its Prime Minister, who was opposed to Nazi expansionism, was assassinated on September 21 by the Iron Guard, Romania's fascists.

In June 1940, Stalin annexed the two Romanian provinces of Bessarabia and Northern Bukovina; in August, the Hitler/Mussolini Axis forced the Romanian Government (by now containing Iron Guard ministers) to surrender Northern Transylvania to the Hungarian dictator Admiral Horthy.

In September 1940, General Ion Antonescu became Romanian dictator and, supported by the Iron Guard and the Germans, forced King Carol to abdicate. His son, Michael, became king for the second time. (In 1927 the six-year-old Michael had succeeded his grandfather, Ferdinand – Carol having renounced his right to succession – but the boy king's reign, in effect that of a regency council, only lasted the three years until he was supplanted by his father in 1930.)

The Nazis invaded the Soviet Union in June 1941 and Romania, principally motivated by the urge to regain Bessarabia and Northern Bukovina from the Russians, found itself at war with all the Allies by the end of the year. When the Red Army counter-attacked at Stalingrad in February 1943, the Romanian army suffered very heavy losses. With the Germans in retreat, Antonescu and Hitler met for the last time in August 1944. By the end of the month, the Communists had established themselves in power in Bucharest; Antonescu and his ministers were arrested (and he was eventually executed in 1946); the Romanian army prevented a Nazi attempt to force a way into the capital and, as in the First World War, turned on the Germans, actually declaring war on Germany on August 23 1944, and with the Soviet forces went on to fight the Wehrmacht in Czechoslovakia and Hungary. (British newspapers splashed on Romania's declaration of war and in January 1945 a BBC commentator said it ranked fourth in the number of troops engaged in fighting the Nazis; 170,000 Romanian soldiers are said to have died in these operations.)

By December 1947 the monarchy was abolished, the King exiled – he made his home in Switzerland and not until 1997 was his Romanian passport returned – and the Romanian Communist Party general secretary, Gheorghe Gheorghiu Dej, was in effect in sole control of the country. Soviet troops remained on Romanian soil for years.

Silvestri's Romanian biographer discreetly makes no allusion to any of his visits to wartime Germany, Austria or Italy. Perhaps this was due to a lack of available information, but a curious omission nevertheless since, for instance, conducting the Berlin Philharmonic aged 29 is hardly an event to be ignored.

Silvestri himself must have approved and was evidently not ashamed of the publicity blurb issued by Columbia Artists in 1959 which included a reference to his visits to Düsseldorf in 1941, to Venice, Trieste and to Berlin in 1942 and to Vienna in 1943. These are presumably what was meant, in a brief sketch of his career by HMV/Columbia prefacing a list of his recordings published at the time of his BSO appointment, by: 'It was during the war years that he made his first appearance in Western Europe,' a transparently deceptive description of cities within the Hitler/Mussolini orbit. Moreover, in another surprising example of political naiveté, at least on the part of his agents, a blurb was issued in 1960 entitled *What The Press Says About Constantin*

Silvestri with 30 excerpts from the journals of seven countries, including one dating from the war years: a 'Press Communiqué' eulogising 'the young Romanian conductor's veritable triumph' during his tour of Italy in 1943. (This was the year in which Mussolini rejected the suggestion of Romanian Foreign Minister Mihai Antonescu that Italy should take the initiative in pulling out of the war, together with Romania and Hungary; the year in which the Allies landed in Sicily and southern Italy followed by the costly struggle northwards through the Nazi-occupied peninsula.) It would surely have been wiser to have omitted this gratuitous information about visits to countries at war with the Allies.

It was following the Berlin visit that he reported the occasion to Florica Musicescu and showed her and young Radu Paladi the photo of himself conducting 'Furtwängler's orchestra' at a concert for the German army. Anatol Vieru believes he also conducted for the Romanian-German Association in Bucharest.

Yet no one in the postwar Romanian Communist hierarchy appears to have thought any the worse of the young Silvestri for having made these professional visits to the Axis countries at the beginning of his career. Dinu Lipatti also played many times in Nazi Germany and its occupied territories, including seven German cities and Prague in January 1941 with Georgescu conducting the Bucharest Philharmonic; and recordings and recitals in Berlin, Leipzig, Bratislava and Rome in 1942 and 1943; and the following year he settled in Switzerland. Presumably, had such a talented young man remained in post-war Romania, these tours would have been overlooked by the regime, as were Silvestri's. It was a different case with George Georgescu.

After studying the cello in Bucharest and Germany, Georgescu had suffered an accident to his hand in 1916 and took up conducting under Richard Strauss and Artur Nikisch. He conducted the Berlin Philharmonic three times during the First World War.

In Hitler's Germany he conducted 15 times up to Romania entering the war in June 1941 and, after that until the end of the war, five times in Vienna (part of the Third Reich after the Anschluss) and also in Nazi-occupied Bratislava and Paris; twice in Mussolini's Italy and twice in Franco's Spain. (One allegation made to me that he had actually conducted in front of Hitler was discounted by two other sources who, independently of each other, maintained he was 'not important enough.') His nine-cities tour of Germany, Vienna and Prague in January 1941 was when Romania was still ostensibly neutral.

Nevertheless, when Georgescu returned from Madrid in June 1944, moves were already afoot to get Romania out of the Axis camp and, after this succeeded in August, he had no more concerts for nearly three years – at first, probably because of air raids on Bucharest and wartime rigours, but later he was officially banned from performing in public – a penalty he shared with Furtwängler, Knappertsbusch, Böhm and, of course, Karajan. The lifting of the ban was published on January 8 1947 under the heading in the Romanian press: 'Georgescu re-enters our musical life.'

There will never be consensus in the debate between those, on the one hand, who adhere from conviction to the view that classical musicians are a species above or at least removed from politics, that their exclusive dedication is to their art and their duty is to perform or compose for saints and sinners alike and all those in between (like Lipatti who once felt it necessary to proclaim: 'I have never been mixed up in any kind of politics') and, on the other hand, those who believe that musicians, too, are earthbound, should have a social conscience, should not feign ignorance of social injustices and state-sanctioned crimes and should abstain from performing before those who perpetrate them or their supporters.

Advocates of the latter view have criticised Strauss, Orff, Böhm, Furtwängler and others for continuing, even advancing their careers in Nazi Germany. Karajan in particular has been excoriated for attempting to conceal or condone his activities under the Nazis; while Erich Kleiber, who resigned as artistic director of the Berlin Opera because of Nazi interference, and Toscanini who took an anti-Fascist stand, have been praised.

However, the majority in all professions find the price for non-conformity under a totalitarian regime prohibitive and even for those who make some gesture of disapproval yet manage to survive, the strain is almost unbearable. Shostakovich said that before he wrote *Lady Macbeth of Mtsensk* he was 'a boy who might have been spanked and later I was a state criminal always under observation, always under suspicion' and even expecting execution, a fate which befell so many of his friends.

It is extremely unlikely that it ever occurred to Silvestri or Georgescu not to conform. Whether or not Georgescu's conducting in countries with fascist regimes, including his own, can be condoned, he was nevertheless penalised for it. No such ban was put on Silvestri who was, admittedly, much younger and conducted far fewer times – a maximum of five such concerts in Germany, Austria and Italy.

The only hint of Costi's political outlook around this time was given by Anatol Vieru:

We talked for six or seven hours in his house in 1946. We were not on the same wavelength as far as politics were concerned: whereas I was very left, he was nothing. He told me, for example, that he was equally attracted to communism as to fascism. For me this was scandalous. I don't know what he really knew about politics. I think he was a pragmatist. Perhaps he understood things I didn't understand.

That was perhaps another example of Costi's Puckish perversity: trying to shock this earnest young student, some-time composer of the hymn:

> *To Stalin, Stalin glory we sing*
> *In his path we surge, higher, ever higher*

Certainly Silvestri had demonstrated his 'pragmatism' in the previous year by taking advantage of an extraordinary change of fortune, one of those occasions just after he had given expression to his feeling of bitterness at his non-recognition by the Establishment. His memorandum to the Musicians' Union, already quoted, complaining that 'the Radio and Philharmonic have closed their doors on me' and 'I was forced to sell my piano,' was dated September 16 1945.

Exactly 34 days later he received a letter from Emanoil Ciomac, director of the Philharmonic, informing him that the Minister for the Arts had approved his appointment as a 'permanent conductor' of the orchestra. By 'permanent' was meant principal and indefinite. (Another conductor called Eduard Lindenberg was also made 'permanent conductor' at the same time but 'defected' to Paris and was not heard of in Romania again.)

Silvestri was 32.

Although the ban on George Georgescu's conducting was a political decision taken on high and for which Silvestri was in no way responsible, he was the one who benefited most from it and one can imagine the chagrin felt by the older man at this young upstart taking his place. It was all the more ironic in that Costi, in a letter to Zeno Vancea five years earlier, had remarked that 'some people, like Georgescu . . . appear to be encouraging me.'

In exactly two years' time the 'permanent conductor' of the Philharmonic would also become its director.

But in his letter to Breazul in 1932, it will be recalled, he had stated his 'ultimate aim' was composition (as well as 'the baton') and his development as a composer had been going on concurrently with these events.

CHAPTER 4

A 'MISUNDERSTOOD AVANT-GARDIST'

Years before Mihail Jora was writing to Costi in the sanatorium and advising him: 'Stand easy!' the wooden-legged professor was stumping across a lecture room floor in the Conservatoire and flinging one of Silvestri's compositions out of the window.

Costi was already a convert to atonality and, since his first opus, a cycle of *lieder* composed between the ages of 11 and 15 to verses of Heine, he had written fugues considered quite beyond the pale by the Conservatoire's professors*. Jora alone had been a little more tolerant, but on this particular occasion, it seems, the young man's latest creation had exceeded even Jora's threshold and he had threatened to expel him from his class. As the offending manuscript landed on the pavement, Jora is alleged to have exclaimed: 'That's the only place where such rubbish is fit for!'

In the opinion of Zeno's widow, Judith Vancea, Jora was one of a handful of 'old guard' composers who had an antipathy for and tried to stifle young and rising composers and it was only tardily that he began to accept Silvestri.

The *lieder* (Op.1, Parts 1–24) were revised six years later and Costi in a letter written to Zeno Vancea in December 1934 seems to have been asking his friend for suggestions which could inspire him to write more. (But, in fact, no more *lieder* would be published for another 19 years.)

> You know that I was always passionately attracted to songs, but up to now I haven't found a poet to my taste so I'll have to wait. You probably know German literature very well – please recommend something. I am only looking for something with a Heineesque atmosphere which I can put in a new setting, plucked from virgin terrain, of course unexplored so far by other composers. Just recently I revised some of my old *lieder* from the cycle of 24 on verses by Heine. They were composed [in 1928] partly in Târgu Mureş, partly when I came to Bucharest. Involuntarily, I was influenced by Schumann and Mendelssohn, with whom one shouldn't risk competition! But, in spite of this, I'll put them 'in circulation' in the hope that they'll be successful, which would be quite gratifying. I'll soon see.

* An analysis of Silvestri's works by Zeno Vancea is to be found in Appendix 2

In 1933, *Dances from Bihor* (a mountainous district in western Transylvania), which he had composed in 1929 when he was 16, were given their first performance in a programme devoted to works by Romanian composers of whom Silvestri was the youngest. The work is a suite of five dances: *Cine în lume nu are . . .* (They who don't have anything . . .), a melody from the village of Beiuş; a Mărunţel (a type of dance) from Beiuş; a Mărunţel from the village of Delan; a Mărunţel from Leleşd village; and *Cintec de joc* (a melody to which one can dance), also from Beiuş. In the same letter to Zeno, Costi explained the genesis of this work:

> Looking for a new formula, I went to a folk source. I took a few Bihor songs from Béla Bartók's collection. I kept them absolutely in their original form, plaiting over their elements the lace of a new composition with a very intellectual content. I attached to these new compositions the rhythms of the original folk songs and, moreover, I also underlined their phrasing. In such a juxtaposition they blend as if by fate. Because the so-called accompaniment is synthesised in a very concrete form, it could stay as an independent entity, with the potential of forming a composition which could be separated at any time from the folk song.

On the frontispiece of the original published Romanian score of the Bihor Dances is an acknowledgement by Silvestri: 'From Mr Béla Bartók's collection.'

Former principal conductor of the Bucharest Radio Symphony Orchestra Iosif Conta considers that Bartók succeeded in breaking down the hypothesis that Romanian folk tunes could not be developed into the classical forms invented by the German composers.

> Bartók knew what to take from folklore that could be transformed into classical form, recreating various folk motifs in, for example, his *Concerto for Orchestra* and *Cantata Profana* in which, incidentally, the names of the Romanian villages where he collected the folk tunes, especially near Turda, are mentioned in the score in Romanian. This proved how much could be done with Romanian folk music and how very rich it is. Bartók, and afterwards Silvestri, Theodor Rogalski and Paul Constantinescu proved that it was possible to develop this folk music in ways that have been appreciated far beyond the confines of Romania.

In contrast, Dvorak created his own tunes for his *Slavonic Dances*.

Judith Vancea remembers how much Silvestri admired Bartók and how for hours on end he and Zeno would analyse his works; in 1956, they went to

Budapest together for the Bartók Festival. Radu Paladi confirmed that Silvestri 'loved Bartók and Janáček.' Anatol Vieru said Costi had told him how his admiration went back to years before Bartók died (in 1945) but that he had qualified this with: 'I have always praised Bartók, but I don't believe he was such a great composer' – a view he seems to have revised in later years. Vieru also recalled a sarcastic remark of George Georgescu after Silvestri had conducted Bartók's *Music for Strings, Percussion and Celesta*: 'This is to Silvestri's taste – he likes music of the bones!' (Vieru added that examples of Georgescu's 'taste', as far as early 20th century composers were concerned, would be confined to works of Richard Strauss and Stravinsky's *Firebird*.)

Unlike the majority of Romanian composers, Silvestri in his later works used folklore only sporadically. The best known of those involving folk idiom are his *Three Pieces for Strings*, composed in 1932 and revised in 1950. The work was actually commissioned by the Union of Composers. The first and third piece have a dance character and the one in the middle is based on a *doina*, a folk song expressing sorrow and which in this case has the form of a *lied* with an exceptionally expressive melody. Although this has a folk character, it does not appear to have been borrowed from folklore but to have been the creation of Silvestri himself.

In another letter to Zeno, written shortly before the one already quoted, Costi informed him:

> A few days ago in the Enescu Prize competition you obtained First Mention with 3,500 lei. . . I can only give you my wholehearted congratulations.

Silvestri himself got joint second prize on this occasion in 1934, with 7,500 lei for his *Five Capriccios* (Op.10) which he dedicated to Jora. Dinu Lipatti got the first (honorific) prize.

George Enescu founded this competiton for composition in 1913 with money he set aside from his concerts. Its purpose was to encourage young musicians who, either from lack of funds or confidence in their own creations or with some other problem, were unable to continue composing. To be a classical musician in Romania required guts since music-making was conventionally associated with the way the gipsies played it; anyone taking it up as a career instead of a more lucrative and 'steady' occupation, was considered somewhat eccentric. The competition – the first prize had prestige value only or, as Silvestri called it, a 'Platonic prize,' but the rest were cash prizes – had given unheard of opportunities to the contemporary generation of Romanian musicians.

Silvestri had already got a first mention in 1932 for *Dances from Bihor*, the composition he did for his diploma; now, this Second Prize in 1934 for the *Capriccios*; then, in 1936, second prize again for his *String Quartet* (Op.16).

When Jora presented him with the first prize in 1937 for his *Cello Sonata* (Op.12), actually composed two years before, he drew attention to the fact that 'this young man was born in the same year the prize was founded.' According to his Romanian biographer, Pricope, he later burned this work because he was not satisfied with it. On the other hand, it is on the list of works which Silvestri himself drew up in Bournemouth, though indeed the manuscript has disappeared.

The same year (1935) that he composed the prize-winning *Cello Sonata*, he also composed the *Wind Quartet* (Op.13 No. 1) which was only given its first performance – not in Romania but by members of the Bournemouth Sinfonietta – in June 1993 as part of the Bournemouth Orchestras' centenary celebrations. So Silvestri got a total of four Enescu awards.

To return to the letter to Zeno: he went on to tell him he was surprised to hear that they had both been competitors and 'I didn't really think I would have such a serious rival.' Neither did he know that Lipatti was also competing.

> As you see, we musicians have started to understand modern music, even if the public hasn't as yet. I presented [for the prize] some *Capriccios for Orchestra and Voice ad libitum*. The music, as you see from the title, is ultramodern. On February 1 [1935] [Ionel] Perlea will conduct them at the Philharmonic and you could hear them on the radio if you are interested. They will be played by the orchestra without a singer . . . the canto remains *ad libitum*!

The *Five Capriccios* were listed as Opus 10 and in his next letter to Zeno he enclosed one of them, 'the shortest and simplest,' as an example, and developed the ideas behind its conception:

> You will see that in the first phrase, *poco joviale*, which becomes a fugato, the sentiment is quite desperate, in accord with the atmosphere of the song as a whole. The first verbal phrase of the song expresses only action, while the musical phrase attempts an ascent it cannot reach, resolving into a rather evasive question (bars 10 to 12).
> The second verse is underlined by an even more depressive theme (from the same element as the first.) Please observe the last hope expressed by the phrase: 'I wish I could escape from slavery' which is followed by the certainty of the impossibility of redemption. You will see that the whole

work represents only the metaphysic expressed so simply (I would say naively) through the folk melody. I said 'naive' because you will note the incoherence between the *poco joviale* of the musical text of the song and the powerful sense of tragedy in the words. As it happens, I played on the irony of this incoherence (in two other *Capriccios*) and it becomes rather grotesque. You will see that my work, played without the canto, will stand by itself very well. In any case, it's only a try!

By this time, of course, he knew about Lipatti getting First Prize and comments on this to Zeno:

Lipatti's composition was *Gipsy Suite for Orchestra*. He is an extremely talented pianist, only 17 years old. He knew the way the prizes were awarded and was very sure that he would get the first prize because last year he got the second. . . I think Lipatti fully merits the prize. Last year I heard his *Sonatina for Violin and Piano* and was very surprised at its maturity; there were only a few mistakes in the construction of the piece which I'm sure will correct themselves very soon. . . The jury consisted of Enescu (whom I heard was thoroughly enjoying himself), Jora, Alfred Alessandrescu, Andricu and Perlea etc.)

When the 20-year-old Silvestri paid his first of many visits to the Vanceas' big estate in Târgu Mureş in 1933, Zeno introduced him to contemporary music, giving him many scores which he had never seen or heard before and which he took back to Bucharest to study. Unfortunately we don't know what these were, but they must have suggested to the young composer new avenues for exploring. The results were to prove controversial, but as Shostakovich would say with the wisdom of maturity:

Real success comes when people argue about your work. . . If everyone criticises it, then perhaps there's something worthwhile in it.

So, when Silvestri's *String Quartet No 1* (Op. 16), published in 1939, was first performed the following year, Jora observed:

The musical sensitivity of this talented young man doesn't appeal to everybody. But it is quite unfair to accuse Silvestri – as is done all too often – of only being able to compose cerebral music. His numerous adagios testify to how erroneous is this view. They are extraordinarily rich in feeling and, as far as Romanian music is concerned, only surpassed by Enescu's.

But even such an ardent admirer of Costi as Nina Cassian had to admit that this *Quartet* was too much for an audience whose cerebration was already numbed in what she called the 'icy Athenaeum,' when he conducted it in the notoriously severe winter of 1946. In her regular *Medalion* feature in the magazine *Rampa* (Stage), she wrote:

> The audience tried desperately to fathom the music that appeared to be so abstruse that even the most intense concentration was insufficient for its comprehension. . . Only a very few are able to appreciate the more profound musical conceptions of Constantin Silvestri the composer.

Unfair or not, this was the kind of uncomprehending reception his next work, *Prelude and Fugue (Toccata)* Op.17 No 2, was given in certain quarters. Originally written for piano in 1938 for Ion Marin Sadoveanu's ballet *Metamorphoses*, it is thought to have been sketched for an *Introduction*, four *Preludes* and *Fugues* connected by three *Intermezzi*. Zeno Vancea maintained in his analysis that only the *Introduction*, three *Preludes* and *Fugues* and one *Intermezzo* were extant. Costi himself played three of these *Preludes* over the radio on February 5 1940. He wrote Zeno in a letter in February that he had heard that the public liked them very much and he had entered them for a prize for young composers. The judges consisted of Ionel Perlea, conductor of the Radio Symphony Orchestra; Alfred Alessandrescu, artistic director of the Bucharest Opera; and Emanoil Ciomac, highly respected music critic, professor of music history and later director of the Bucharest Philharmonic. Costi remarked wryly:

> They declared them chaotic and disjointed. So you see I am in the position of presenting my music to the musicians, who then fail to understand it!

In Anatol Vieru's opinion:

> As a composer he was advanced and alone. On the other hand, he had an inferiority complex. He told me once that he had spoken to Mihail Jora about how disappointed he felt with the new style of composing and Jora had advised: 'Don't be put off, you must go your own way.'
>
> Though Silvestri's relations with Jora and composer Paul Constantinescu were excellent, his taste was not that of his generation and they considered him eccentric. His ideas were more advanced than those of the Romanian composers of his generation. While they praised his talent, they considered his works were not down-to-earth or in the tradition of Romanian ethnic music. He was too open-minded for them. In fact, he was very traditional but critics didn't consider him so.
>
> Silvestri remains a great figure in Romanian contemporary music, a complex figure: a great conductor and distinguished composer. His works

are and will continue to be performed. Now, they don't seem so eccentric as 50 years ago. I welcome all means, such as the Silvestri International Festival, of keeping his name alive.

When Silvestri did a radio interview in his Paris flat prior to a concert with the ORTF in December 1966, he told French listeners:

> At the time I was composing I was a misunderstood *avant-gardist* and no one would perform my music. I was either appreciated or detested. That happened all the time. When I come here now with my music composed some 30 years ago, it could be said that it is already out of fashion if you compare it with the 12-tone technique of today.

(When in the Sixties he showed some of his works to the Paris publisher Salabert he was told they were too conservative.)

Asked by the interviewer whether he had ever composed serial music, Costi replied:

> Yes, I started with serial music, but I got really fed up because of the severe criticisms. In those times, I was considered mad and when you hear everyone saying it, you come to believe it must be so!

The interviewer interposed: 'Nevertheless, you were in good company: Schoenberg, Alban Berg, Webern. . .'

'But in Romania,' Costi explained, 'these were just names in a music lexicon. Schoenberg was considered something fantastic that had escaped from a menagerie!'

In 1956–57 Silvestri revised the material of the original version of his Op.17 No 2 and made substantial changes. It now became a single *Prelude and Fugue (Toccata)** and he himself orchestrated it for a large orchestra, with augmented brass and percussion. He described it as

> a kind of ballet, on a subject more tragic and dramatic than brilliant. Even if the first impression is that it is a bravura piece, it isn't. It's a piece with which to start or end a concert.

Elsewhere, Silvestri explained that it was modelled on fugues from J.S. Bach's *Art of Fugue* and that 'much of the material stems from Romanian folk music and the orchestration is in the tradition of Romanian symphonic music.' The *Prelude* evoked the spirit of Transylvanian dances and even the subject of the *Fugue* has the style of a dance melody from Ardeal; from which anyone unacquainted with the work might well wonder why in 1940 Messrs

---

* For Zeno Vancea's explanation see Appendix 2 – page 000

Perlea, Alessandrescu and Ciomac found it so unorthodox. However, from the impressions it made on American critics when Silvestri conducted it in 1960 – with the Chicago Symphony and the following year with the Philadelphia Symphony Orchestra – it is clearer why 20 years earlier Romanian musicians found it 'chaotic and disjointed.' To the American critics it was 'a brilliant study in insistence and intensity; exceedingly complex; a well-scored composition'; it was written in 'a strongly personal, vigorous and' (even in 1960) 'distinctively contemporaneous idiom.' To another, it was 'distinctly percussive and rhythmic, thickly dissonant, polytonal and masterfully manipulated.' One of them thought it was 'derived from the French Impressionists, with a seasoning of middle-period Bartók and of Mossolov's *Iron Foundry*.' This was an allusion to the work of Soviet composer Alexander Mossolov, originally a ballet composed in 1927 entitled *The Factory* and in its concert version was known as *Music of the Machines*; to add 'realism' to its performance metal sheeting had to be rattled in the percussion department.

If Silvestri read this particular review – as in all probability he did – surely the irony must have struck him that, only 16 months before in an interview over Radio Bucharest, he himself had been mildly sarcastic at the expense of another 'machine' ballet, and now someone was making a like comparison with his own *Prelude and Fugue*. He had been describing the music scene in London during his 1958/59 visits. The English, he maintained, were no longer interested in Janáček or *Carmina Burana* (which he claimed was given the bird), but in 'Wozzeck onwards' and 'if there are shrieks and rattles and uproar they consider it modern and like it.'

He went on to describe a concert which included George Antheil's *Ballet méchanique*

> written for four pianos which make a racket for half an hour with each of the players trying to hit the keys as hard as possible – plus another 14 players with different instruments, including eight xylophones, 20 timpani, including tam-tam, two electric doorbells, a car horn and a tape of an aeroplane propellor – an infernal noise for half an hour. After three minutes, as far as I was concerned, the composer had finished everything he had to say and the rest of the 27 minutes he just battered the audience. He knew his métier, but it's like someone who sets out to write a short piece of three minutes, like a divertimento or a prelude, but gets involved in writing a symphony instead.

Even if the American critic was being extreme in comparing Silvestri's *Prelude and Fugue* with the *Music of the Machines* (or *Iron Foundry*) and even if

Mossolov's work has not much in common with Antheil's *Ballet méchanique* except its title, yet both the French and Russian works were written in the Twenties, Silvestri's in the late Thirties, and all three shocked conservative elements in their respective music circles. (Mossolov's was inevitably dubbed 'decadent.')

If Silvestri was considered 'mad,' to use his own epithet, for composing these early *avant-garde* works, it did not deter him from having a bit of fun 20 years later at the expense of such experiments as that of Antheil or of Edgard Varèse's *Ionisation*, composed between 1929 and 1931, which he also heard performed in London. Written for 13 percussion instruments with limited pitch, it was one of the experiments in rhythm by this French-born American scientist turned composer who incorporated Philadelphia factory sounds in his works. 'The whole thing lasts seven or eight minutes and is only percussion,' Silvestri told his no doubt astonished Radio Bucharest listeners,

> except there is a piano on stage and about 20 bars from the end someone puts his elbows on the keys and this produces a sort of chord. [In fact, three chords which are exchanged between the piano, glockenspiel and tubular bells.] I have heard other pieces of this kind and this one is well done, working up to a climax. But I couldn't say whether it is comedy or drama or lyrical. Perhaps where the electric bells ring for 15 seconds on their own, that is supposed to be the lyrical part. There were all kinds of big barrels, probably specially constructed for this piece, and other things from which jungle sounds were produced. That was alright with me – I'm used to seeing jungle films!

His conclusion from all this was cautious and non-committal:

> Of course, it's difficult to lay down levels of musicianship. It takes decades until one knows what is of real value in a particular era until you sift the wheat from the chaff. So, these days people just don't know what is of value in contemporary music.

This view was developed by Silvestri in a quotation the Romanian critic and broadcaster Iosif Sava used when drawing attention to the maestro's interest in 20th century music from Schoenberg to Stockhausen and to his impatience with works he considered had no value, even to the point of believing they were the products of musical charlatans. Silvestri wrote:

> I believe only an extremely small number of works are perfect – that is, ones that from beginning to end do not have a single superfluous or ill-conceived bar or which could be considered *chefs d'oeuvre* of our times. Among

such works, in my opinion, are: first of all, Béla Bartók's *Quartets Nos 5* and 6 which nobody has surpassed; Stravinsky's *Sacre du Printemps*, Alban Berg's *Wozzeck* and Bartók's *Music for Strings, Percussion and Celesta*. As far as the creations of Arnold Schoenberg are concerned, although I promoted his music 25 years ago, I must admit I cannot understand it fully. This means that even today I cannot tell if the author of these works is a composer of genius or just a great theoretician. But that is solely due to my own limitations.

Sadly, modern music reduced its expressive palette, in a way, and it is no longer capable of expression, because of the means it uses; it can only express some emotional states.

This modern music can astonish you, provoke consternation, bizarre emotions or an atavistic anxiety; call it 'metaphysical' if you like. But only in exceptional cases are we able to experience the calm, the profound serenity Beethoven can induce or the tranquillity of Brahms.

This doesn't mean that modern music, which has undoubtedly achieved new and invaluable means of expression, won't survive or will not go on developing. I am convinced that at a certain moment, through the accumulation of ever new experiences, this music will enlarge its expressive palettes and find room for those feelings which in the past constituted the glory of music and will again find the means of expressing the entire range of human emotions.

For his next work following *Prelude and Fugue*, but before he had received the 'chaotic and disjointed' strictures from the prize judges, he had changed his style. This was *Sonata for Oboe and Piano* Op. 19 No 1 composed specially for the biennial Seventh Venice International Festival of Contemporary Music to which he had been invited to represent Romania. 'I finished it only yesterday,' he wrote to Zeno Vancea (still living in Târgu Mureş) on May 30 1939.

> If you could listen to it on Monday June 5 at 9.35p.m. on Radio Bucharest or Radio Romania, I would be very glad to hear your opinion because I tried in this work a new style, as simple as possible and with a nearly 'linear' character. Actually, I wrote the whole work in 10 days, but copying it took me three weeks. That always happens with my works because I am obliged to copy all the movements myself and in this way I take five or six times longer than I need for composing a work.

Because of the war, the Venice Festival was cancelled 'though announced with cymbals and trumpets,' as Costi put it.

Nine months later he was explaining to Zeno:

All my works are really written in the Christmas, Easter or summer holidays, but these are short and should be for resting. Anyhow, since in these holiday homes' (he was writing from the Bruckenthal Sanatorium) 'I don't have a piano, essential to me for composing, you can imagine what little time I give to composition. Because of this, all my works, with very few exceptions, are written in a matter of days. This time before going away I wrote a *Sonata for Violin and Piano* [Op.19 No 3] which lasts approximately 30 minutes. I think next May I will do it on the radio. I believe you will be interested in it because it is written in quarter tones, but these are used as a melodic and not in a harmonic sense.

Zeno's widow remembered:

Costi was always sending us large parcels with his compositions. He couldn't afford a copyist so that is why he did the copying himself – very beautifully and meticulously. He composed so fast and spontaneously that he would say that he could not get the same feeling of relief when the task was at last done as when he had finished the copying, which nevertheless he enjoyed doing.

But copying his own manuscripts was not the only chore which held up the creation of new works; he also spent much time correcting orchestral parts and scores of his friends. For instance, in a letter to Zeno Vancea he provided specific evidence of the kind of correcting he had to do:

I have been four days sitting here correcting. I am really devastated by the state of the material: there are no dynamics – almost non-existent – and they are also missing in the score. The slurs vary from instrument to instrument; there are whole bars missing or too many bars; some of the bars written in the orchestral part don't correspond with those written in the full score. . . I have been correcting in the last four days to the limit of my patience, yet it's still only done superficially. Believe me, I have already done over 1,200 corrections (yes, one thousand two hundred!) Some of the errors I left as they were because I really didn't know how to correct them. The autograph corrections in the score are so many that I would really have needed pages to ask you about them, so I just corrected them as I thought fit. . .

In a previous letter he was even more specific. Referring to the autograph of Zeno's pantomime ballet *Priculiciul* (The Goblin), Silvestri wrote:

I need to know the following: In the first dance (what is its name?), in the third bar after H in the cor anglais I suppose you have B natural; in the third dance, *The Dance of the Bear*, the seventh bar after A, the viola part is written still in the C clef ! The first bar after I, also in the third dance, in the double-bass part, do you have E or D sharp on the second beat? In any case, please indicate in the most precise manner your metronomic indications as they change throughout the score. . .

In November 1939, he corrected Enescu's *Third Orchestral Suite* Op.27, *Suite Villageoise*, composed in 1937–38 and described by his most recent biographer, Noel Malcolm, as Enescu's 'last large-scale work for full orchestra.' The correcting Silvestri described as 'an operation that took me nearly a month to do. Only five minutes ago I finished the last line of the thousands of pages which I had revised. . .'

The multitude of errors to which Silvestri was alluding were presumably made, in each case, by the Romanian copyists of what were often sophisticated works scored for many desks; some original mss may not have been easily decipherable and evidently some copyists were not as 'meticulous' as Costi was in copying his own creations. In one instance he refers to 'material that is not ideally written and, of course, there will be further dozens of errors in the parts, which will upset the players enormously.'

At a later stage in his career, Silvestri did not hesitate, not only to correct wrong notes, but even to make improvements in at least one new work before its first performance. This, naturally, was after discussion with and the consent of the composer who generously conceeded: 'He showed me one ingenious piece of counterpoint that both worked perfectly and much improved the passage concerned; it was hurriedly incorporated' before Costi conducted it.

There is no indication that he received payment for any of this correcting and it is most unlikely that he expected any. It was probably a labour of friendship, of esteem for another's talents or Euterpean dedication and should be weighed on the scales balancing the kindness and generosity which he received from benefactors like Jora. As will be apparent later, Silvestri's kindness was a characteristic to which many would pay tribute and in this correspondence with Zeno Vancea it is evident that the young Costi was generous with his time, his praise and the counsel which he gave to his friend and in the efforts he made to promote his works. 'You have been unanimously appreciated and your new works have aroused everybody's curiosity,' is an example of his encouragement; and the following words of wisdom were proffered by the 27-year-old Silvestri to the man 12 years his senior:

I see you have started to be more prolific and I congratulate you; experience counts as much as talent, which one obviously has to have in certain measure, but experience comes as the result of continuous training, so you should start writing as much as possible. After creating many, many works, in the long run you can choose what is of lasting value, both as far as content and form are concerned.

And when Vancea was worrying about whether his *Priculiciul* was going to be put on at the Opera (it was – in 1942), Silvestri told him: 'The only thing you need is patience.'

Costi dedicated to Zeno his *Sonata Breve A Due Voci* Op.13 for piano, for clarinet and bassoon or for viola and cello. When he told his friend that he would be able to hear it for the first time when he played it himself over the radio, together with other piano pieces he had composed, he added: 'If I don't play my own pieces, my chances are very slim of ever hearing them.'

This feeling of composing for a void, of total lack of feed-back, could have been a factor discouraging him from composing more than he did and he would certainly claim that this was one reason for him not doing so. Though, as has been mentioned, he won the Second Enescu Prize in 1936 for his *Quartet for Strings*, four years later he still had not heard it performed, at least in public. 'The other day, Teodorescu promised to play it with his quartet, but I asked him to do only the adagio and, for the rest of the time, to play your quartet,' he told Zeno in March 1940. (Alexandru Teodorescu was the leader of the Bucharest Philharmonic for 45 years.) He went on to explain the current situation in Bucharest:

You see, not only are [contemporary] orchestral works not often played, and then only with difficulty, but this also applies to chamber music. Whenever more than one player is needed, there is a problem. If I don't play my works myself, do you think I can find someone else to do it? Jora and [Theodor] Rogalski are the only people who played one or other of my orchestral works and for this reason I have three big works for the orchestra with the material already copied, but all of them have been four, five or even six years 'in the warehouse': a *Sonata for Cello*; one for *Clarinet and Bassoon*; a *Trio for Winds*; a *Quartet*, a *Quintet* and so on. This is also why I don't write and why I don't feel Romanian. That I have got where I am is only due to Jora. From the others, big or small, I only met with sabotage, mistrust or utter disinterest. . .

That there was a sound basis to Silvestri's plaint is borne out in an article in

December 1936 in *Muzică și Poezie* (Music and Poetry), the monthly journal of the Bucharest Philharmonic and published by the Royal Cultural Foundation. One of its regular contributors, Virgil Gheorghiu, claimed: 'Our composers are becoming whitehaired while waiting for recognition.' Audiences would tire of the hackneyed repertoire 'at Thursday night concerts' in the Athenaeum, he warned. Someone should take the initiative of offering a Romanian composer once a month an opportunity to conduct one of his own recently composed works. Specifically, he mentioned the 28-year-old Paul Constantinescu and Nicolae Buicliu, a year younger, who had got a first mention in the Enescu competition.

> Who will go to Mr Buicliu's home, shake him warmly by the hand and offer him an orchestra to perform his works? There are people around of sufficient intelligence to be aware of the situation. Their silence is reprehensible.

Nikolai Gogol is supposed to have set fire to some of his early creations; Tchaikovsky said he destroyed a partly composed symphony (reconstructed as the Seventh by another composer) as well as a third piano concerto; a young Dvorak, his self-doubt redoubled after his second opera proved unperformable, indulged in wholesale destruction of his early works; and Shostakovich confessed that, 'like a silly young fool,' he burned a lot of his mss, including an opera, when he was going through a period of 'doubt and despair.'

Whether or not Silvestri was aware of any of these illustrious examples, he made a similar claim, first to his friend Zeno in this same letter of March 1940:

> Some years ago, in a moment of profound moral depression, I consigned my works to an *auto da fé* so that, up to Op. 10 [the *Five Capriccios*], apart from a few early *lieder* and Romanian dances, I destroyed everything. So all that is left of my compositional heritage today is merely what I have composed since then, amounting to about 20 works. The majority of these I have never even heard and therefore they cannot be considered definitive. But their style is quite uniform because they were written over a short period: approximately three years. . .

This claim will be examined later, but three days before this letter to Zeno, he had written to George Georgescu, then director at the Opera, telling him the same story, specifying that this burning of his works had been in 1938 and explaining: 'The negativism which had dogged me all the time reached its climax, stifling all my youthful enthusiasm' and 'after months of neurasthenia I reached a point when I no longer hesitated to make an *auto da fé* of my works'.

At the very end of a letter he wrote to Zeno on May 14 1942 – that is 17 days before his 29th birthday – he disclosed two pieces of information in curious juxtaposition and the second almost mysteriously laconic:

> Last summer I composed a *Sonata for Bassoon and Piano* and another for *Clarinet and Piano* and since then I have become very quiet. On the other hand, we have got married and we live all together at the old address. . .
>
> I embrace you,
>
> Costi

No name of his wife, nor has her existence been mentioned in any of the previous 10 letters to his good friend Zeno from which these quotations have been taken. 'All together' presumably means he and his bride were living in his mother's flat.

'Since then I have become very quiet. . .' and he would become increasingly so. But however dispirited he may have felt at the indifference to his works, it was not the principal reason for the post-war non-productiveness of Silvestri the composer. (After 1944, he only wrote another two string quartets, Op.27 Nos 2 and 3; and, finally, *Three Songs* to words by Rainer Maria Rilke, published in 1953.)

Rather, it was due to a conflict of priorities, in which indifference to his compositions no doubt contributed, but in which the sudden opportunity for full-time conducting offered by the ban on George Georgescu was the paramount motivation. Anatol Vieru saw it as a personal problem for Silvestri:

> He was more and more involved in conducting and less and less with composing and this was his problem. In one of our last talks – actually, when we had quite a long walk through the Bucharest streets – I asked him why he wasn't composing.
>
> I, myself, had returned from Russia where my views had changed. When I first went there to study, in 1950, I thought I was a Zhdanovist*, but when I came back for my vacations I had already become another man, because in Russia I came face to face with the truth; all the people I saw there said that, on the contrary, I was an *avant-gardist* – not that I considered myself one. But I had imbibed all this music of Shostakovich, Prokofiev, Stravinsky, Hindemith and so on. So I asked Silvestri: 'Why don't you compose more? Is it because of Zhdanov?' And he told me: 'No, that's not it. It's my own problem. I cannot accuse anybody else.'

* For an explanation of Zhdanovism see Chapter 6 page 172

In fact, he already had been very successful as a conductor. Composing and conducting are very different things and you must be able to concentrate on one or the other.

In April 1945, Silvestri had the gratification of having the first performance of one of his works conducted by Romania's pre-eminent musician. In a concert in the Athenaeum commemorating the 25th anniversary of the founding of the Society of Composers, George Enescu conducted works by contemporary Romanian composers. The culmination of the concert was Silvestri's *Toccata* which he had orchestrated in 1939 (and which, as previously noted, he would change substantially in 1956.)

Perhaps if George Enescu had stayed in Romania after the war he would have persuaded Silvestri not to forsake composing entirely. If others were indifferent to his compositions, the doyen of Romania's composers, who had praised the boy in Târgu Mureş and who in 1932 had 'expected great things of him,' still had high hopes of him as a composer when he himself left the country for good. Enescu's friend Romeo Drăghici (the man who received the 'North Pole Express' card from Silvestri) received another from him with 1958 New Year greetings, this time from Holland. Romeo replied:

> Dearest Maestro Costi: I was so happy to receive your letter from Amsterdam and to be alive to see the prophecy of our great lamented friend, George Enescu, fulfilled. On September 10 1946, after I had accompanied him to Constanţa when he was leaving for America, he said to me as we parted: 'I am leaving Romania with my mind at peace because I am leaving behind a gifted composer in the person of Constantin Silvestri who will bring fame to our country if he is allowed to do so'.

And when three composers – Ion Dumitrescu, Alfred Alessandrescu and Alfred Mendelsohn – went to Paris in a vain attempt to persuade Enescu to return, apparently Silvestri was the only name from back home he mentioned and asked them to give him the message: 'Please go on composing!'

But let Silvestri himself have the last word on the subject. In a radio interview in Paris in December 1966 he was asked to say something about himself as a composer. His reply was: 'In recent years I have myself forgotten that I was a composer.'

That was not literally true because he was still conducting his own works. However, he was speaking metaphorically, as he was when he continued:

> Even a composer has to have a routine: working with a pencil in his hand. Now, it's no longer a pencil – it's a baton.

CHAPTER 5

'PERMANENT CONDUCTOR'
TO 'PEOPLE'S ARTIST'

In an article on Silvestri in *Record Review* in the early Sixties, an enthusiastic admirer stated: 'He has not had even one single lesson in conducting.'

In a second article in another journal, the same author expanded on this, claiming: 'He is the only conductor to get right to the top of the tree who is entirely self-taught.'

Yet we have already noted that Costi himself in a letter to George Breazul in 1932, after giving the musicologist his *curriculum musicae* up to that time, wrote: 'At the moment I follow the necessary courses in composition and *conducting*.' [My italics J.G.]

Eugen Pricope also had one brief reference to him attending the piano classes and theoretical and pedagogic course after entering the Bucharest Conservatoire in 1930 'which included courses for conducting and composition.'

Silvestri was not necessarily embroidering the truth in the conversations he had (in French) with this British friend. First, we do not know how many of these classes at the Conservatoire he attended, nor for how long; nor what was the nature of the conducting tuition in them. What is known is that when Silvestri began teaching conducting at the Conservatoire – which he did for nearly 10 years, becoming the doyen of the conducting professors there – he had to invent a method and create a study course himself. From which it can be assumed that conducting tuition hitherto had resulted in what a Bucharest Opera conductor described, with an undulating sweep of the arm, as the 'manual exhibitionism' of some Romanian conductors at that time.

'Silvestri became a teacher of conducting without having been taught himself,' is also the view of composer Radu Paladi. 'I don't believe very talented musicians need to learn stick technique from others. Who taught the cellists George Georgescu or Toscanini to conduct?' (Another Bucharest conductor maintained that Georgescu used to come to rehearsals at the Opera and learned by ear as the *répétiteur* played operatic scores on the piano.)

As for Silvestri being the only self-taught conductor to 'get right to the top of the tree,' that would have been challenged by others besides Toscanini and Georgescu – by Karajan, for instance, whose conducting experience before his début with a hired orchestra in Salzburg seems to have been beating time in the Vienna Music Academy to orchestral scores played on the piano; or by Boulez who said he taught himself in two years; or by Karl Böhm who claimed he had never had a lesson in his life.

The point was developed by George Hurst who was a guest conductor of the Bournemouth Symphony Orchestra several times in the Silvestri era, when he himself was principal conductor of the BBC Northern Symphony Orchestra, and who became adviser and conductor of the Bournemouth Sinfonietta:

> Many of the greatest conductors never had a lesson in their lives. Toscanini was one, Pierre Monteux another. And whoever taught Hans Richter or Artur Nikisch? None of them ever had conducting lessons. Does it have to be taught? It comes down to the old maxim: 'There's no such thing as teaching, there's only learning.' What was important was not what they were taught but what they learned – if you have intelligence, perception and discrimination you learn.
>
> In most cases these people played in orchestras for a large part of their lives – Richter was a horn player, Nikisch and Monteux violinists; they saw whom they considered great conductors – it was Wagner in the case of Nikisch – and whom they considered charlatans and decided whom and what to emulate. Toscanini played the cello under all the worst and best conductors in the world; so did Monteux, who played with the Opéra-Comique in Paris and Edouard Colonne's orchestra – under all the riff-raff as well as under Mahler and Nikisch – and he learned.

Composer Anatol Vieru also maintained that Silvestri 'as a conductor was really self-taught' and explained why he thought so:

> He was the first in Romania to realise the importance of long-playing records which only appeared here after the war and he was the first to think about comparing different performances. Together we published a monograph about this. He would write notes on the score of an orchestral work – for instance, in red as Furtwängler interpreted it and green for Toscanini's interpretation. He had a pocket radio which he took along with him when he went fishing and he used to stay up all hours of the night listening to orchestral music being played from abroad over the radio.
>
> It was also at this time that magnetic tapes were introduced here and night after night he would cut tapes, smoking and drinking the while. He had enormous patience.

Compare this with Costi's lifestyle in Bournemouth a decade later as described by the BSO's then assistant conductor, James Loughran:

> He was a great student. He had reel-to-reel tapes and he recorded not one in seven-eighths, which I used to do and which was bad enough for the quality, but he would go one lower than that so you would hardly see the tape-recorder moving. So, on one side of some of these tapes he would have all Mahler's symphonies or the complete Ring cycle. He was always taping, always listening to what was new. He studied very hard, but the trouble was he found he could only study at night when the phone didn't ring. So he would arm himself with a bottle of wine to keep himself company, though he wasn't in any way alcoholic. He would work until five o'clock in the morning and we would see this little figure coming down half asleep at 10 a.m. for a rehearsal. . .

The availability of records in Bucharest in the Fifties was limited and somebody who knew him well said he used to spend hours with a restaurant waiter called Cima who had a big collection and they would listen to them together and compare different versions of the same work.

Silvestri's notes on scores had already been observed (at least 10 years before Vieru knew him) by Teodor Bălan when he saw exercise books in Costi's room with 'his own markings which no one else understood' and, throughout Silvestri's career, this meticulous habit would surprise those who came across the scores he had studied.

The importance he attached to this method was illustrated by an amusing recollection of one of the first pupils to finish his conducting course. As a teenager, Constantin Petrovici was studying theoretical musicology and composition at the Bucharest Conservatoire; he was in his second year when Silvestri started teaching in 1948 with 50 pupils (of whom only six would finish the course in 1952.) But because Petrovici was fascinated by Costi's reputation, especially for improvising, he decided to switch to conducting. (In 1959 he himself began conducting at the Opera and was still doing so in 1998.) One of the pieces he had to do for his conducting course with Silvestri was the overture to Glinka's *Ruslan and Lyudmilla*. He used to go to Costi's home for lessons and it was there that he took his score of the opera with him. But when he opened it and Silvestri looked at it Petrovici remembers the maestro registered shock/horror and exclaimed: 'What's this? It's in virgin condition – not a mark on it!'

Over 40 years on, and Bournemouth Symphony Orchestra archivist Raymond Carpenter in an eloquent appreciation of Silvestri recalled:

An inspection of his scores and recording catalogues show an unusual curiosity in listening and analysing the interpretations of the world's leading conductors and soloists. His knowledge of the fingerprints of professional musicmakers was encyclopaedic, from the vast differences in the tempi used by the great artists to their phrasing, the editions of their scores and the variants from the composer's wishes. His working scores are littered with blue, red and green markings – noting the *modus operandi* of conductors from Furtwängler to Toscanini.

When the BSO went on its European tour in 1965, manager Ken Matchett used the unconvertible currency which they earned in Leipzig (then in the German Democratic Republic) to buy Mozart, Beethoven and Brahms scores from Breitkopf and Hartel to build up a library for the orchestra – making sure there were duplicate copies for the maestro. It later became the exacting and unpaid task of Doug Morris, BSO cellist who doubled as librarian, to copy all Costi's markings into the other scores.

Conductor Nicholas Braithwaite also remembers Silvestri handing him his own score of the Shostakovich *Tenth Symphony* to study and being surprised at the markings 'in various coloured crayons in which he had noted different performances and things like the metronome speeds of different conductors'; and an observant soloist remembers:

> I saw him put the different markings in colours. He had definite ideas with rubatos and slide tempo changes, which made them sound incredibly inspirational at the moment of being played in a concert.

In the post-war period of Silvestri's conducting career he never used a score in a concert performance. A Bucharest reviewer as late as 1956 was impressed by Silvestri 'conducting always by heart' such works as Beethoven's *Missa Solemnis*, Mozart's *Requiem Mass* and his *Great Mass in C minor*, Tchaikovsky's *Manfred Symphony* and Britten's *Young Person's Guide to the Orchestra (Variations and Fugue on a Theme of Purcell)*. One reason was that sometimes in Romania full scores were unavailable and relying on a miniature score would have been a considerable visual strain. (Also the instrumental parts of many works were not printed but hand-copied. The reason for this was that the foreign publishers' copyright for many scores – by composers such as Ravel or Honegger, for example – were beyond the means available to Romanian orchestras. There were copying offices in Bucharest which the Philharmonic used where these scores were copied by hand. Even Enescu's works composed in Paris, as we saw in the last chapter, had to be corrected by Silvestri himself before they could be performed in Romania. Some of Enescu's and Silvestri's works still, in the Nineties, cannot be printed in Romania because the copyright is held by French or American music publishers.)

By the time Silvestri came to Bournemouth and with no such handicaps, he preferred always to conduct with a score; and players were surprised to learn that this had not always been his custom. He would explain that conducting with a score was 'better for the music' and that Otto Klemperer had once said to him: 'Why should I conduct from memory? The score is there to use.' Later Klemperer would remind young conductors that neither Mahler nor Strauss would conduct without a score; that it was vanity to flaunt their knowledge of a work before the audience; and a conductor should not become 'a slave to his memory.'

Teodor Bălan has recorded the various stages of Silvestri's preparation prior to conducting a work: he would first sightread it on the piano with great facility; then listen to various recordings, comparing and analysing them; and when he was satisfied he had memorised the work he would stand in front of the loudspeaker and conduct, carefully monitoring his gestures.

But Anatol Vieru said that though Silvestri

> learned to compare the interpretations of other conductors, he couldn't learn their techniques. He had a personal technique which was very embarassing for the orchestra. After the war he got the chance to conduct very many concerts. But he was not satisfied with the Bucharest Philharmnonic, nor they with him.

Vieru, who began his own career as a conductor, was a pupil in Silvestri's conducting class and was at many of his rehearsals.

> There was a lot of tension during some of these. I remember in particular a rehearsal of the *Coriolan Overture* where Silvestri had his ideas about the sounds the players should produce, but when he had to put these theoretical ideas into practice, he had to fight the orchestra and it was very awkward.
>
> He was a pioneer, a revolutionary in conducting as far as Romanian orchestras were concerned. He wanted to produce more refined sounds such as those produced by a chamber orchestra.

That is just what he would eventually achieve with the Bournemouth Symphony Orchestra or, as one of its principal players put it: 'What Silvestri did was to make an orchestra sound like a solo instrument.'

'He was trying out ideas as in a musical laboratory,' said Vieru, using a metaphor also used by a Romanian broadcaster in 1967 who attributed

Silvestri's propensity for experimenting to his alleged 'study of chemistry at Bucharest University.' Or, as conductor Iosif Conta put it:

Silvestri's conducting class was like a laboratory; he was an analyst, a scientist in music. He instituted for Romania the analytic way of looking at a score and of conducting it.

Vieru regretted

I never did meet Silvestri again after he went abroad, though I was curious to hear him. But I did hear the records for which he won prizes. I think they were wonderful, but he had changed: he had succeeded in training the orchestra!

The level of playing in Romanian orchestras at this time and the basic reason for misunderstandings between Silvestri and the players was explained by veteran conductor Mircea Cristescu who, as we have seen, used to turn the pages for Costi at his uncle's soirées. He studied conducting and the viola in parallel and graduated in both. Cristescu was also in Silvestri's first conducting course and performed with the Philharmonic as a student conductor and later as a viola player.

I was impressed by his musicality, his refinement and sensitivity; the colours he drew from the orchestra, the tensions he could build up, and his ability to master the smallest details of the score. . . But the orchestras of those days didn't have the technique of orchestras of today and their concert aim was 'round sound and round phrasing.' So, when Silvestri came along with his insistence on analytical details, shaping and colouring, the orchestras were getting very confused. Their need to concentrate and their equipment as players had to be 100 per cent better in order to be able to do what Silvestri required. And that is why his recordings at this time were not impeccable from the point of view of orchestral performance and why so many were erased by the Radio. At the same time, he was experimenting with ideas and he had a very broad vision for the repertoire of the orchestra. . .

That Silvestri often ran into troubled waters with the Bucharest Philharmonic was confirmed by a player who said:

Some of my colleagues were quite hostile to him because they couldn't understand his diligent attention to the works to be performed and his musical demands on them. So, in turn, he became hostile to them. Musically speaking, they were amateurs.

For all his improvisations on the piano, from the moment Silvestri took over the Philharmonic there was nothing extempore about his concerts: all had to be well prepared and his *cri de coeur* about insufficient rehearsal time was made as early as September 1946 when he actually handed in his resignation to the Philharmonic management because there were not enough rehearsals and also on account of the indiscipline and 'bad habits' of the players. He did not mind being its guest conductor from time to time, he stipulated, but in the prevailing conditions he did not want to be 'permanent,' that is principal, conductor any more.

His resignation was rejected. Nevertheless, the following month, he wrote a long letter to the management detailing all of what he considered to be the orchestra's 'bad habits.'

Whatever transpired in rehearsal, Radu Paladi said he felt personally that Silvestri's concerts 'invariably radiated happiness, they were always an "event" and he had an extraordinary effect on the audience.'

Another regular member of that audience both at rehearsals and concerts was Edgar Cosma who was impressed with Silvestri's conducting of the *Pathétique*, in spite of not being a particular admirer of Tchaikovsky's music. Cosma has been living in Paris since 1960 and became a frequent conductor of the Bournemouth and other British orchestras. He discovered:

> Suddenly, here was a conductor who not only researched the score but understood it and paced it wonderfully. It was an exceptional performance, everything was in its right place. There was life in what he did. Up to then [1945] I had only heard conductors who were 'impersonal,' the work they had done on a piece was superficial. Silvestri changed my mind about Tchaikovsky that evening and opened up a new world for me.

Radu Paladi also suggested reasons why the players were not happy with Silvestri:

> It had something to do with the conflict between him and George Georgescu. After Silvestri became the Philharmonic's director in the autumn of 1947, 'Gogu' intrigued against him. There were whispered criticisms to the effect that Costi was good, but his stick technique was not so explicit as Georgescu's. Nevertheless, the results were superior and those players who were dedicated musicians were happy with him. But many did not like Silvestri and, in the end, the orchestra's judgement was: 'We must have a conductor with Gogu's hands and Costi's brain.'

Another cause of dissent was that Silvestri would invite his students from the Conservatoire to the rehearsals and the players resented being criticised in front of them. Some of the players were themselves teachers of these same pupils and felt they were losing face.

By the time Costi conducted his last concert with the Philharmonic before he went to the Radio and the Opera in December 1953, the players wanted to break his head because he was so demanding!

This last concert was the occasion when the orchestra applauded as Georgescu embraced his young rival and Costi is said to have remarked drily: 'I don't know why people are always very happy when I come – and when I go!'

Silvestri's frustration in not getting the ready response he wanted from the Philharmonic players and the ensuing resentment, was of a different order to the reluctance to do his bidding on the part of some Western orchestras which he would also experience in due course. Players in the West were probably better trained in long established academies than their Romanian counterparts; familiar with a far wider repertoire and usually excellent sight-readers. But because of their experience of performing works in the standard repertoire in a certain way, they would resent innovating guest conductors.

The Romanian players also had a tradition behind them: the Bucharest Philharmonic Society had been founded in 1834 and George Enescu himself during the First World War had helped to convert the orchestra run by the Ministry of Education into a professional philharmonic. The string players, especially, were talented, with a time-honoured tradition behind them of rural fiddling, but with it a strong soloistic virtuoso tendency which militated against ensemble playing – and it was this that contributed to clashes with Costi.

Silvestri, a conductor as exigent as he was unorthodox, was bound to meet some measure of hostility from players both in Romania and the West, even if reasons for it were not identical. He no doubt had the Bucharest Philharmonic's bad habits in mind when he used to give this advice to the students in his conducting sessions:

The attainments of the individual players and the conductor's artistry only to a certain extent determine the quality of a performance. This depends primarily on working as an ensemble and without individual players either becoming infatuated with their own performance or being unable to master the purely technical side of the music.

Despite these internal problems, Silvestri conducted at least 70 concerts during his six years as director of the Philharmonic. In the just over eight years he was its principal conductor, October 1945 to December 1953, he won ever

*The 28-year-old Silvestri (second from right) with Professor Musicescu (far right),
Dinu Lipatti (far left) and friends at the wedding party after his first marriage,
to Viorica Vasilescu*

increasing audience acclaim as well as official recognition by being awarded a
State Prize in 1952; while the orchestra was promoted to the status of the
Bucharest State Philharmonic in October 1953 by a decree of the Council of
Ministers, Romania's supreme ruling body at that time. The Athenaeum was
designated its official residence.

When he took up his appointment as principal conductor, Silvestri
declared:

> I need a prodigious repertoire and I must know all these works perfectly,
> that is, by heart. A single concert can make or break one.

Included in his repertoire would be many Romanian works – among them
first performances of his less well-known contemporaries – some of which he
promoted throughout his career both within Romania and worldwide. It
was, therefore, significant that in his first concert after his appointment as the
Philharmonic's director, he conducted at Christmas an outstanding first
performance of the *Nativity*, part of the *Byzantine Oratorio* of Paul Constantinescu, who was another of Jora's pupils and acknowledged as a major composer. The *Oratorio* was not performed again until 1968. Silvestri also did first
performances of Constantinescu's *First Symphony*; his *Triple Concerto for*

Piano, Violin and Cello (with the brothers, pianist Valentin and violinist Ştefan Gheorghiu and cellist Radu Aldulescu); his *Piano Concerto* (with Valentin Gheorghiu which they recorded abroad); and his *Concerto for Strings*, which was also recorded.

But conducting the works of his contemporaries did not necessarily mean Silvestri approved or liked them. On at least two occasions, others noted the opposite was the case. Paladi was at a concert where Silvestri was conducting a piece by a well-known contemporary, but with such a patent lack of enthusiasm that he was astonished.

> It was completely out of character. He was treating this work with such manifest indifference that he gave the impression he was doing it because he was obliged to. In contrast, next on the programme was Claudio Arrau playing the Brahms *Second Piano Concerto* which Silvestri conducted magnificently. For me, this showed that he was a genuine artist, not a hypocrite and if he didn't like a compositon he couldn't become involved, but if he liked it he identified with it.

> On another occasion, Costi was rehearsing the score of a work of another contemporary which was to be played in the first half of a concert. The players noticed he was getting more impatient by the minute, until he reached a point where he threw aside the score and declared: 'It's an insult for such a work to be dedicated to George Enescu!'

Other landmarks during his eight-year reign with the Philharmonic included persuading an initially reluctant government to provide for the formation of a Philharmonic Choir, the first fruits of which were a performance of Mozart's *Requiem* on the 160th anniversary of his death; four performances of the *Missa Solemnis* in 1952 for the 125th anniversary of Beethoven's death (repeated three times in April 1957, as has been mentioned, before he went to London to conduct it in the Royal Albert Hall); and at the end of every season he conducted the Beethoven *Ninth* which concertgoers facetiously referred to as 'The New Symphony' because of his unfamiliar interpretation.

He conducted in the Tchaikovsky, Kodály and Dvorak festivals; and a concert of Hungarian, Bulgarian and Romanian music in celebration of the Bucharest Conservatoire's 90th anniversary. In addition, he did special concerts for students; others for children; and proms in a park – an innovation for Bucharest. Silvestri was also responsible for the formation of an excellent vocal quartet whom he coached either at his home or in a room at the Opera House.

Acknowledging applause with Soviet pianist Iakov Zak in 1955

He had another somewhat bizarre assignment: having written only a few years earlier: 'I owe nothing to my country' and 'I don't feel Romanian,' Costi, who seems to have had a well-developed sense of irony, must have appreciated the paradox of conducting the finals of a competition, initiated by the Central Committee of the Communist Party, for a National Anthem. He conducted all five entries in the small hall of Radio Bucharest, but in the event the judges did not like any of them – and eventually chose a sixth.

Trial runs were given as early as the Bucharest Philharmonic's 1949–50 season to works that would later cause considerable interest, in Britain and the US for example, either because they had been rarely performed, as in the case of the *Manfred Symphony*, or the way he interpreted them, as in *Bolero*, or both. The *Manfred* by December 1951 was performed no less than seven times. Edgar Cosma remembers: 'When *Manfred* was first performed the concert had to be repeated three times, with the hall packed on each occasion.'

Bolero was performed three times in March and June 1951. When a Romanian journalist, who in his youth was a regular attender of Silvestri's concerts, described the effect his conducting of *Bolero* was alleged to have had on certain female members of the audience, I thought he was exaggerating and intended to dismiss it as a sexist irrelevance; that is, until a second person, quite independently and without any prompting, referred to it in similar terms. The journalist recalled:

(Above) Conducting the Leningrad Philharmonic, and (below) the 'Great' Mass in C minor *in Bucharest on the bi-centenary in January 1956 of Mozart's birth*

Although below medium height, Costi was extremely handsome, with classical Greek features. He was very sure of himself and I had the impression he liked indulging the audience a little – and especially the ladies. Whenever he conducted *Bolero* they were aroused to a state of ecstasy and for years there was this general erotomania among the ladies of Bucharest's *haut-monde* who flocked to his concerts. It was extraordinary.

It should be borne in mind that Ravel's technical experiment was a complete novelty in Romania in 1950 as it had been for Western audiences 20 years before. When it was first performed in Paris, one observer noted that people clutched each other and crumpled their programmes into lumps of perspiring pulp. The effect of that terrific change to E major was that of a pricked bubble. One could hear the gasp as the tension was released.

So the reactions to it in Romania may not have been so extraordinary after all. (But it would have been interesting to know if they were the same when Silvestri conducted it as on the one occasion when the 'old school' George Georgescu did it, as late as 1958. While it still had a place in Silvestri's repertoire after he left Romania, Georgescu dropped it immediately from his.)

The second person who commented on his *Bolero* was poetess Nina Cassian. She had had a few lessons in harmony with Costi when she was 16 and, later, used to play some of his piano pieces – his *Chants Nostalgiques* (Op.27 No. 1) was the *pièce de résistance* of her repertoire with which she delighted herself and her friends. 'I had the biggest ecstasies imaginable seeing him conduct,' she said (in our Heathrow interview),

> for instance, the *Pathétique* – though Tchaikovsky is by no means my favourite composer – or *Manfred*, which was masterly. But what I remember even better – perhaps because it is frivolous yet so relevant – is the way he conducted *Bolero*. Neither before nor since have I heard anything like it. In the climax he goaded the whole orchestra into an incredible frenzy. It was like a demagogue whipping up a crowd into a state of revolt.

What would Costi have made of these alleged 'erotomanic' effects of his painstakingly prepared performances – would he have been horrified or tolerantly amused?

To counter any accusation of sexist bias, Silvestri's conducting of *Bolero* could have an equally startling effect on men, judging by a Bournemouth Symphony Orchestra performance in the Royal Festival Hall which produced ecstatic applause, with one man in particular actually standing on his seat, brandishing his programme and yelling at the top of his voice.

But on another occasion it was greeted, not by near-swooning ladies or frenzied gents but by what sounds suspiciously like proley rasberries. 'It was at an open-air concert for factory workers in Romania,' Silvestri himself once recalled,

> after a few bars [of *Bolero*] a factory siren gave a blast. I paused. There was another blast. I carried on – and a whole passage was punctuated by factory whistles.

It will be recalled that the ban imposed in 1944 on George Georgescu's conducting, ostensibly because he had performed in countries with fascist regimes, was lifted in January 1947. From then until the end of 1953, he conducted 109 concerts with the Bucharest Philharmonic, the orchestra of which he used to be the principal conductor and director prior to the ban. Silvestri had been principal conductor of the Philharmonic for almost two years when the ban on Georgescu was lifted and, as noted previously, became its director the following autumn. It requires little effort to imagine the gall Georgescu must have felt every time he stepped on to the rostrum for those 109 concerts, knowing that a man 26 years his junior now bore the very titles, with their prestige and power, which had once been his. In another sense it was even a reversal of roles since Georgescu had been director at the Opera when Silvestri was a mere *répétiteur*, occasionally permitted to conduct.

It may be, as some maintain, that Georgescu had a paranoid streak which made him jealous of anybody whom he conceived to be a potential rival and that, whenever he had the opportunity to do so, he would prevent him – whether it was Ionel Perlea or Silvestri, for example – from conducting the Philharmonic. One conductor contemporary claimed: 'Georgescu was viciously jealous in general – something unbelievable.'

Be that as it may, given Georgescu's invidious situation *vis-à-vis* Costi in which circumstances beyond either's control had placed him, it is hardly surprising he intrigued to change it at the earliest opportunity. That he did intrigue is corroborated by several sources. 'I don't want to say anything about someone who is no longer with us,' said another conductor, 'but George Georgescu knew how to pull the strings so that he could regain control of the Philharmonic.'

It was a situation similar to Furtwängler's intrigues against Karajan and barring his younger rival from the Berlin Philharmonic and State Opera and afterwards from the Vienna Philharmonic and Salzburg Festival.

With hindsight there could be significance in the fact that over the same period that Georgescu conducted the Philharmonic 109 times, its principal conductor and director did so only 96 times. Both men had engagements during this period in the Soviet Union and Czechoslovakia and probably Silvestri was abroad more frequently – in Hungary for example. In any case, Georgescu had plenty of opportunity to regain his former popularity with players and public and, as the more conservative and conformist of the two, to insinuate himself into the good books of the all-powerful party.

Whatever were the particular strings Georgescu was able to pull, Silvestri, apparently without warning, received a notice in writing from the woman Minister of Culture, Constanța Crăciun, to the effect that 'your function as Director of the Philharmonic ceases as from December 13 1953.'

The function of orchestra director in those days was considered secondary in the hierarchical pecking order to that of principal conductor who, nevertheless, by being given the additional appointment, benefitted from the extra salary. It is now considered that Silvestri's dismissal as director was a political move on the part of the Central Committee of the party, where such decisions were invariably made, and the Minister of Culture was merely the executioner.

It was a measure which was probably intended to go some way towards appeasing Georgescu and to make partial amends for his bruised feelings over the ban: he was appointed director while Costi was to retain his position as principal conductor. After all, Silvestri could hardly be dismissed from this, the more prestigious post, since it was only about a month before, on October 1, the Council of State had conferred on the Philharmonic the honour of being pronounced the highest musical institution in the country, to receive all the material help from the state it needed and the Athenaeum henceforth was proclaimed its official home, fulfilling the dream of three generations of players.

But Silvestri was so shocked and disgusted at the brusque manner in which he had been relieved of the post of director that he tendered his resignation as principal conductor.

This certainly pleased some of the old diehards in the orchestra (in the 50–70 age band) who had never been able to accept the new broom regime of Silvestri (now aged 40) whom they still considered a 'young' upstart. The First Trumpet, for instance, a man called Adamache, got so fed up at one rehearsal where, typically, the conductor had insisted on going over and over certain passages of a work, that he is reputed to have walked out with his colleagues, observing as he went: 'Dear Costi, drop it – we've had enough!'

According to the Philharmonic's records, after his last concert as principal conductor on November 1 1953, Costi did not conduct it again until the following March; did a total of nine concerts in 1954; only four in 1955; none in 1956 and the last time was when he conducted the *Missa Solemnis* in April 1957 (after his first London visit.)

Silvestri, at 40, was without a job. Ironically, he was offered the post of artistic director at the State Opera – Georgescu's old post. He had been only too glad to leave the Opera for the Philharmonic because it had seemed a dead end and he initially turned down the offer, perhaps because of memories of his erstwhile frustration, but more likely because of bitterness at what he probably considered Georgescu's usurpation of his Philharmonic kingdom and the indignity of doing what was virtually a job swap.

Iosif Conta, who had been one of Silvestri's first conducting pupils in 1948, remembers how he went to the chairman of the Radio, Ion Pas, and told him it would be a disgrace to the country if Romania failed to give Costi a permanent post. Pas then went to see Silvestri at home and persuaded him to accept the post of artistic director of the Radio Symphony Orchestra.

Costi changed his mind about the Opera offer and accepted that post as well.

If Silvestri produced a state of ecstasy in sections of his Bucharest public, more surprisingly some players in the Radio Symphony orchestra used even more rapturous expressions over 40 years later about the effects on themselves of the sounds he conjured from them.

Radu Zvorişteanu, a violinist in the orchestra who became its leader, recalled: 'He was hypnotic for the players and the public. We had the feeling it was not just music any more: it had a supernatural quality.'

His violinist colleague Aniela Beldi maintained:

He gave me the feeling that I was disembodied and felt like floating in space. I couldn't feel the chair or my legs any more and I was producing sounds which were really his sounds. He was captivating, fascinating. The players never looked anywhere except at his eyes, at the score, and back again to his eyes.

(Eight or nine years years later, Principal Clarinet Raymond Carpenter in the Bournemouth Symphony Orchestra would be particularly conscious of the clarity of Silvestri's eyes.

The whites were very white and if he looked at you, you knew you were being looked at! He could do it in such a way as to make you feel extremely uncomfortable. But when he smiled, the whole face lit up. It was really a beautiful smile and showed you that underneath all the biting sarcasm, the scathing wit – which could absolutely decimate you in his relentless pursuit of the style of music-making he wanted – there was a great warmth of personality and character.)

The two Bucharest violinists were agreed that when Silvestri came to the Radio he had a different attitude to their orchestra from what he was reputed to have had to the Philharmonic and this was reciprocated by the players. 'They appreciated him and it was the best time they had,' Beldi remembers.

He also conducted the Radio Studio Orchestra which consisted of players with little knowledge of music and was augmented with players from the Philharmonic. The first time I played under Silvestri was with this

When Enescu was leaving Romania for good, he told his life-long friend Romeo Draghici (seen here in 1979): 'I am leaving behind a gifted composer, Constantin Silvestri, who will bring fame to our country.' It was Romeo's postcard that chased Costi through six countries and finally caught up with him in Lapland

orchestra. There were two weeks of hard rehearsing because he had to teach the players the A to Z of playing and musicianship. He said to them: 'If you do well I'll give you a present.' The concert was a success and he made us sound like a big orchestra.

The 'present' turned out to be an encore: Corelli's *Badinerie* from his *Suite for String Orchestra*, which Beldi described as 'out of this world.' Zvorişteanu said that whenever this piece was played, Silvestri would turn around towards the audience as the echo of the last three notes faded and step off the podium 'in a drooping way as if he was almost falling off. The public loved it.'

According to one eye-witness there was an occasion when Costi got so carried away when conducting the Tchaikovsky *Fifth* that he did actually stumble and fall off the podium, to the alarm and concern of my informant, but quickly climbed back again. Should sceptics find this an unlikely story, there are at least two precedents: it happened during a London Philharharmonic concert in Blackburn to a British conductor – 'a stout cheerful extrovert known to the orchestra as "The Stepney Slasher",' according to bass clarinetist and Royal Opera House librarian Richard Temple Savage who recalled that after the 'Slasher' fell off the platform the LPO 'played stolidly on until' (like Silvestri) 'he rejoined us, fortunately not much hurt.'

A Bournemouth player also remembers a guest conductor who fell off the podium and did himself an injury. So even conducting has its occupational hazards.

After the Studio Orchestra, Beldi joined the Radio Symphony Orchestra and on this, too, Silvestri worked hard to improve the quality of playing. For the players this meant work of a kind they had never before experienced.

'Janáček's *Sinfonietta* is a very difficult piece and when Silvestri put the parts on our desks we despaired,' Beldi recalled. 'However, he worked so well with us it was a resounding success and we had to repeat part of it as an encore.'

Enescu, who had left Romania in 1946, died in Paris in 1955 in comparative poverty after a long debilitating illness and, finally, a stroke. Largely thanks to Silvestri, in Romania his works were played more often than in his lifetime. Edgar Cosma remembers how, although his *Rhapsody No 1* had been performed innumerable times, when Silvestri conducted it he had 'never heard it done with such power and verve and with such a personal approach, yet with such strict adherence to the text.' It was the same with Enescu's *Symphony No. 1 in E flat major*.

But the only works which the Radio orchestra had played were his *Third Orchestral Suite* and the two *Romanian Rhapsodies* (which Silvestri would record together with the *Concert Overture on Romanian Folk Themes*.) So, when Silvestri began rehearsals for the first performance in Romania of concert excerpts from Enescu's opera *Oedipe* in June 1956, 20 years after its première in Paris, Beldi recalls:

> Again we were in despair when we saw the score for the first time. We couldn't make head nor tail of it, it seemed so chaotic. But Silvestri took every section, phrase and motif and worked on them with us like a jeweller. We could see the diamond taking shape as it was cut and polished from the original carbon. All of a sudden it started to make sense. We heard things then which today are not heard any more when it is performed.

For Enescu's *Octet*, Silvestri took eight players from the orchestra and they were absolved from playing in other programmes for two months while it was rehearsed and performed. Vieru described it as a most important but very difficult work, composed in 1898 when Enescu was 17 and sometimes compared with Schoenberg's *Verklärte Nacht* (Transfigured Night), a sextet composed a year later.*

Composer Pascal Bentoiu recalled that when Enescu's *Chamber Symphony*, which he was just finishing when he suffered his second and semi-paralysing stroke in 1954, was again performed in the Enescu International Festival in

---

* Noel Malcolm: *George Enescu His Life and Music*: 'Occasionally there are superficial harmonic resemblances to Schoenberg's *Verklärte Nacht* . . . but the two works are fundamentally far apart.'

Bucharest in 1958, Silvestri conducted it twice in the same concert. When it was given a somewhat tepid reception after the first time, Costi came back on stage and spoke to the audience, most of whom were already on their feet moving towards the exits. He said in effect, according to Bentoiu:

> This work is a *chef d'oeuvre* of maestro Enescu. It is more difficult to understand than his other works because of its very modern language. For this reason we will play it again from beginning to end.

On hearing it a second time, its for those days novel idioms were clearer to the audience who also found it more harmonious. It was acclaimed a great success.

Enescu, who expressed regret that it was popularly assumed that the two *Romanian Rhapsodies* were all that he had composed, would have particularly appreciated Silvestri's promotion of this and his other works; in 1958 Silvestri said people in Britain knew about

> Enescu, the great violinist, good conductor and composer of the two *Romanian Rhapsodies*, but only now is there starting to be a growing interest in the works of the mature period of Romania's greatest composer.

Yet it would still be with the *Rhapsody No. 1* that he would win optimum audience acclaim for an Enescu work.

Silvestri conducted all the Beethoven symphonies with the Radio Symphony Orchestra and Zvorişteanu claimed that the Philharmonic became jealous of the RSO's marked improvement:

> Georgescu started sending 'spies' to Silvestri's concerts to find out how many times he was recalled to the platform to acknowledge applause. Actually, more people came to Silvestri's concerts than to those of Georgescu who, from the purely visual point of view, was fantastic – with beautiful but empty gestures – and would get the orchestra to make a big noise, with emphasis on the timpani. With Silvestri it was the opposite: he was looking for colour and expression. I'm sure he felt he was better than Georgescu and was disappointed that the musical hierarchy gave the older man precedence.

Former Philharmonic conductor and director of the Opera Constantin Bugeanu thought

> the salon-type public in Bucharest were impressed by the flamboyant gestures and charisma of George Georgescu, who had noted the way other conductors performed in Germany, and not so impressed by Silvestri who, nevertheless, was the real musician.

Silvestri was disarmingly magnanimous and disingenuously self-mocking in his own appraisal of Georgescu:

> He is the type of conductor made for the rostrum with his charming presence. He doesn't look at all the details, but there is breadth in the way he conducts, in the atmosphere, in his scope and style. But when he records, the effect is not the same any more. Of course, what helps him on the rostrum is his stature, eminently suited to conducting, whereas I am small and plump and lack presence.

Damnation with faint praise could not have been delivered more deftly.

Though the personal revelations of audience and players' reactions to the results of Silvestri's conducting may sound hyperbolic, there is no reason to suppose that they were any less genuinely felt than his own intense and sometimes uninhibitedly emotional reactions to certain works. It would seem a reasonable assumption that, through the catalyst of the music, his intensity of feeling was transmitted to players and audience alike.

Aniela Beldi said she was 'obsessed for years' as a result of the impression left on her by Silvestri's conducting of Mozart's *Mass in C minor* K427, The Great Mass, which the Radio Orchestra gave its first Romanian performance in the Athenaeum on January 26 1956, followed by two more soon afterwards and which became the RSO's first record. 'Every time he arrived at The Crucifixion,' she recalled,

> tears rolled down his face, which showed how he himself was suffering. His stature was not impressive – he was small, with a stoop – yet he was so persuasive that, at the approach of The Resurrection, as if he were preparing for the moment, he would stretch his arms out wide – and players would feel the cupola of the Athenaeum was opening.

There would be further instances of Costi's emotional reaction to sacred music.

It is odd that Silvestri, the conductor of *The Great Mass*, several times of Beethoven's *Missa Solemnis*, both in Romania and London, and the founder of the Bucharest Philharmonic Choir, should apparently have been reluctant to conduct choral works when he came to Bournemouth. He did, in fact, conduct a very successful performance of Dvorak's *Stabat Mater*, but manager Kenneth Matchett claimed: 'I always had trouble persuading him to work with a choir. He wasn't in the British choral tradition.'

Matchett was therefore delighted when he managed to persuade Silvestri to agree to do Elgar's *Dream of Gerontius* with the Bournemouth Municipal Choir. In fact, as long ago as 1947 after Silvestri had become director of the Bucharest Philharmonic, *The Dream* was announced in the programme for the forthcoming season but seems to have been dropped for whatever reason, no doubt to Costi's intense disappointment. Now, 16 years later, it was scheduled for the eve of Good Friday, April 18 1963, part of the BSO's 70th anniversary festival. Matchett then explained what happened:

> I think he asked at first for 24 hours rehearsal time, something enormous which we managed to cut down to 18 hours. We had to pay the choir for these extra rehearsals and engaged a good trio of soloists: Helen Watts, Kenneth Bowen and Thomas Hemsley. After about 12 hours of rehearsing, Silvestri came to me and, pleading ill health, announced: 'I can't do it.' That was two days before the performance. Luckily, Charles Groves was free and after a further three rehearsals conducted it in the Winter Gardens.
>
> Silvestri sat in the stalls with his head bowed throughout. There was tremendous applause at the end. I looked across at Costi: tears were pouring out of him. He sat there for about 20 minutes after the hall had emptied.

Sir Charles Groves remembered Silvestri

> was very bowled over by that piece. We all had supper afterwards and he could talk about nothing else. When I was asked by the BSO to do at least four performances in a week of Britten's *War Requiem* he came to the one in Bournemouth and was very interested in that, too.

The scene changes to a rehearsal in Winchester Cathedral, two Easters later. Southern Television is to present a Good Friday Meditation programme. Raymond Carpenter (recalling the event 30 years later) sings the cello part in the *Motif of Longing* in the *Tristan Liebestod* that 'comes from nothing and, as we all creep in, I can see Silvestri's baton quivering and hear him saying: "Don't watch my hand – it's nervous!"'

Then it is time for the *Prelude* and Good Friday Music from *Parsifal*, with the TV cameras panning across the cathedral's interior and focussing on architectural features as the new Dean of Winchester talks about The Cross.

As usual, Silvestri is insisting on getting the sounds from the orchestra he wants, but there is the additional complication of the music having to be co-ordinated with the camera sequence and cues. He gets increasingly involved

Southern Television filming Silvestri conducting the BSO for a Good Friday 1965 programme – for Costi an intensely emotional experience

in this religious music and there are no less than three 'takes', each longer than the last. . . 'We would either have to speed it up or make a cut,' Matchett recalls.

> Everything was getting slower and slower – it always seemed to be that way: the more he got involved in the music, it would slow down as though he were enjoying every second of it, wallowing in it.

On this occasion, before the final session was concluded, at least to the apparent satisfaction of the producer, there was a crisis.

> Silvestri was totally overwhelmed by the music and the whole situation and broke down in tears. We had a 15-minute break during which we just couldn't talk to him at all. He was totally out of control. The break over, we did the final 'take' and just managed to get everything in.

With sacred music and the drama of the crucifixion involved on both occasions, Matchett hazards a hypothesis to explain Silvestri's reaction:

> I noticed that whenever he went into a cathedral or was in the presence of a cleric his whole demeanour changed: he became very subdued as if he were overawed. I sometimes wondered whether, deep down, he had guilt feelings about being a non-practising Catholic.

Possibly. But the complexity of human motivation allows for other inter-pretations of why the wellsprings of Costi's emotions were released by partic-ular music. It would be surprising if love/death associations were not aroused when he was conducting the *Prelude and Liebestod* in Winchester, although it is unlikely that the immediate exigencies of conducting would have allowed him to be conscious of them – buried memories, possibly of the traumas associated with the deaths of his father and step-father and in his youth of a girlfriend who died in one of Bucharest's several earthquakes. Or unconscious associations with past performances of the same work could also have played their part: in this case the sobbing of people in the audience when he first conducted the *Liebestod* in Bucharest when, eventually, the post-war ban on performing the works of German composers, especially Wagner, was lifted.

Though some music may leave its hearers indifferent, generally the listen-er's emotions react to it in some way and the more intently it is listened to the greater the stimulation. It is not surprising that the emotions of the con-ductor, who almost by definition is the channel through which the written score is transmuted into sounds, should vibrate with particular intensity. Silvestri was not unique in these visible manifestations of feeling; other conductors have admitted to having to make supreme efforts of self-control during passages that moved them (for unexplained and probably inexplicable reasons) in order to avert such manifestations. Karl Böhm confessed he once nearly lost control during the love duet in the second act of *Tristan and Isolde*; and at the end of conducting Strauss' *Tod und Verklärung* (Death and Trans-figuration) he did actually 'break down' in tears – a commonly used but essentially Protestant expression with its connotation of something shameful. Colin Davis was on the verge of doing the same at Covent Garden, he has admitted, towards the end of the *Liebestod*.

As director of the Romanian State Opera, Silvestri is remembered for his respect for the score and for his patience. 'He treated the score quite differently from more conventional conductors who used it to express their own personalities,' said Constantin Petrovici.

> Silvestri respected all the composer's instructions and so brought it to life. He was profoundly analytical. If the minutist part of a computer is missing the whole machine breaks down. Similarly, Silvestri tried not to ignore any little articulation in a work because to do so would damage the work as a whole.
>
> But not only was he a fabulous analyst, he was able to get wonderful

results from an orchestra; whereas other conductors, no matter how they spoke to the players, were unable to evoke the same response.

Which would seem to indicate that Silvestri himself had developed a *modus operandi* with his fellow musicians in the Opera (and in the Radio) more successful in terms of mutual relations than had been those with the Philharmonic. That Petrovici was not alone in his assessment is borne out by the recollections of other members of the Opera orchestra. Tuba player Nicolae Ionaşcu said Silvestri had

> the patience of iron. If he had to tell a player seven times how to do something and if the same musician wanted the same help in the same place, he would do it again and again without becoming impatient. But because he treated us so well in rehearsal, we felt obliged to work at home. We neither dared nor wanted to come to a rehearsal unprepared.
>
> He was always so friendly to everybody and you could discuss anything with him, especially during the breaks in rehearsals or in the corridor. He would listen to any problem, be it personal or to do with the music. We didn't have to ask for an appointment to talk with him as we did with other maestros.

Yet, as far as being artistic director was concerned, Costi would claim that administration wearied him – 'I am a musician, not a clerk. I only want to make music – that is the life I need,' he would say.

When Lorin Maazel, like Silvestri, held simultaneously positions as music director of the Berlin Opera and principal conductor of the Berlin Radio Orchestra he acknowledged the combination had provided great opportunities for 'a broad overall musical development.' No doubt Silvestri benefitted likewise, but it is curious that later in his career in the West he would say he detested opera and would only be persuaded to return to conducting it if it were a production of Enescu's *Oedipus*.

In fact, he did conduct just one opera at Covent Garden in 1963: Mussorgsky's *Khovanschina* – but the critics were not enthusiastic. He had an odd little technical problem with this opera, which it had been decided would be produced in English from the Shostakovich version. The microfilm of the score and Russian libretto was sent from Moscow to Covent Garden; it was printed, enlarged and the libretto translated by Edward Downes. Only one copy of this was photographed, but Silvestri not unreasonably insisted he too must have a copy of the English text with his score. He finally got it – in red ink! This was the only way it would show up on the glossy photographic paper.

Significantly, even with the enhanced reputation Silvestri won during his Bournemouth era, British players also testified to his accessibility and kindness. Principal Oboe Roger Winfield had already had 13 years professional playing behind him when he came to the BSO, including 'six hard years under Barbirolli' and as a cor anglais player under Karajan during the Philharmonia's US tour.

> When I first met Silvestri I was already 28 and inclined to be sceptical, if not a cynic. Yet he fairly knocked me for six. I just couldn't believe that a conductor could get such results out of an orchestra in such a pleasant way. It was quite a remarkable performance and I'm afraid he has been the criterion by which I have since judged conductors. After leaving the BSO in 1968, just before he died, I played with some of the world greats but there's been none to match Silvestri.

Throughout this period of his career, that is from 1945 to 1957, Silvestri was also building his reputation abroad, mainly in the self-styled 'Socialist' countries of the Eastern Bloc. His most spectacular triumphs seem to have been in neighbouring Hungary where the unique phenomenon (from today's perspective) of carrying a conductor through the concert hall as a token of appreciation seems to have occurred at least twice. Teodor Bălan quotes from the Hungarian newspaper *Vilag*, undated but apparently in 1947, when Silvestri, hitherto unknown in Hungary, made his first visit. Commenting on his conducting of a Bach *Oratorio* (*Christmas* or *Easter* is not stated) it declared:

> It is no wonder that the audience gave him a standing ovation, stamping their feet and eventually carrying the maestro in triumph on their shoulders. And three times they insisted on an encore of his own *Toccata* – something quite unprecedented in our musical life.

On January 16 1947, Cella Delavrancea (who died aged 103 in 1991), a piano teacher as renowned in Romania as Musicescu, wrote in *Rampa*:

> I have just returned from Budapest where Silvestri achieved a great triumph after one of his concerts and was carried shoulder-high by his admirers. . . It was at last Sunday's all-Beethoven concert which consisted of the *Fidelio Overture*, the *Piano Concerto No. 4* and *Symphony No. 4*.

The following month, Nina Cassian referred to this again in the same journal:

> As a conductor, Silvestri's every concert is a unique experience, as exemplified recently in the Hungarian capital where the critics gave him rave reviews and he was carried shoulder-high.

The paper *Magyar Ujsag* wrote:

> Silvestri's concerts were a bomb for our capital. His triumph was all the
> more authentic because the public in Budapest never allow themselves to
> be carried away by international celebrities. In Budapest, where Kubelik,
> Gigli and Galli-Curci had flops, Silvestri had triumphs, only equalled by
> those accorded to Nikisch and to Toscanini during his tour with the New
> York Philharmonic 12 years ago.

The Hungarian honeymoon continued into 1948, with the journal *Hirlap*
maintaining:

> Not since Willem Mengelberg have we heard a *Pathétique* like Silvestri's;
> since Nikisch, such a Dvorak; since Bruno Walter, such a Mozart; since
> Furtwängler, such a Brahms;

while over the radio he was lionised as 'one of the great conductors of our
time'.

He did not expect the same reaction from the Czechs and was apparently a
little apprehensive before his first visit to Prague the same year. But even the
dauntingly fastidious Pragiotes seem to have been won over. The *Rude Pravo*
reviewer wrote

> Even though he only conducted one concert, everybody was in agreement
> that he should be considered one of the greatest conductors of our day –
> one among the four or five greats,

Another recorded that this first visit was extraordinarily successful for
Silvestri, both as conductor and composer. He returned to Czechoslovakia in
1953, 1955 and 1957 but, as we have seen, the exile from Romania was unable to
share in the BSO's success there in 1965.

He was fêted in Dresden, in the German Democratic Republic, in 1955 'with
indescribable enthusiasm' for his 'titanic' interpretation of the Beethoven
Ninth, for his 'masterly technique and for his memory which retained the
smallest details of the score,' according to one reviewer.

Anatol Vieru was a student in Moscow when Silvestri prepared and conducted the Shostakovich *First Symphony* and recalled:

> I went to the rehearsal and Shostakovich was there too and seemed very
> pleased. But at the performance in the Tchaikovsky Hall some people got
> up and left – his *First Symphony* was not a very popular piece and Shosta-
> kovich himself was under a cloud at the time.

At home in Bucharest at the peak of his career in Romania

Radu Paladi said that the *First Symphony* was given its first postwar performance in Bucharest by Silvestri and was a work which particularly fascinated Romanian audiences. Although he himself was not there, Paladi had heard from other musicians that Shostakovich had gone backstage after Silvestri had conducted a performance of the symphony with the Moscow Radio Orchestra and told him: 'I relived the creation of my symphony during this performance. If I were to conduct it myself, I would probably do it in the same way.' Shostakovich had, in fact, written it for his graduation from the Leningrad Conservatoire when he was 19 – the scherzo even earlier – and it had been an immediate success. One Western critic, after reviewing his works up to and including the *Seventh Symphony*, remarked as early as 1943 that, since his *First Symphony*, 'something has gone out of Shostakovich which he has not yet succeeded in recapturing,' thus anticipating by nearly 40 years the composer's own revelation of his revulsion for Stalin.

As for Silvestri, he considered Shostakovich a genius, according to Vieru who remembered

> seeing in the Romanian Society for Cultural Relations with the USSR one of Silvestri's own compositions which he had sent to Dmitri with a handwritten dedication expressing his deep admiration.

This esteem appears to have been mutual and, according to Bălan, Shostakovich was moved by Silvestri's interpretation and surprised at his understanding of his works. In 1956, Silvestri conducted in Bucharest the *Eighth* – 'declared counter revolutionary and anti-Soviet' in the words of its composer years later – and *Tenth Symphonies* on the occasion of Shostakovich's 50th birthday. He also made a Soviet recording of the *First*; an HMV recording of the *Fifth* (the 'Soviet artist's reply to just criticism,' Dmitri's tongue-in-cheek sub-title) with the Vienna Philharmonic; and the *Tenth* with the Romanian company, Electrecord – but, of course, too soon to know that Shostakovich intended it to be 'about Stalin and the Stalin years.'

In a Bucharest broadcast in 1958, Silvestri compared the *First* and *Tenth Symphonies*:

> The *First Symphony* is the most unified, the most Tchaikovskyan of all Shostakovich's symphonies. He wrote the *First* at an age when he decided: 'I have to say what I know' and in the *Tenth* he says: 'I have already said what I knew then, but now that I have time, I can say it in more detail.' So he repeats it, on a larger scale but not with as dramatic a conclusion as in the *First Symphony*.

But, like the Shostakovich *First*, Russian audiences had mixed feelings about Silvestri's interpretation of the Tchaikovsky last symphonies. Both Cristescu and Paladi said the Leningraders disliked his conducting of the *Fourth* 'because he broke with tradition'; the musicians were 'stuck in their old habits' and preferred the more conservative George Georgescu who, according to Paladi,

> became very good friends with Svyatoslav Richter who was often invited to Romania – the first postwar country outside the Soviet Union in which he played.

The performance of the *Mass in C Minor* on the bi-centenary of Mozart's birth in January 1956 (which so affected Amelia Beldi) made waves that reached inside the Great National Assembly in Bucharest during its eighth annual session. One of the deputies answering some criticism of the state of Romania's culture declared:

> The basis of our culture, far from shrinking as some maintain, has been consolidated. Can't these people hear the echoes of Mozart's sublime *Mass*? Never was music more popular and working people are starting to be musically educated, beginning to like it and understand it. . .

In November, the announcement appeared in the press:

> For exceptional merit in the realm of artistic activities, the Praesidium of the Great National Assembly has conferred the title of Artist of the People on Constantin Silvestri.

The following month, the Radio devoted programmes to this newly honoured People's Artist, playing four of his own works and performances of works, like the *Missa Solemnis*, which had helped exalt his reputation as a conductor.

At 43, the once impecunious Costi now had a handsome flat in the Calea Victoriei, almost next door to the Romanian Academy and close to what would become the Enescu Museum and today houses the Union of Composers (after Ceauşescu's son Nicu had designs on it for himself.) Costi and his wife Viorica had two cars between them. He had built up a collection of 110 paintings, including a Vlaminck, and his Romanian canvasses, he would boast, rivalled those in Bucharest's galleries. Persian carpets were also among his acquisitions. He came by these assets through a combination of what must have been by this time a substantial salary; the sale of the records he had made; and because of the low prices of the paintings and carpets which the dispossesed bourgeoisie were obliged to sell. He also claimed to have 3,000 78-rpm records and 2,000 LPs as well as a considerable collection of stamps.

His collecting urge was not necessarily wholly or even in part that of the parvenu: he had been a philatelist since boyhood; his record collecting was an integral part of his music-making; and his fascination with graphic art extended beyond his collection, to discussions in his home with art students and artists, especially about the Romanian Impressionists.

Materially, Silvestri was now well-endowed by the standards of his time and place, his moderate acquisitive ambitions sated. In the 11 years since his appointment to the Philharmonic, his reputation was established and he was the recipient of high honours. He had reached the peak of his career – at least in the country of his birth.

CHAPTER 6

FULL TO THE BRIM

In the autumn of 1956, Romanian newspapers announced that People's Artist Constantin Silvestri had been invited to conduct the London Philharmonic Orchestra.

Under a regime where travelling beyond the national frontiers, even to those countries considered by the authorities ideologically kosher, could only be done with their say-so, one can imagine there was a good deal of behind-the-scenes debate about the wisdom of granting a visa to a man, admittedly brilliant, but who had shown a suspect independence of spirit and unorthodoxy – just the type to succumb to the blandishments of an open society. He would surely be seduced by the crass liberalism of a city which was home to both that monument to Mammon, the Stock Exchange, and to a monumental bust of Karl Marx dominating his grave.

On the other hand, some of the wetter *apparatchiks* must have argued: to refuse Silvestri a visa would result in bad publicity worldwide, which could have a knock-on effect on Romania's tourist trade. There could even be a positive side to granting him a visa: a boost for Romania's prestige, the reflected glory of a successful concert tour in the West.

The wets won; the exit visa was granted.

This is not entirely suppositional: Silvestri in the past had either been refused visas to travel to the West or – what amounted to the same thing – such had been the bureaucratic procrastination that a visa had become useless by the time it was granted. Once, when a Spanish tour had been arranged with Costi conducting a foreign orchestra, the exit visa never arrived and the tour had to be cancelled.

One of the most powerful men in Romania after Gheorghe Gheorghiu-Dej at this time was Chivu Stoica who became Prime Minister and would become President of the Council of State when Dej died (but who would shoot himself in 1974 after a quarrel with Ceauşescu.) Stoica got impatient with Silvestri's repeated importuning for exit visas for foreign concert tours and is alleged to have exploded: 'Why does this ass keep trying to force my hand to let him go?'

Although Silvestri had gone to Paris in 1956 to pay respects at Enescu's grave, he had been in the company of Jora and Ion Dumitrescu (Perlea who had already defected joined them at the graveside.) So there was really no precedent for letting him go West on his own and permission could not have been granted lightly.

Two questions beg to be answered: first, how did the management of the LPO hear about this Romanian conductor whose reputation admittedly extended to Budapest, Prague, Warsaw, Berlin, Leningrad and Moscow but was confined to behind the Iron Curtain?

Secondly, a question requiring a far more analytical answer: when and why did Silvestri make the fateful decision to stay in the West?

A brief allusion has already been made to the meeting in Bucharest between Silvestri and Malcolm Rayment, London music critic of the *Glasgow Herald* who had called Costi's 1957 début in the Royal Albert Hall 'the most memorable concert in London since the war' and who, seven years later, dedicated his own symphony to the maestro and to the BSO. The circumstances of that meeting are worth recording because the result would indeed be 'memorable' for Silvestri.

On a visit to Romania in December 1955, Rayment had been invited to look over the Radio Bucharest building. He recalls:

> When I heard a truly electrifying account of part of the Shostakovich *Tenth Symphony* coming from the Radio's concert hall, I refused to move until it was all over. It was then that I met Silvestri for the first time. We discussed, in French, tempos and their relationships in the final movement of this symphony which he was preparing for its Bucharest première. This was of especial interest to me since I had gone through the work with Sir Adrian Boult prior to his giving its British première.
>
> Subsequently, Silvestri came to my hotel and invited me to a party in his flat, which I afterwards realised he had organised for my benefit. I know the exact date because it was there that he gave me a copy of his *Second String Quartet* Op.27 with a little inscription in Romanian showing our strong *rapprochement* and the date. It said:

> 'I encountered in you, Malcolm, a new friend. If friendship means communication through words, they were not necessary – our eyes spoke for us! We feel about de Falla and Bartók in the same way – and probably about the whole gamut of the arts as well. Please accept this score as a token of my regard.

'[Signed] C. Silvestri

'11.XII.55'

Our mutual understanding grew at that party because there were English-speaking Romanians there who were able to translate for us.

I was determined to introduce him to London. I thought there would be an uphill battle when I got back but, although I did a bit of prodding in the initial stage, the opportunity came sooner than expected.

I had strong connections with, and did quite a lot of work for, the LPO and, in fact, they asked me to choose three really outstanding conductors from Eastern Europe, but unknown in this country, for an adventurous series of concerts they were planning for 1957 and in which I was involved. Apart from Silvestri, I suggested Janos Ferencsik from Budapest, who also came, and a conductor from Brno who, however, never received the invitation because it wasn't passed on by the agency in Prague.

My recommendation of Silvestri I still think was my best service to music.

Negotiations began directly between the LPO and Silvestri or through a London agent, Julius Finzi, who in July 1956 wrote asking him for his biographical details. In August, the LPO was asking Silvestri what programme he wanted to conduct for his London engagements at the end of January 1957.

In the five months between receiving this request for his programme and Silvestri actually leaving for London, he went to Budapest for the Bartók Festival, from where he wrote to a friend that in a couple of days he would be returning to Bucharest to conduct five concerts – two of them with David Oistrakh; back to Budapest for two more with the Hungarian Philharmonic; north to the GDR with concerts in Dresden and Leipzig; and six more in Moscow, Kiev and Leningrad.

Sandwiched between his two visits to Britain in 1957, he had two concerts in Brussels, more in Greece and Switzerland and, as we already noted, the *Missa Solemnis* was recorded in Bucharest. He also managed a rest in a secluded spot at the foot of Mt. Retezat in the Western Carpathians.

At this distance in time it has not been possible to ascertain whether George Georgescu – his reputation restored and now fully in charge of the Bucharest Philharmonic – really did block Silvestri's chances of conducting Romania's most prestigious orchestra, as some aver. Even Costi's two Oistrakh concerts were not with the Philharmonic.

There is a curious story which, if true and depending on the interpretation put on it, shows Georgescu in a more generous light than those who stressed his alleged jealousy would have us believe, unless it was a theatrical and

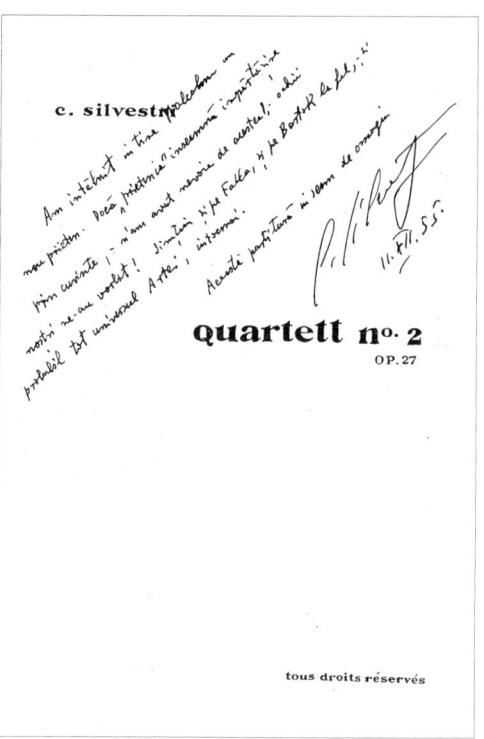

c. silvestri

quartett n°· 2

OP. 27

tous droits réservés

'Please accept this score as a token of my regard' – Silvestri's inscription on a copy of his Second String Quartet *which he presented to a new-found British friend. This meeting in Bucharest Radio led to his first visit to England in 1957 to conduct a series of concerts with the London Philharmonic and, subsequently, 13 records with the Philharmonia*

hypocritical display of magnanimity. Unfortunately, after 36 years there was no confirmation from any other source, but my informant was adamant he was an eye witness of at least the first part of what he related.

It was at what must have been at one of two Bucharest concerts in April 1955 when Silvestri conducted the Philharmonic and included in the programme was Liszt's symphonic poem *Tasso, Lamento e Trionfo*. George Georgescu was in the audience with his wife, Tutu, and Gita Mendel Schapira, who had been a close friend of Enescu. To the surprise of all those who took for granted rumours of Georgescu's jealousy of Silvestri, the older man strode up to the platform and embraced Costi. At which – and this must have been hearsay – Gita turned to Tutu as they both joined in the applause and exclaimed: 'How wonderful! Now we have two great conductors!' To which Mme Georgescu is purported to have rejoined: 'Really? I only know of one.'

But it would have been of no great consequence if the stories about the Georgescu/Silvestri rivalry were apocryphal and, especially, the rumour that went the rounds in Bucharest in subsequent years that it was the prime reason for Silvestri leaving Romania for good. Since Georgescu had never conducted a work of Silvestri before, and had actually handed him the baton in 1942 to conduct his own *Concerto Grosso*, certainly the prescient Fates must have been playing a merry jape putting it into George's mind to include Costi's *Prelude and Toccata* in a Bucharest Philharmonic concert on September 18, 1958. Six weeks later, Silvestri had shaken off the dust of his native land for ever. But there were certainly other more compelling reasons than this alleged rivalry for him doing so.

'I heard,' said Anatol Vieru,

> that Silvestri wanted to leave Romania as early as 1947 but the frontiers were already closed. I think in this phase of his life, in spite of him having given me, as an example of his contrariness, his 'attraction' to both fascism and communism, he really felt threatened by both. After the war, because he was so involved in music, he wanted only a musical career and he felt he was a prisoner in Romania. I was very politically orthodox at that time, so I was shocked when he referred to Petru Groza [the Prime Minister and later Head of State 1945–1952] as a pig. In fact, the new regime helped him very much and he reached the top. It was a very dramatic period; while the regime did a lot for music, all was not well ideologically – everything was mixed-up, ambiguous, unclear.

Someone in the Radio who, as a young man, used to vet cultural (including some musical) programmes before they went out over the air, claimed

> artists didn't suffer, only the writers, philosophers and historians; not the actors, musicians and graphic or plastic artists. Nevertheless, although the Soviet troops left Romania in 1958, the Russian 'advisers' remained until about 1960. They were in every field, not only in security and the armed services, but in agriculture, industry and commerce; in every corner of life: in the railway stations, the airport, the Health Ministry – you name it, they were there. And, of course, in the Radio. Our adviser there had the rank of general in the Soviet army. His office was close to that of the president of the Radio and he was present at all the management meetings. He either had an interpeter or he had learned Romanian. He was the one who made the final decisions.
>
> There has not been enough time since the revolution to make an in-depth analysis of this period, but these things will surface in due course.

These were the conditions that appertained when Silvestri was director of the Radio Symphony Orchestra. Even if artists in the pre-Ceauşescu era were privileged in having a degree of immunity from direct repression not afforded some other professions, there were those who were affected indirectly because their relatives were penalised. A case in point is that of Pascal Bentoiu, who in the course of giving his recollections of Silvestri, explained why he himself had turned down an offer to become director of the Philharmonic. His father had been a member of the National Peasant Party, forcibly dissolved by the Communists in July 1947 for 'anti-state activities,' and he was jailed in 1948 when Pascal was a 21 year-old student of composition. His father was released in 1956, found 'not guilty' of whatever he was accused, but re-arrested the following year (in the repercussions throughout the Soviet bloc following the suppression of the Hungarian uprising) and given another prison sentence of 25 years. After five years, he died in prison – having spent a total of 13 years in jail. His family were thrown out of their house. Neither Pascal nor his sister were allowed to continue their studies nor to go to any public function. When the Philharmonic offer was made in the Sixties, Pascal Bentoiu felt he was only qualified 'to be the Athenaeum's porter' and refused.

Silvestri probably knew little about the physical repression of these early years of the regime. Judith Vancea said she only learned later of the persecution in Gheorghiu-Dej's time, which included thousands of political prisoners being sent to build the Danube-Black Sea Canal, or those, like the elder Bentoiu, dying in prison. 'The arts were given the full support of the state,' she said.

> Before Ceaușescu [i.e. pre-1965] there were many concerts and the philharmonics thrived on state subventions. Only as living conditions worsened and heating and lighting were progressively reduced did the audiences dwindle.

As we have seen, in the comparatively short period of a decade since his appointment with the Philharmonic, Silvestri also thrived. His circumstances were very different from those that had irked him under the old regime – about which he had complained in the memorandum that never reached the King; that had brought him to the state of contemplating 'abandoning the lyre' and of evoking the bitter 'I don't owe my country anything.'

In May 1959, that is eight months after he had left Romania for the last time, he told an Australian journalist the government in Bucharest did not impose any restrictions on the work that could be performed and it encouraged composers by commissioning work from them. What he did not mention were the restrictions that had been imposed on his own foreign travel. These had meant not only that he had been unable to make a reputation outside of the Soviet bloc, but also that he could not savour at first hand the musical milieux and developments which, tantalisingly, he was aware of through his radio monitoring.

Moreover, perhaps because he still wanted to keep his options open or for fear of reprisals against those he left behind, neither did he mention the Big-Brotherly 'advisers' who must have been very irksome (to put it mildly) however discreet they were supposed to have been in the musical compared with other fields.

Conductor Mircea Cristescu:

Silvestri was always experimenting with new ideas. He had a very broad vision for the repertoire of the orchestra, from the pre-classics to the moderns, but he had to fight for the inclusion of certain composers. In the early post-war period it was Wagner and Strauss because of the anti-German bias. When I joined the Philharmonic as a viola player, Wagner was taboo and I remember the day when Silvestri announced: 'We can play Richard Strauss this year!'

Furthermore, as the director, Silvestri had to take part in meetings where there were not only trade union representatives but Soviet advisers as well and he couldn't stand it when they were interfering with his artistic programmes. His brother-in-law was the distinguished violinist Mircea Vasilescu; they had many things in common and so were very close. Mircea learned from Costi how suffocated he felt because his considerable potential was not being realised.

As an illustration of this suffocating atmosphere and an example of the straightjacket of ludicrous jargon and sycophantic hyperbole in which even intelligent music critics were constricted, here is how the section headed 'Musical Life' – which included reviews of concerts conducted by Silvestri and Georgescu – appeared in the April 1951 issue of *Muzica*, organ of the 'Union of Composers of the People's Republic of Romania':

After the table of contents there followed three full-page portraits of 'Comrade Gheorghe Gheorghiu-Dej, Secretary-General of the Workers Party of Romania,' of Ana Pauker, secretary of its Central Committee, and of Vasile Luca, another Central Committee secretary. Then there were five pages devoted to: 'The Party – Our Music Mentor' from which the following choice excerpts are gleaned:

Our aim is . . . to create ever more numerous compositions . . . new works on a grand scale – operas, symphonies or oratorios – which will reflect all the many facets and inner resources of the Communist fighter [which, presumably, smaller works were not worthy of doing]. We must make a strong battlefront around our Party, mobilise and enthuse the working masses in the fight against the enemy of peace and Socialism. This is the pledge all honest musicians must make on the occasion of the great day: May 8 [the 30th anniversary of the party's foundation].

This was followed by the verses of songs composed after the party was banned under King Carol by ones dedicated to the anniversary; by a list of Stalin Prizewinners for 1950; by the titles of music that had been awarded state prizes; a list of signatories of 'Composers for Peace'; and a report of a symposium of Soviet composers on Shostakovich's *Song of the Forests*.

'Our composers,' it ran,

will discover in this work many reflections of their own striving to find a clear musical expression . . . in the spirit of the Party. It is sufficient to remind them of just one theme of burning relevance today which is awaiting its artistic fulfilment: The Plan of Electrification within the framework of the great task of Socialist Industrialisation. This is how Shostakovich understood his mission as artist and composer. . . The subjugation of the blind forces of Nature is no longer a dream in the era of Stalin. When Stalin says: 'It is!' then it must be. And then we can answer joyfully: 'We have accomplished it!'

At last there is presented: 'Symphony Concerts Conducted By Constantin Silvestri' – not an unqualified eulogy, however. After praise for his choice of programmes, his conducting and 'great attention to Soviet composers,' our man is taken to task. For he also gave 'too much attention to works which belong to an outmoded phase of the music in the Land of Socialism' and

did not present any of the new works linked to the activities of Soviet life and illustrative of the new orientation of music composition following the historic Decision of the Central Committee of the Communist Party of the USSR on Problems in Music,

(about which more will be said later.)

The final sentence of this 'review' is a classic example of the arrogant impertinence and veiled threat by the party *apparatchiks* when dealing with a brilliant and popular artist: 'We do not doubt, though, that all these deficiencies will be remedied by this eminent musician. . .'

Having taken full advantage in 1957 of being granted his exit visa to make concert tours not only in Britain but to other West European countries, and without any sign that the Romanian authorities would not grant him such freedom in future – as indeed they did – it would be reasonable to assume that one major cause of his spiritual 'suffocation,' or ideological and professional claustrophobia, had been removed. Now he could escape from it at will, while retaining his Romanian domicile and citizenship.

But there would be two potent factors which would have a crucial influence in bringing about his final decision to reject this option and stay in the West. The first was a very personal one that had nothing to do with politics or Georgescu or suffocation.

Apart from his public concerts in London during his first visit in 1957, Silvestri spent a full week in mid-February in the Kingsway Hall, Holborn, recording the last three Tchaikovsky symphonies with the Philharmonia for EMI. It was during a break just after listening to a playback that he was approached by a Romanian journalist friend resident in London who had quietly entered the studio together with a young lady dressed in black.

'Sorry I'm late,' apologised the journalist, 'but as compensation I've brought you your cousin from Târgu Mureş.'

Costi appreciated the joke. He had no cousin in Târgu Mureş . . . and the lady was certainly attractive.

'Well, well! What a nice idea!' said the chivalrous Silvestri and invited them to sit down, just before the bell sounded for the second part of the recording to start.

The journalist impressed on the 'cousin' what a great honour it was, not only to have met the maestro, 'the greatest conductor in Romania' – she just about recalled once having heard his name being announced on Radio Bucharest before a concert was broadcast – but also to be allowed to remain in this Holy of Holies, a recording studio during an actual recording.

When this was over, Silvestri took the The Lady in Black to lunch in the Piccadilly Hotel. There he learned that she was Mme Regina Meisner, widow of a Hungarian businessman who had died from a heart attack in Munich when they were on their way back to their home in Paris after a holiday. Now, she was visiting London with a lady friend.

For her part, Regina – known to all her friends as Pupa – noted the wedding ring on her luncheon companion's finger. 'I thought he was a nice man, but I was not all that impressed with him,' Pupa recalled 40 years later in her Paris flat.

But Silvestri certainly was with her and pressed his suit with all his natural charm. But after escorting her back to the Vanderbilt Hotel in South Kensington, whether or not his intentions were strictly honourable, he got no further than the doorstep where, to his persistent: 'When do I see you again?' he was given the reply: 'You are a person *très sympatique* and, as an artist you must be very sensitive and therefore able to understand my feelings better than most. You see me dressed from head to foot in black and you know why I am in mourning. And that mourning,' pressing her hand to her heart, 'is nothing in comparison with what is here. I lost the man I adored. I thank you for all your kindness and insistence on wanting to see me; but I am immune. It is really not possible. I hope I don't offend you.'

Soon after she got back to Paris, Pupa got a letter from Costi which ended: 'I'm still thinking of you.'

And he still was exactly one year later, the end of the requisite period of Jewish mourning. (Pupa was the daughter of a Romanian rabbi.) Exactly to the day, Pupa received another letter:

> I am in Paris. I have respected your wish and left you alone for a year. Now, if you still remember me, I am staying in Hotel —— . It will be a great pleasure to meet you again.

Only a mental identikit impression can be built of Viorica (Romanian diminutive for a violet), Costi's first wife whom he married when he was 29, from the brief and sometimes contrasting references to her.

When he was a 17-year-old violinist, Pascal Bentoiu remembers her as 'a very pretty woman'; Constantin Bugeanu said her father was a prosperous lawyer and her stepbrother, Mircea Vasilescu, was 'a handsome violinist at the Philharmonic.' (It was probably through him that Viorica and Costi met.) 'She was a splendid wife who took on all responsibilities so that Silvestri was free to concentrate on his work.'

Radu Paladi said Silvestri did not have to do his improvising concerts too often 'because he had a rich wife.'

Judith Vancea seems to have known her best:

> She was a beautiful Romanian who nursed Silvestri in a villa in Sinaia when he had TB. She was a sensitive, generous person and at first the marriage went very well and we invited them to stay with us many times in 1948 and 1949. But Silvestri was always surrounded by women and had many conquests. Viorica was humiliated many times. He was a passionate man. . .

Less appealing was Nina Cassian's description of Viorica: 'A rigid beauty with no expression, without warmth,' but Nina admitted very frankly that her appraisal may have been influenced by jealousy.

Pupa never actually described her predecessor, but told a strange story of how Viorica insisted on meeting her and how, only after extreme pressure during a long-distance phone call from the first Mrs Silvestri did she agree to meet her in a Vienna hotel. Silvestri himself was also present and a pact was made whereby Viorica agreed to free Costi from his marital bonds provided he got her out of Romania. All three then travelled back to Paris, apparently the best of friends. The collusion aspect of this affair (which would have made any British divorce lawyer's hair stand on end) does not seem to have occurred to any of the parties concerned. Because Viorica had come from Bucharest in a hurry and left essential clothing behind, Pupa even bought her a mink coat . . . and Silvestri continued to support her.

Viorica soon got homesick for Romania and several times commuted between Paris and Bucharest. She eventually became hospitalised in Paris with leukaemia and died – Costi attending her to the last.

As she looked back down the years, the last word on this subject by Pupa (who herself had survived the deaths of three husbands) was: 'So, I married a widower, not a divorcee.'

A year after he first met Pupa in London, Silvestri was back in the UK where, in January and February (1958), he did seven concerts with the LPO in London and on the south coast; recorded Hindemith's *Mathis der Maler* symphony, Bartók's *Divertimento for Strings* and Liszt's symphonic poem *Tasso* and *Les Préludes* with the Philharmonia; and there were more concerts in Paris at the end of the month and in March.

Then he returned to Romania. So far our suppositional wets who had argued for giving Silvestri a visa were justified; he had made three separate visits to the West and returned; Romania had a new peripatetic ambassador enhancing his country's prestige.

In April he gave an interview for the Radio to a journalist in his study at home in the Calea Victoriei. On the wall behind his desk was a painting, *The Kobsa Player*, by the Romanian Impressionist Ștefan Luchian (a *kobsa* is an ancient stringed instrument resembling a lute) and on his desk the latest type of recording equipment playing one of the Tchaikovsky symphonies he had recorded with the Philharmonia the year before.

He admitted to the interviewer that he had had a tiring schedule in Britain and that at one rehearsal with the LPO 'one of the best English conductors,' Sir Adrian Boult, had offered 'to take over for half an hour so that I could get a rest.'

In view of how events were to unfold, the conclusion of this interview dealing with his future plans, is significant:

INTERVIEWER: So now you are having a rest?

SILVESTRI: It's normal isn't it? I feel I need at least six weeks. But I must also resume the conducting lessons with my students. I would be very happy if, before the end of the concert season, that is before the end of June, I could do one of Paul Constantinescu's *Oratorios* which I have been planning to do for some time.

INTERVIEWER: And next season? I see on your desk folders from Australia and America.

SILVESTRI: Yes, I received some very insistent proposals from there and from other places, like Israel. But, I tell you in confidence [*sic*], I declined all offers for this autumn such as to conduct in Berlin and Vienna, at the Edinburgh, Besançon and Montreux festivals and to open the Concertgebouw season in Amsterdam.

INTERVIEWER: Why?

SILVESTRI: I can answer that in one word: *Oedip*! I would like this autumn during the Enescu International Festival for everyone to be able to hear Enescu's *chef d'oeuvre*, his *Oedip*.

What he did not tell the interviewer – unless it was, indeed, 'in confidence' and therefore not over the air – was that he had accepted the Australian Broadcasting Corporation's offer for a tour in 1959 and also, probably as early as this, the Chicago Symphony Orchestra's offer for 1960. Had he already made up his mind that these would be tours from which he would not return to Romania?

George Enescu had started to work on his opera, *Oedipus* * during the First World War and finished it in 1922, but the orchestration was not ready until 1931. The first performance was at the Paris Opera in 1936 and in a radio interview in Romania Silvestri mentioned 'the great success' of its Brussels production which he had seen in April 1956, either on his way to or on his way back from his visit to Enescu's grave in Paris. But not a note or word of *Oedipus* had been heard in Romania itself until Silvestri, who had brought back photocopies of the score from Paris, conducted Act IV in a commemorative concert for Enescu in Bucharest three months later, when the principal soloist was Gabriel Naruja, a doctor by profession.

In the Bucharest Radio interview he explained how the Swiss-born libret-

---

* The libretto of Enescu's opera was written in French and the title as *Oedipe*, which in Romanian is spelled *Oedip*. The English *Oedipus* is used here throughout except when a Romanian is being quoted.

tist Edmond Fleg had followed the narrative of two plays in the Sophocles trilogy, *Oedipus Tyrannus* and *Oedipus Colonnus*, and adapted it in the form of four acts. He went on to give a résumé of the opera version of the plot which is repeated here because of its significance regarding the events that followed the first staging of the opera in Bucharest and the impact of these on Silvestri.

In Act I, the Prologue, the celebrations after the birth of Oedipus to Queen Jocasta and King Laios of Thebes are interrupted by the blind prophet Tiresias predicting Oedipus will commit parricide.

In Act II, Oedipus having escaped the attempt of his father to have him killed as a baby, and having been fostered by King Polybus and Queen Merope of Corinth, tells his supposed mother that he has learned of the prophesy that he will kill his father and, to escape this fate, he will banish himself from the kingdom. In a chance encounter with King Laios he kills him, not knowing he is his real father. Oedipus, later, confronts the Sphinx which declares Destiny is so powerful it even controls the fate of the gods themselves and poses the riddle: 'What puny creature in the whole vast Universe could eclipse Destiny?' Oedipus cries: 'Man – Man is bigger than Destiny' and the monster which had been devouring those Thebans unable to give the correct solution, expires. Oedipus is crowned King of Thebes and marries Jocasta, unaware she is his mother.

Twenty years later, in Act III, Thebes is devastated by a plague. Jocasta's father, Creon, consults the Delphic oracle and learns that only if the murderer of Laios is found will the plague-ridden city be redeemed. Oedipus initiates an inquiry and when Tiresias and the shepherd who witnessed the killing testify, Oedipus gradually realises the truth about himself. Jocasta commits suicide and Oedipus pierces his eyes. Protesting that he is not guilty since his fate was sealed even before he was born, at Creon's behest backed by popular demand, the blinded Oedipus leaves the city together with Antigone, his (and Jocasta's) daughter.

In Act IV, the Epilogue, Oedipus and Antigone arrive at the spot where he knows the oracle has predicted he will die in a grove sacred to the Eumenides, the protectors of Athens, and thereby redeem himself and bring prosperity to the city. He explains his resolve to Theseus, King of Athens; the gods restore his sight and, declaring (in the Fleg version): *'J'ai vaincu le destin'* (in the Romanian translation by Emanoil Ciomac: 'I triumphed over my destiny, I conquered Fate'), he walks, unaided, to a cave and is engulfed in a blaze of light. It is decreed that none may witness this act of immolation and the assembled Athenians cover their eyes.

Just as he said he intended to do, it was Silvestri again who would prepare and conduct the first performance in Romania of the entire opera. That was on September 24 1958 as part of the first Enescu International Festival.

Silvestri was tremendously impressed with the opera and here he explains why:

> Because of its dramatic value – the combination of text and music – I consider that with *Oedipus* Enescu realised a theatrical masterpiece, surpassing opera and, through reviving Greek drama, combined drama with lyrical theatre. In this way, *Oedipus* ranks with the most valuable 20th century operas: Debussy's *Pelléas et Mélisande*, Strauss's *Salome* and Berg's *Wozzeck*.
>
> I would say that with *Oedipus* Enescu was the initiator of something quite new in music. He is absolutely original in this creation: no other influences, no borrowing from other composers. I am referring particularly to the scene with the Sphinx in Act II and to the scene with the blinding of *Oedipus*. The way in which he uses the chorus, the link between the chorus as commentator and the *bel canto*, is unique. The orchestral colours, enriched with the special timbres of various combinations of instruments, including some never used in this way before, bring to *Oedipus* a palette hitherto unsurpassed. The melodic substance is infinitely rich, as it is throughout Enescu's works. The unity between the counterpoint, melodic material, construction and text is total.
>
> But because of the extraordinary complexity of the work, these things are not easily perceived at first. It needs a rather more musically knowledgeable audience to appreciate all of its subtleties. But I think that, through the skill with which the opera was conceived, the public will be won over and will come back to listen to the work and slowly, slowly will be able to understand its musical substance.
>
> Even today, after so many months of rehearsing and when I know this work pretty well, my emotions are as spontaneous as ever – for this is the effect Enescu has on one: it is like being in a labyrinth with hidden places which, when discovered, move one to tears.

Aniela Beldi has already been quoted expressing how difficult the players found the score of *Oedipus* in 1956. In 1958, the baritone David Ohanesian, a professional who in this Bucharest première and many times over 26 years played the leading role and has sung alongside such world top-rankers as Luciano Pavarotti, Placido Domingo and Leontyne Price, maintained:

> From the musical point of view this is the most difficult score I have ever come across in the whole operatic repertoire. In all the opera houses in

which I have appeared from Athens to Los Angeles, whether as Scarpia or Iago, I kept on thinking of Oedipus and his destiny. The great Enescu provided me with this role, which became my life and determined my destiny. I am happy to have been born with the capacity to sing *Oedipus*. I believe it is the most difficult and, maybe, the most important lyrical work of the 20th century,

an opinion he shared with Silvestri and with Arthur Honegger, who is said to have declared *Oedipe* was without doubt the work of one of the greatest composers and its place was 'among the highest summits of opera.'

Ohanesian, who had already retired from the operatic stage, was living modestly compared with his renowned colleagues. His Mercedes-Benz, his only visible status symbol, was parked on the unmetalled and at night unilluminated track outside his bungalow near Băneasa Airport on the outskirts of Bucharest. A well-built, ruddy-cheeked, unassuming man in his 60s with a lively intelligence and dry humour, he was glad to take refuge from the inevitable stresses, pollution and clamour of the metropolis, to tend his garden, poultry, pigs and their litter; to reminisce with friends, over his wife's home-made cakes washed down with home-brewed Kirsch, and even to enter into televised polemics on behalf of his beloved *Oedipus*.

He expanded on the difficulties of the role:

It is a long role and the interpreter, apart from having to be equipped with a robust voice rich in harmonics, faces ever new demands: alternations of restraint and tumultuous explosions; indications like *poco sforzando, ben sforzando, poco rinforzando, ben rinforzando, feroce* and so on, which one rarely encounters in other scores; and I had to sing in quarter-tones and declaim in tones. The quarter-tones are written to express a wail or lamentation.*

* Pascal Bentoiu in his *Capodopere enesciene* (Enescu's Masterpieces) says the quarter-tones appear at moments of extreme stress, desperation or evil throughout the opera as for instance when Oedipus sings of the virtues of poison as a remedy to end his sufferings; in the diatribe of the Sphynx; in Oedipus's self-mutilation and, in Act IV, these quarter-tones occur a few times, as when Antigone is frightened by Creon. Sometimes there are not just quarter-tones but three-quarter tones and Bentoiu gives as an example:

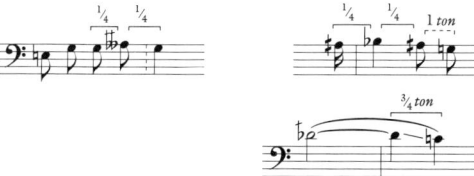

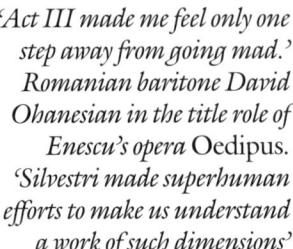

'*Act III made me feel only one
step away from going mad.*'
Romanian baritone David
Ohanesian in the title role of
Enescu's opera Oedipus.
'Silvestri made superhuman
efforts to make us understand
a work of such dimensions'

The alternation between feebleness and forcefulness presupposes a perfect technique in the singer and considerable experience. It makes tremendous demands on one's stamina.

Also from the acting point of view it is, I think, the most complex role I have ever encountered. Act III made me feel only one step away from going mad. More than once I felt I was suffocating.

The extent of Ohanesian's emotional input into the role can be gauged from this description of an episode in Act III by a contemporary reviewer:

In his anguish, Oedipus pierces his eyes and the dreadful, almost inhuman groan which is sung in Ohanesian's thrilling baritone, freezes the blood in our veins.

Opera conductor Constantin Petrovici said the score was in Enescu's handwriting and he remembers Silvestri looking through a magnifying glass as he perused fragments of it. For three months before the first rehearsal, Silvestri had himself copied the parts for each instrument. 'He was a great conductor,' Petrovici said,

and, in a way, a great philosopher because he was telling the players what accents had to be attached to a phrase, the feel of it, so that the audience would have the best possible reception. It is the conductor who has to work out how the audience hears the music the way the composer wanted it to be heard.

Four percussionists were needed for *Oedipus*. One of these was Ioan Maxim whose accomplishments included playing the glockenspiel, tam-tam,

Silvestri at the apex of his career in Romania poses with Oedipus *producer Jean Rînzescu (left), David Ohanesian (back row right) and two other leading members of the 1958 cast*

xylophone and guitar; he had even been invited to Paris to perform in Boulez's *Le Marteau Sans Maître*. But for *Oedipus* he had been chosen for his prowess on the flexatone or saw which, in the words of Enescu's biographer, Noel Malcolm, 'takes over from the last shriek of the dying Sphinx and continues upwards in an unearthly *glissando*.'

Maxim recalled:

Silvestri would rehearse each department separately and individual players could be involved in as many as 50 rehearsals with him altogether. Other famous conductors I had played under would use substitutes to conduct the earlier rehearsals and would take the percussion department for granted, not worrying very much how they played their instruments. But Silvestri had a very clear idea how every instrument, including those in the percussion, should sound, the colours they were capable of producing. He would say to us that for such and such a passage you should use metal or perhaps it would be wood, narrow or wider sticks, and he knew within a centimetre or two the place where each instrument should be struck.

Enescu had given very precise instructions in the score as to how loud or soft each instrument should sound so, if it didn't produce the right sound, Silvestri would insist that it should be replaced. The colours produced by a

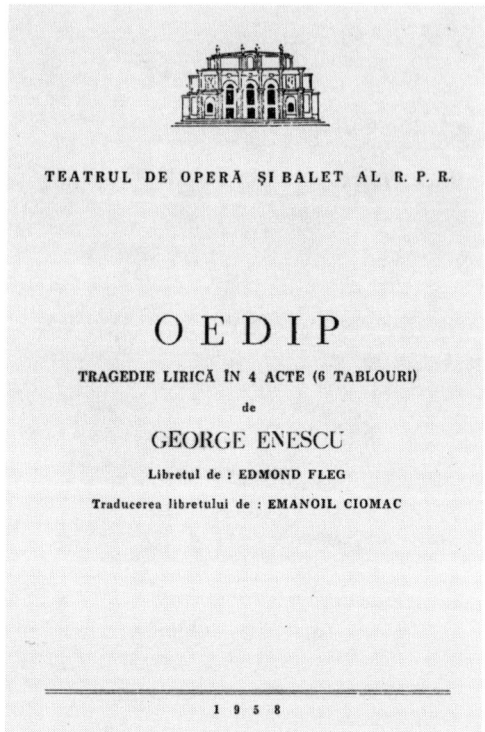

TEATRUL DE OPERĂ ŞI BALET AL R. P. R.

OEDIP

TRAGEDIE LIRICĂ ÎN 4 ACTE (6 TABLOURI)

de

GEORGE ENESCU

Libretul de : EDMOND FLEG

Traducerea libretului de : EMANOIL CIOMAC

1 9 5 8

Front cover of the 1958 Oedipus programme. It contained the synopsis of the plot which is supposed to have caused censorious comments in Gheorghe Gheorghiu-Dej's box at the preview for the government hierarchy, two days before the première

certain instrument had to be 100 per cent and if they didn't correspond to what he imagined the sound should be he would make a grimace and cry: 'Don't strike it in that spot, but here. . .' and he would indicate where it should be struck. And somehow it worked out right.

Some conductors learned new things about the various instruments in the course of rehearsing – but not Silvestri. He seemed to know everything about each instrument and was teaching the players how to use them. He never got into a temper or quarrelled with or shouted at any of us. Yet we felt he was like a doctor examining each of us under a stethoscope.

(This view was mirrored by Ivor Pemberton, for four years sub-principal double bass in the Bournemouth Symphony Orchestra under Silvestri:

He was quite capable of pulling up a xylophone player for being too lazy to play in octaves – amid the welter of sound of the full orchestra playing *fortissimo* he had noticed that this particular individual was only using one stick. Similarly, he surprised someone who for years had been much in demand as a cimbalom player, especially in Kodály's *Hary Janos Suite*,

YEHUDI MENUHIN (U. S. A.)

„C'est la première fois que je me trouve en Roumanie seul, sans Georges Enesco, l'homme qui représentait si bien les qualités du peuple roumain.

La dernière fois que je me suis trouvé dans votre pays, il y a onze ans, j'ai joué, aux côtés du maître, sept jours durant, et j'ai été heureux.

Maintenant, je suis ému de pouvoir prêter moi aussi mon concours à ce Festival qui honore sa mémoire. Le Festival a été merveilleusement organisé, à tous les points de vue. Mieux encore, on n'y sentait pas l'organisation, mais la chaleur, les sentiments et l'émotion de tout un peuple, qui apportait de la sorte un hommage de plus au génial artiste et à son oeuvre immortelle.

Je n'ai malheureusement pu assister au Concours, mais je suis heureux d'avoir pu entendre quelques-uns des lauréats, qui ont fait sur moi une forte impression. Le violoniste roumain Ştefan Ruha, premier prix du Concours de violon, m'a beaucoup, beaucoup plu. C'est un artiste doué d'un tempérament remarquable et, s'il continue de travailler avec sérieux et persévérance, nul doute qu'il remportera de gros succès.

J'ai été très heureux d'avoir pu revoir, vingt ans après sa première à Paris, „Oedipe", cette oeuvre exceptionnelle du grand Enesco. La musique de cet opéra est si profonde, elle est issue de l'esprit et du coeur d'un artiste si généreux, qu'elle offre et offrira pendant longtemps encore une inépuisable source d'inspiration.

Je me souviens d'Enesco comme d'un grand musicien, un grand chef d'orchestre, un violoniste et un professeur sans pareil, mais surtout je me rappelle le compositeur. Parce que, avant toute autre chose, il aimait composer. Il désirait léguer à son pays et à son peuple tout ce qu'il y avait en lui de meilleur, de plus précieux. Sa vie tout entière a été l'expression de la modestie incomparable qui le caractérisait. Enesco pensait avant tout à sa patrie, qu'il aimait par-dessus tout. Malheur à qui eût tenté de dire quelque chose contre son pays !

Il a aimé son pays pour tout ce qu'il avait de plus authentique et de plus expressif. C'est pourquoi, sans doute, il attacha tant de prix au folklore roumain,

The 42-year-old Yehudi Menuhin was one of eight leading international musicians, including David Oistrakh and Sir John Barbirolli, asked by La Roumanie Nouvelle *to give their opinions for its October 1958 issue on the first George Enescu International Festival. He praised* Oedipus *as an 'exceptional work' whose music would be an 'inexhaustible source of inspiration' for years to come*

when he insisted on telling him how to play his instrument 'correctly.' I personally have never known a conductor who made so much effort to prepare himself to face the orchestra with a clear idea of what he wanted.)

Not all the players in the *Oedipus* rehearsals invariably took the same rosy view of the maestro as Maxim did, however. One of his colleagues in the percussion department was over hasty in assuming Silvestri was not according his department the respect due to it. In Act II, Scene II, where Oedipus reaches the crossroads and during a storm kills King Laios, Enescu's score calls for much activity on the drums to simulate thunder. After one rehearsal break, Silvestri lightheartedly ordered: 'Right, let's start at the timpani aria, shall we?' To which the affronted timpanist retorted: 'And when are we going to start from the baton aria?' Costi was apparently embarrassed by the player's

*Discussing a point with David Oistrakh behind the scenes at the first Enescu
International Festival in 1958*

inability to take his little joke. It didn't deter him, however, from making a
similar one later: there being no bar numbers, he said – to the tuba players this
time: 'Let's start from the aria of the bears!'

One observer, journalist Eva Molho, sat-in on a rehearsal when Silvestri
was instructing one of the timpanists called Ştefanov how to imitate a heart-
beat:

> Ştefanov listened very intently and after that the timpani did indeed start
> beating like the actual beating of a heart. Everyone taking part in this opera
> has to understand Silvestri's intentions and correspond accordingly.
> Everything is patiently explained.

Here is her description of the scene during one of the rehearsals in the Opera
House:

> It is bare apart from the podium. There are desks at which the company is
> sitting like schoolchildren, taking part in the rehearsal which they call a
> 'sitz-probe.' In front of the podium, along it, on the real stage, the compact
> mass of the Greek choir forms one integral element. Silvestri, on the
> rostrum in the orchestra pit, makes the same total demands on himself as

Acknowledging applause with Claudio Arrau after a performance of the Brahms
Second Piano Concerto *at the first Enescu International Festival in 1958*

he does on the players, on every member of the choir and every soloist, in order to achieve what he wants from each bar, even from each note: not only skill, artistry and virtuosity, but their very soul. Under his baton, people seem to be absolutely spellbound.

Ohanesian said there were over six months of rehearsing during which Silvestri

made superhuman efforts to make us understand a work of such dimensions. We were studying phrase by phrase and scene by scene many times over. One of the problems was the choir which was getting terribly bored and disorientated rehearsing on its own the short and separate responses – sometimes on one single note or with repetitions of the same rhythmic pattern. That is, until Silvestri began rehearsing each act right through and the choir began to understand the meaning of their part in the context of the opera as a whole.

Ohanesian explained that the role of the choir varied significantly in the course of the opera, from the Greek choir in Act I, which provides the ambience of the legend; the more complex choir required for the coronation

'I triumphed over my destiny. I conquered Fate' – David Ohanesian
in Act IV of the Oedipus *première*

scene; to the richly expressive choirs of the venerable Athenian sages, of the Thebans and of the Eumenides. Only on a few occasions in the opera did Enescu use the whole choral potential.

Incidentally, the Bucharest Opera at this time had a most impressive corps of principal singers, formed by Silvestri and two other conductors, Egizzio Massini and Jean Bobescu, consisting of 22 sopranos, nine mezzos, 18 tenors, 12 baritones and eight basses.

Silvestri had a short break in the mountains after the preliminary rehearsals but resumed rehearsing in August. As well as *Oedipus*, he also had to prepare for the other works he was going to conduct in the Enescu International

Festival which included, as has been mentioned, Enescu's *Chamber Symphony* and the Brahms *Second Piano Concerto* with the Chilean pianist Claudio Arrau.

The *Oedipus* first-night audience was, in his words, completely 'won over.' Judith Vancea and her daughter Ioana were there and remembered how the Opera was packed and what a great success it was. Pascal Bentoiu said it was 'really wonderful and caused a sensation in contemporary society.' Yehudi Menuhin, who was playing in the Enescu Festival, said he was 'very happy to see *Oedipus*, 22 years after its first performance in Paris' and had been 'very moved when attending a rehearsal of this immortal work which Enescu left as a legacy to his country and to posterity.'

With *Oedipus*, Silvestri had reached the apex of his career in Romania – a triumph he shared with the producer Jean Rînzescu, with the designer Roland Laub, with Ohanesian and all the other soloists, chorus and orchestral players. It was appropriate that this was achieved conducting an 'immortal work' by the man who had foreseen a brilliant future for the little boy in the navy blue cravat he had heard playing in Tîrgu Mureş and who, later, had again predicted: 'We expect great things of him.'

But 48 hours before the opening night of *Oedipus* there occurred the first of two events which would immediately precede the *dénouement* of this act in Silvestri's own drama: his final exit from the Romanian stage.

With his increasingly heavy schedule abroad during 1957, someone had to take over direction of the Republic's State Opera and Ballet and this fell to Constantin Bugeanu. The Ministry of Culture evidently had doubts as to whether Silvestri would return in time from abroad to start rehearsals for *Oedipus* or even for the performance itself. But when Bugeanu was asked if he would conduct the opera instead, he replied it was a Herculean work and would take months to learn; in any case he was already preparing Enescu's *Third Symphony* which would take up six weeks of the summer.

One of Bugeanu's tasks as the new Opera director was to ensure that the *Oedipus* programme contained a synopsis of the plot. At the special performance laid on for the government hierarchy on September 22, two days before the première, Bugeanu maintains he saw Gheorghiu-Dej and his cousin in the box studying the programme notes and animatedly discussing them. Afterwards, Minister of Culture Atanase Joja, a philosopher of some repute, was ordered to have a word with Bugeanu to see how the mystical element in this operatic conversion of Sophocles' plays, written over 2,400 years before, could be expunged to bring it more into line with the tenets of dialectical materialism (or at least as these were interpreted by Zhdanov).

References have already been made to 'Zhdanovism' and for a generation not familiar with the term a brief explanation may not be out of place since Silvestri was a victim of its stifling effects, at least peripherally.

Long before Andrei Zhdanov, Leningrad Communist Party chief and at one time tipped as Stalin's successor, there had been much discussion – in fact ever since the 1917 Russian revolution – about the role music should play in furthering the aims of the state, about the creation of a 'Marxist musicology' and between advocates and opponents of learning from such Central European contemporaries as Alban Berg or Paul Hindemith. The views of the diehards invariably predominated and discussion was finally scotched when in 1936, after two years of an acclaimed run of Shostakovich's opera *Lady Macbeth of Mtsensk*, Stalin himself (with Molotov) attended a performance, called it 'a farrago of chaotic and nonsensical sound' and banned it.

But repression of this kind reached its zenith in 1947 when Stalin ordered Zhdanov to make a mass purge of the arts. This affected scores of writers and composers and included criticisms not only of Shostakovich again, but of Prokofiev, Khachaturian and Kabalevsky. The purge had to be given a simulacrum of intellectual justification, so a Conference of Soviet Music Workers was convened in 1948 which was harrangued by Zhdanov in his notorious speech entitled *On Music*. In this, he advocated 'a serious spring-cleaning . . . to purify the air in the composers' and musicians' organisation' (the Union of Composers); condemned 'a small group of select aesthetes' who were gratifying their 'individualistic emotions;' likewise the 'formalists' who were composing music 'which is ugly and false, permeated with idealistic sentiment. . .' and also the 'passion for, and even certain orientation towards, contemporary Western bourgeois music, the music of decadence.'

Silvestri himself, in conversation with Anatol Vieru, condemned the 'Zhdanov resolution' passed at the end of the conference, as 'a conspiracy of the mediocre majority opposed to the gifted few.' He also held strong views about the obligations of the state to create optimum conditions for the creative artist.

Zhdanov died in 1948, Stalin in 1953 and though there was a partial thaw under Khrushchev, a sneeze in the Kremlin could still produce a bad cold in the Eastern Bloc satellites. In any case, the paternalism endemic to these Soviet-modeled regimes was so ingrained that a critical eye was kept on all cultural activities and a censorious view taken by the party pundits of anything that smacked of 'mysticism' or of humanity not being in complete control of its destiny. Presumably the Romanian *apparatchiks* could do no more than criticise the libretto of Act IV of *Oedipus*; even they did not dare

In the official Album of the State Opera and Ballet of the People's Republic of Romania, *published after Silvestri's final departure from the country, there was no mention of him conducting* Oedipus. *On this page his name on the programme was obscured by a picture of a scene from the opera*

accuse the country's most renowned musician of 'formalism' or of any other transgression of the Zhdanov code. Otherwise, Enescu's augmentation of the percussion department for the opera would surely have brought down the wrath of the disciples of Zhdanov who had himself demanded rhetorically: 'Is it not true and right that in musical compositions the sound of cymbals and drums should be an exception and not the rule?'

The second event – or rather non-event – which may have been the 'final straw' for Silvestri concerned the scheduled recording of *Oedipus*. There are various versions as to the reasons why a recording of *Oedipus* was not made at the time, and the definitive one remains unresolved. Pascal Bentoiu said it had been intended to record the opera towards the middle of October with Electrecord in Bucharest. On the day the recording was due to take place, Silvestri, all the players, soloists and chorus assembled as scheduled, but he was met by a deputation from the musicians' union who refused to allow the players to perform because of the terms of the recording agreement. Silvestri said he would do his best to improve the players' conditions under the contract but meantime, since everybody had turned up and all were eager to do it, would they keep to the arrangement and allow the recording to go ahead? They refused.

Pascal Bentoiu inferred that this was a contrived dispute concocted by the party, which did not want a recording made of the opera in its existing form.

The State Opera tuba player, Nicolae Ionaşcu, remembers four days of rehearsal with the recording engineers setting up their paraphernalia for the planned recording. Everything went well and, at the end of the four days, Silvestri himself announced it was going to take place. Ionaşcu could not be sure of the reason for the cancellation, but thought it was because the recording company, Electrecord, could not or would not pay the extra money demanded by the soloists – the orchestra, chorus and the rest of the staff would not have been paid more anyhow. Whatever the reason, said Ionaşcu, Silvestri was furious. So was everyone else 'because a recording would have been a way of promoting the Bucharest State opera, *Oedipus* itself and Romania.'

For his part, Ohanesian explained:

> I was very young and shy, I had come from Cluj and was new to Bucharest and didn't like to ask questions. But I was observing everything very carefully. I remember how at a certain moment when we were on stage ready to record, someone came in from outside the Opera. He and the maestro had a very long discussion. In the end, Silvestri got very red, threw away his baton, asked us all to disperse, and the recording never took place. [Subsequently, records were made: the first conducted by Brediceanu and, in the early Nineties, by the Romanian-born American conductor Lawrence Foster.]

In all, there were eight performances of *Oedipus* in September-October 1958, six of them conducted by Silvestri, the last two by Mihai Brediceanu (which lasted 10 to 12 minutes longer than Silvestri's). Bugeanu had told the Minister, Joja, that he could see no way in which the 'mysticism' objected to in Act IV could be exorcised. The scheduled tour with the opera to Brussels, Paris and London was cancelled. Indeed, *Oedipus* was not staged in Bucharest for another three years and when Brediceanu conducted 10 performances between August 31 1961 and January 13 1962 changes had been made both to the libretto and to the *mis en scène* in the Epilogue. Pascal Bentoiu gave the following examples:

Oedipus in the revised version no longer talks about oracles and gods; and Creon reports, not Apollo's prediction, but what the *hoi polloi* predict.

In the original Fleg version, when in the final act the blind Oedipus, led by his daughter, reaches the spot (Colonnus in the Sophocles play) close to the walls of Athens which is destined to be his last resting place, he asks Antigone to confirm that she can see certain objects so as to identify the place the gods had designated for him, such as a spring, a glistening rock, an altar. However, the hacks employed by the party were asked to improve on Sophocles and Fleg with some thinly veiled contemporary propaganda; so, in the revised version, Oedipus asked instead: 'Is it here where Theseus combines under the one wreath of laurels justice with power, giving the city its glory?' And when Antigone affirms this, Oedipus declares ecstatically: 'Yes, at last, we've arrived!'

Again, in the original Fleg version Oedipus makes his farewell speech to Theseus, ending with the words: 'I will walk serenely towards my last hour and I will die in light.' In the revised version, however, he addresses, not Theseus, but the people of Athens with the following gibberish:

> Stay, happy and good people, sources of springtime,
> And when your last hour catches up on you don't forget
> You should be the ones who pass away in full light! (*Să treceţi voi in plină lumină*)

Ohanesian told a story about the post-Joja Minister of Culture, Constanţa Crăciun, a cultured and perceptive woman who was not too happy with the changes but nevertheless felt obliged to carry them out. She attended dozens of rehearsals at which numbers of these were tried out for the 1961 production, until Ohanesian asked her: 'How many more rehearsals for God's sake before we do the performance?' To which Constanţa replied with a twinkle in her eye:

> Well, I don't think we can be far off – after all, we've practically brought collective farm tractors on to the stage, so we can assume it's almost 'ours' [the party's] by now!

Of course the printed programme had to be changed as well. Whereas in the 1958 version it contained only a synopsis of the plot, the 1961 and subsequent versions were prefaced by four pages of notes. These enlightened the audience with:

The conception of the 1958 production was inadequate, resulting in the central idea of this noble opera not being given sufficient emphasis, especially in its sublime climax. In the present [1961] production, *the producers strove to correct the deficiencies which were justifiably criticised at the first performance* [My italics J.G.] and have stressed the fundamental aspects of the Sophocles tragedy which are so relevant for us today: humanity, optimism and belief in Man's potentialities. To underline the greatness of Man, Enescu made some modifications. In Sophocles, the Sphinx's question was a simple riddle and in the opera the question formulates the spiritual problem of existence: 'Who is stronger than Destiny?' And Oedipus answers without hesitation: 'Man is stronger.' This idea, full of optimism and closely related to the understanding of Man in our epoch is expressed very eloquently. But it is not only declaimed – on hearing the words of Oedipus the Sphinx collapses, demonstrating in this way that the mystery was revealed and so, indeed, Man is stronger than fate. . .

That was the cut-and-dried, repletely optimistic moral of the work which it was intended the audience should accept; it made no allowance for an alternative more equivocal interpretation, namely, that only the future would tell whether the dying Sphinx was weeping because of its defeat or laughing because of its triumph.* In a society where in every sphere not to be successful was regarded as shameful, dramatic portrayal of even possible human failing was unacceptable.

How soon after that special preview for the government functionaries on September 22 did the criticisms from on high reach Silvestri's ears of the opera to which he had devoted so many months of intense effort? Why did he not conduct the last two performances, on October 11 and 26? Had Brediceanu been his 'understudy' ever since Bugeanu had refused to do it and was he now brought in to conduct these two performances because Silvestri was protesting at the criticism?

Here are two opinions. First, Anatol Vieru's:

Silvestri had worked very hard on the production. I spoke with him about the score and he told me he considered its complexity was akin to that of Alban Berg's *Wozzeck* and that it was a very important work in the pantheon of Romanian music. When the ideological arguments began and Leonte Răutu, the propaganda chief, said it was too mystical, he took it

---

* Noel Malcolm: *George Enescu His Life and Music*, pp. 143–44 makes some interesting observations on this point.

personally and was deeply hurt. That is why after the first performances he left for concerts abroad and never came back.

And Radu Paladi summed it up pithily:

> There were restrictions on what Silvestri wanted to do and the last drop which filled his glass of frustration to the brim was the party's insistence on cutting or altering part of *Oedipus*.

Or was there a more prosaic explanation: that Silvestri already had an engagement in Moscow in mid-October and Brediceanu had all along been scheduled to do the last performances?

Silvestri certainly did have engagements in Moscow and Leningrad immediately after leaving Bucharest; he was in Brussels for two concerts the following February (1959); was recording works by Humperdinck, Mendelssohn, Rimsky-Korsakov, Borodin and Glinka with the Philharmonia in London in March and started his Australian tour in April. He never returned to Romania.

On returning to Paris in January after the Soviet tour, he reported to the ailing Edmond Fleg about the Bucharest production of the opera for which the poet had conceived the libretto. On the 18th, Silvestri received a letter from Fleg's wife, Madeleine, expressing their happiness in having met him and how Costi's 'profound affinity with *Oedipus* had created a bond' with the poet, who 'felt just as passionately about the musical side of the work. We had the impression we were welcoming an old friend. . .'

To sum up the reasons for Silvestri finally quitting Romania: first, from the favourable reactions to his 1957 conducting in London and Paris he was confident he could at least continue (and probably develop) his career in the West. That experience, however, had shown him both the disadvantages as well as the advantages of working in a milieu where the state subventions for the arts were minimal compared with in his own and neighbouring countries; where, in consequence, the arts had to be self-supporting, where commercial viability was paramount and therefore competition to attract audiences was intense; where there was an ongoing struggle to attract corporate and private sponsorship, the 20th century equivalent of patronage. He was certainly aware, from his experience in London alone, that there was nothing like the rehearsal time available his artistic perfectionism required.

On the other hand, immediate contact would be possible with all the latest cultural developments, in the widest sense, including the availability of cassettes and scores of contemporary works. He must have calculated, should he succeed in getting his own orchestra, that he would not have to conform to any politically-orientated bias towards or away from certain composers or musical trends; no indirect or actual governmental or party censorship; no foreign 'advisers'; there would be freedom of expression, to criticise if needs must, without fear of reprisal; and freedom to travel whither he wanted (except for his self-imposed ban on going behind the Iron Curtain for fear of the consequences).

Somewhere in his mental abacus he must have ranged other pluses and minuses: the Georgescu factor, for instance, as against the loss of his magnificent collection of paintings, carpets and records (though he seems to have 'defected' with his stamp collection)and the exchange of material security and relative prosperity for an uncertain future.

Not least of the gravitational pulls were those engendered by his emotions: a sense of guilt at leaving Viorica behind and probably even deeper sorrow at parting with Ana, his mother, knowing in his heart he would never see her again – but both outweighed by the attraction of his new love in Paris.

It was the regime that was to blame for the finality of departures of this kind: the lack of freedom for an individual to choose to emigrate with the option of making return visits to his or her homeland and without being branded a 'defector,' with its implication of disloyalty, even treachery.

We are largely in the realm of conjecture about the reactions within Romania to his 'defection.' We do not even know when it was realised, either by the authorities or by his relatives, friends and acquaintances, that he had decided not to return. Iosif Conta relates how Viorica and her family invited some 200 guests for a 1959 New Year's eve party and Silvestri who, as we have seen, had been on his Soviet tour, was expected to arrive in time for it; instead, he phoned – the friend did not know from where – and spoke to several of the guests, giving them the season's greetings.

Judith Vancea was convinced that, once he left the country 'there was no possibility of him returning because he was considered "an enemy of the state".' Nor did he write again to his old friend Zeno, though he did correspond from time to time with Jora.

There was still an occasional article about Silvestri in the Romanian press – the last appears to have been in May 1959. Then for the vast majority of Romanians the line went dead for 10 years – until his death in London was announced.

CHAPTER 7

A BOURNEMOUTH LOVE AFFAIR

Silvestri had just lowered his baton after the final bars of the blazing climax to Brahms D major symphony when to the first ripples of applause was added a ringing voice from the midst of the audience declaiming against 'this stupid and criminal act by a lot of morons.'

This was not, however, some disturbed person's denunciation of the interpretation and execution of the Brahms by Silvestri and the Bournemouth Symphony Orchestra. Rather the opposite: an expression of a young man's wholehearted approval of what he had just heard and regret and exasperation knowing he and the audience would not be able to listen to the BSO again, here in the Knightstone Theatre or anywhere else in their town.

The theatre had gone silent during the young man's protest; then the audience rose to its feet and applauded his outburst as well as Silvestri and the orchestra.

It was, in fact, an unprecedented demonstration against municipal parsimony, a malaise all too typical of official attitudes to the arts in the UK. It was

Sir Dan Godfrey who founded in Bournemouth the UK's first permanent professional orchestra. Silvestri carried on his tradition of championing British music

April 1962, not yet a year since Silvestri had taken up his post as the BSO's principal conductor. The place, Weston-super-Mare, a resort on the Bristol Channel (though when the tide is out promenaders almost need binoculars to see the Mare) and where the council's bounty to the BSO had receded to the point of withdrawing its £200 annual grant. This was the 'criminal act' against which the young man was inveighing during what would be the BSO's last concert in Weston.

Not that Bournemouth had set any better example in the past. From the time Dan Godfrey founded a band of 30 players in 1893, this, the first permanent municipal orchestra in the UK, had suffered vicissitudes that more than once threatened it with extinction – right through its conversions, first into the Bournemouth Municipal Orchestra; then, in 1954 when the town's Corporation withdrew its financial support, into the independent Bournemouth Symphony Orchestra whose first concert as such was conducted jointly by Charles Groves and Sir Thomas Beecham.

As archivist Raymond Carpenter explained:

> The orchestra had been for years embattled by civic parsimony and public indifference, had suffered crisis after crisis, and couldn't even call its traditional home, the Winter Gardens, its own concert hall. For 10 years the late Sir Charles Groves had fought tooth and nail to save the orchestra from bankruptcy and, after he left, the dark clouds of ignominious defeat loomed over the only professional orchestra in South West England.

Actually, there was a nucleus of public spirited townspeople who in the Fifties formed the Winter Gardens Society. When the Corporation refused to accede to a Musicians' Union demand to bring pay and conditions into line with other provincial orchestras and withdrew its support, the Society, in order to keep the 1954 concert season going, offered to pay the difference between the Corporation rate for the players and what the union was demanding.

It was at this point that the Arts Council asked Kenneth Matchett, business manager of the Carl Rosa Company, to do a report on the Bournemouth Orchestra. 'So I packed my bags, never dreaming that the fortnight this was expected to take would become 21 years,' he recalled.

In October 1954, it was Matchett who formed the Western Orchestral Society (WOS) and took over the orchestra, together with its conductor Charles Groves and most of the musicians after auditioning them. Groves resigned after six years and went to the Welsh National Opera. Matchett recounted:

So we had to find a new principal conductor. This was not going to be easy because we never had enough money to do all that we wanted to do. I also felt the orchestra needed something a little different – while it was very good and safe, there was nothing special about it. Ever since Sir Dan Godfrey's day, the orchestra had been supporting British artists and composers, so I was under great pressure, particularly from the Arts Council, to make it a British appointment.

However, I decided that we would have at least 12 months when we would have a look at different people. We probably had 20 to 30 conductors over this period, British and foreigners, some of them old friends. But the time came when I, as manager, would have to make the appointment and I was getting anxious – having all these different guest conductors popping up was not all that popular with an orchestra that traditionally had always had a resident conductor. My choice would have been Jascha Horenstein, the Russian-born conductor who had done a marvellous Mahler *Eighth* a couple of years before, but he declined. [Horenstein died in London in 1974.]

It was the Romanian conductor Edgar Cosma, living in Paris, who told me about his compatriot and fellow refugee Silvestri. I got a favourable opinion about him from Eric Bravington, manager of the London Philharmonic. So we engaged Silvestri a couple of times. Though I liked him from what I saw and heard of him performing, taking him to supper afterwards and talking to him in the car – a sure way of getting to know somebody – I relied on sounding out the orchestra on what they thought of these guest conductors – and then adding my own judgement. Without a shadow of doubt Silvestri was a hit with the orchestra.

So I went to Paris to see what he thought about being principal conductor and we had – there is no other way of describing it – an extremely alcoholic 48 hours. I wasn't particularly a wine drinker but we seemed to drink wine from the time I arrived until I finally staggered on to the plane to come home. We got along famously.

I insisted on his coming to live in Bournemouth and that he must be prepared to conduct up to 70 per cent of all performances. For his part, one of his demands was for rehearsals far in excess of what was normal. We had the standard six hours plus three on the day of the performance, a total of nine. Silvestri wanted twice that – I think we compromised at 12.

Matchett was not only staking his reputation by appointing a foreign conductor against tradition and in the teeth of vehement opposition in certain quarters, but he compounded the gamble by steadily building up the orchestra from its original established 63 players to 92, despite the 'looming clouds' of bankruptcy.

Although these bold policies did pay off in terms of raising the BSO's prestige to heights that probably only Silvestri himself had thought attainable, it was going to be an ongoing struggle to keep the ship financially buoyant. Despite the Western Orchestral Society's sometimes unorthodox methods of raising money (such as a raffle with a Morris Minor as prize which raised £13,000); or the Bournemouth Corporation partially redeeming its reputation by doubling its subsidy; and the Arts Council making a sevenfold increase in its grants over the years, by the end of 1966 the orchestra was still in troubled waters. Lord Goodman's report in 1965 on the London orchestras had a knock-on effect resulting in pay increases for provincial orchestras – an estimated £90,000 anually in the case of the BSO. While this was very necessary to stop the drift of players from the provincial to the far better paid London orchestras (which in the case of the BSO had led to 25 resignations), Matchett had to make strong representations for increased assistance. When it came, this was again offset by the government's Prices and Incomes Policy and by spending curbs.

In his pleas, Matchett pointed out:

> We are being supported as a national symphony orchestra and not as a local town band. It is internationally recognised that Bournemouth and Monte Carlo – with their comparatively small populations – are unique in the world in having a weekly performance of symphonic music by professional orchestras.

In fact, as WOS chairman Sir Alan Cobham stressed in an emergency meeting of the Society, the BSO was doing 'four concerts a week plus long rehearsals and travelling which often meant lengthy coach journeys and returning home through the night after concerts ended' – conditions which are overlooked by the majority of concertgoers.

With his well-tried method of tackling problems head-on instead of retreating, Matchett eventually persuaded the WOS board that the only way of alleviating the financial problem was to form an addition to the BSO: a chamber orchestra, so that major works could be performed relying solely on their own personnel and thus avoiding the expensive practice of engaging extra players. Certain modifications would have to be made within the BSO, but for large works – by Bruckner or Mahler, for example – the necessary extra strength would be available from this enlarged pool of some 114 players.

Matchett explained:

I got a favourable decision from this board meeting by telling them it was no good saying 'reduce the orchestra' because ultimately that would mean the end of the BSO. What we had to do was to enlarge it because in that way I could plead for more money from the region by guaranteeing them concerts.

Silvestri took some persuading because he felt the unity he had been at pains to build might be put in jeopardy. But in the end he agreed and the Bournemouth Sinfonietta was born at the end of 1967.

It must have been with some distaste that Silvestri was inevitably drawn into such mundane extra-musical problems and he probably had a sneaking nostalgia for the days when he only had to put in a phone call to the Minister of Culture to get whatever support for a musical venture he required. And not only musical: he once went to a Communist Party panjandrum – he liked to boast it was to Gheorghe Gheorghiu-Dej himself, which is unlikely – and said:

Look, after every rehearsal my silk shirt is soaking with sweat and it gets torn as well. It means I have to buy a new shirt every time at a cost of about 300 lei. [In the 1990s, after multiplying that figure 10 times, it would be equivalent to about one month's state pension.] So I need 10 shirts a month. If you want me to continue conducting, you'll have to provide me with a dress allowance.

And apparently he got it. He himself gleefully told the story to a group of journalists during a rehearsal break at the Radio in Bucharest.

The situation was somewhat different now. Matchett regrets

we were never able to pay him top money and I felt we never paid him sufficient for all that he did for us. But there was nothing very much I could do about it, although I made sure we were always very generous with his expenses. He had absolutely no idea about money and we never had a contract. We kept saying we would draft one, but never got around to writing it. Actually, though I had to have contracts with the players because of the union, I never had a contract with any artist or conductor. My word was my bond.

So it was certainly not material gain that tempted Silvestri to Bournemouth nor the kudos of association with an internationally famous orchestra. Inevitably the question was asked (and still is) why did someone who had already been the guest conductor of some of the world's most renowned orchestras –

the Berlin and Vienna Philharmonics, the Concertgebouw, five of Britain's most prestigious and two in the US – each time attracting audience enthusiasm and mainly favourable reviews, why did he choose to become principal conductor of a provincial orchestra, however worthy its reputation, and in a country with whose language he was barely acquainted?

The Guardian music critic, looking back on Silvestri's career in England, thought it strange that 'so dashing a figure should want to find refuge with a provincial orchestra' and that it had not been expected – presumably by himself and fellow critics – that Silvestri would have been content with the 'arduous, often humdrum job of raising the orchestra's standards.' But he concluded that

> in fact, his appointment was a success on every count. He built up the orchestra's confidence in itself as a group of international standard. . .

What can be gleaned of Silvestri's motives when this question was put to him?

'Having travelled around the world so much, are you glad to have a permanent orchestra again?' he was asked on Southern Television when his appointment to Bournemouth was announced in September 1961. To which he gave the somewhat abstruse answer: 'I think I must have one again. I was a teacher for 10 years and a conductor is also a teacher.' There were missing links in this syllogism and his meagre knowledge of the language at that time was probably the reason why he did not make himself more explicit.

But his reply to the next question put by the interviewer: 'And what do you hope to teach the Bournemouth orchestra?' was clear, confident and prophetic: 'This orchestra has a national reputation, but I think in two or three years it will become internationally famous.'

Five years later, in a radio interview in Paris, the question was put directly: 'Why did you choose Bournemouth when you had offers for more spectacular orchestras?' His answer was indisputable and devoid of false modesty: 'I managed to make a spectacular orchestra of it, too.' But this still left no one the wiser as to why he had made the decision in the first place.

Was it, as these brief replies of Silvestri indicate, just because he had an urge to teach and at the same time to mould a 'safe' into a spectacular orchestra? Mstislav Rostropovich has also spoken of the great challenge and stimulus to his creative and educative urge which he experienced when he chose to conduct an allegedly third-rate orchestra; and this motivation to improve, essentially to mould, a hundred-odd people to one's own conceptions, must be a very natural component of a conductor's psyche.

Someone who had spent many hours in conversation with Costi because he had played with him and the BSO more than a dozen times since they first met in 1965, provided a more lucid explanation which complements Silvestri's own. He is Hungarian-born pianist Peter Frankl (who, incidentally, became a British citizen in 1967, the same year as the Silvestris.)

Using an analogy once coined by Sir Georg Solti – 'Good orchestra-conductor marriages . . . are highly desirable and should start as a love affair; preferably love at first sight,' Frankl opined:

> Silvestri had this love affair with the Bournemouth orchestra because he was the type of conductor who needed his own orchestra. Nowadays there are perfect technicians who know exactly how to beat and it's more or less a technical achievement. That is why many of them, are successful now and can go globetrotting because they are immediately understood by all orchestras; whereas Silvestri had a personal style: he belonged to the older generation of conductors, of Furtwängler and Klemperer who, with their inner personalities, could convey music to the orchestra with something more than beats. I think as a purely guest conductor he couldn't achieve that with only one or two rehearsals. He needed time so the orchestra could get to know him intimately.
>
> I remember places where he had been as a guest conductor – in Australia and South Africa, for example – where they told me they really couldn't grasp his personality, they couldn't follow him, couldn't catch his big forte. I feel he absolutely needed his own orchestra.

Conductor James Loughran made a similar assessment of Costi's motivation:

> He knew the English temperament: very orthodox, good discipline and concentration, quick sightreading, not necessarily better than that of any other nation, but quick because they had to be, owing to the few rehearsals. He knew he didn't want that kind of orchestra. He wanted one that would make people forget, just listen to the music, be swept away by it.
>
> This unorthodoxy paid off, though some sniffed at it, they thought it too gipsy. But, oh, it was so much more musical! It was a code of his musical life that he wanted this freedom – he didn't want bar lines, and every good musician would agree with that. We don't want time-beaters, we want music to speak naturally, at its own pace.

Edgar Cosma believes that Silvestri the composer was an integral component of Silvestri the conductor who 'went to the heart of the music, unlike conductors who just conduct.' In conversations with Silvestri when Cosma was a student at the Bucharest Conservatoire

> I understood his principal concern was fidelity to the score – nothing should be distorted, added or changed, but one should try to find everything in it, like the right tempi.

This does not necessarily conflict with what Silvestri would later tell Malcolm Rayment, that he had no time for those critics who

> apparently go to work with pocket metronomes, telling conductors that their tempi are either faster or slower than those specified by the composer – as if they were not perfectly aware of it!

In one work Silvestri's timing varied between 14 and 22 minutes according to the accoustics of the hall and to the quality of the players, but in this case, since the work in question was his own, Silvestri the conductor had every reason to take liberties with the creation of Silvestri the composer. Once, when Shostakovich did the same, it was the conductor who got the blame. Dmitri was at a rehearsal of his *Ninth Symphony* at the 1962 Edinburgh Festival and emphasised to Sir Charles Mackerras that the slow movement should be played slightly rubato and not exactly as he had originally written it. After the performance, Shostakovich actually praised Mackerras for having done just as he had wanted – but a critic, unaware of the composer's eleventh-hour instruction, complained that the slow movement had been played at the wrong tempo.

Rayment remembered Silvestri quoting Debussy's reply to a conductor who questioned the metronome mark at the beginning of one of his works: Debussy insisted that it was absolutely correct – as far as the first bar was concerned!

Not that Silvestri was averse to sometimes using a metronome; in a rehearsal of the last movement of the Prokofiev *Fifth Symphony*, he is reputed to have peremptorily instructed the First Viola, who had failed several times to play a phrase as he wanted it to be played : 'You . . . you take lessons from this metronome!'

Silvestri was in the tradition of such great composer/conductors as Mahler, Strauss and Elgar, but his composer's analytical treatment of the score was sufficiently exceptional to be widely regarded in the Fifties and Sixties as unorthodox. And although there have been composer/conductors – Boulez or Bernstein for example – who, like Silvestri, stressed the importance of fidelity to the score and identifying with the composer coincidentally with a degree of freedom of interpretation, Simon Rattle laments that the 'whole tragedy of the conducting scene now is that virtually none of us are composers . . . You get a glossy style of surface conducting.'

To illustrate the latitude of interpretation Costi considered was permissible, here is a composite of several versions, differing only in detail, of another story in the Silvestri hagiography:

On a tour of Northern England, the BSO had performed the Brahms *First Symphony* at five concerts in various towns but on each occasion the performance was different. Silvestri – who usually travelled with his players in the same coach – in the course of chatting to a group of them on the long journey back to Bournemouth, asked which version they had liked best: the Viennese Brahms, the French Brahms, or the Italian Brahms. 'One day we might even do a Japanese Brahms,' he quipped. (And, judging from an enthusiastic review of the same symphony when he conducted it with the Queensland Symphony Orchestra, perhaps he also had an Australian Brahms in his pouch.)

He also conducted two versions of a work in the same concert (in Bournemouth on February 6 1964), the *Overture to Iphigenia in Aulis* – first, in Gluck's original, then in Wagner's re-edited version.

With hindsight of the multinational Brahms legend, we are in a better position to understand what the maestro meant when he asked Moura Lympany whether she played the Schumann *Piano Concerto* the German or the French way. After 30 years she was still not absolutely sure of what was behind the question. 'I suppose he meant like Cortot. I replied that I had learned it with Mathilde Verne, Clara Schumann's pupil.'

In Vladimir Ashkenazi's opinion, 'Silvestri was best with the Romantics.' He was certainly a great admirer of Brahms as can be assumed from the carnivorous analogy he used to give for the delectation of the Bournemouth players:

Beethoven is like roast lamb, bounding and full of energy; Tchaikovsky is like roast beef, immensely strong and massive. But Brahms is like pork. . .

and the flabbergasted orchestra – Silvestri pausing for effect – wondered whatever was coming next.

You can eat all of a pig, from head to trotters. So in Brahms, [he explained] every section is given a part of the action: the viola, second bassoon, double bass, even the triangle. He hands all the beautiful melodies around the orchestra – not just to the violins and cellos.

But, apart from being an illustration of Silvestri's flexibility of interpretation, Nicholas Braithwaite saw the multinational Brahms story as an example of how Silvestri trained the orchestra.

One of his principles was to rehearse a piece in every possible way so that players couldn't be sure they were going to do what had been done on the Thursday morning or whenever, but had to respond to what the conductor was up to at the actual performance.

Or, as Alun Francis put it (he was a young horn player in the BSO at the time and would one day become principal conductor of the Berlin Symphony Orchestra):

> Often Silvestri did not conduct at all; he made some gestures and just let it happen. This produced a very good sense of ensemble; he made people do things for themselves. But we were on tenterhooks all the time. We never knew what was going to happen.

Again, in Kenneth Matchett's version:

> He had a real mischievous streak in him and there would be a twinkle in his eye as, up there on the stage in a rehearsal, quite po-faced, he would suddenly change everything. He made the orchestra hang on to the end of his baton.

But however entertaining for the mere observer at a rehearsal, this particular kind of Silvestri mischief could be unnerving for the players. Although BSO sub-principal double bass Ivor Pemberton found

> Silvestri's baton technique was the most expressive I have ever seen – almost every nuance in the music was reflected in the movements of the stick; it had an almost mesmerising effect and there was no excuse for not knowing exactly what he wanted,

he has also never forgotten a rehearsal of Bartók's *Music for Strings, Percussion and Celesta* 'which must have put 10 years on the life of every player and the leader had to ask him to beat more clearly – most embarrassing for all concerned.'

Raymond Carpenter recalls:

> If he had a Bruckner symphony with its huge canvas, he would go through the first movement so that we got the general idea. Then he'd go back and do sections here and there. He would sometimes rehearse in a seemingly casual way, nonchalantly smoking his cigarette. If he got to the last movement before the concert and hadn't covered every inch of the ground, it never worried him. But it did worry us because there would probably be a passage that we hadn't actually played before and didn't even know how it went. It did wonders for our concentration. But he did that on purpose:

to keep us on our toes. He had great faith in his orchestra, which he called 'his family.' Everyone somehow knew what was expected.

That was one of the reasons – Braithwaite drew the moral – 'why the orchestra reached such a high standard: they had to listen – to play as an ensemble.'

Nowadays, it is almost axiomatic that, while conductors should not impose their own concepts on those of the composer and should keep faith with the directions in the score, nevertheless they do have a certain latitude in how they interpret it. Few would go so far as the literal adherence to the composer's scoring as Toscanini passionately advocated (and himself ignored at will.) The degree of success which conductors achieve in seeking the golden mean between freedom of interpretation and fidelity to the score is a prime consideration in assessing their reputation.

But even if the conductor's freedom to interpret is conceded in principle, when a custom has grown up of playing a work in a certain way, such is the potency of tradition that in practice there are always some who regard any other interpretation as heterodox. A contemporary said Silvestri shocked the purists by his drastic personal editing of familiar scores, changing note values, phrasing and dynamics,

> but his command was so authoritative and his performances so compelling that the complaining purist stopped grudgingly to listen and the professional musician admitted to finding fresh pleasure in playing music he had known for a lifetime.

Silvestri's conducting of the Tchaikovsky *Fourth Symphony* is a case in point. In Romania, in Russia, in the UK or wherever he conducted it – or, indeed, any of the last three symphonies – amid the general audience approbation there would be an element of disapproval of his departure from what had long been taken for granted as the norm. Even laudatory reviews spoke of his 'audacious tricks of interpretation' or his 'bravura reading' and at his first concert in Bournemouth (before his appointment) local reviewer Kenneth Williams 'formed a love-hate relationship with the reading' of the Tchaikovsky *Fourth* –

> hatred for the quirks that seemed at times to amount to a revision of the original, as familiar phrases limped almost unrecognisably along; love because of the almost physical thrill imparted by the stupendous climaxes.

(Incidentally, as a matter of historical interest, the *Fourth* was given its first British performance in Sir Dan Godfrey's Bournemouth in 1898, that is, 20 years after it was composed.) Whatever orchestra Silvestri conducted, the first reaction of the players to his interpretation of the *Fourth* was sheer incredulity.

The rehearsals for these first concerts of Silvestri in Bournemouth are engraved on Raymond Carpenter's memory:

> We only knew about the maestro through his recording reputation, that he had just brought out some very fine recordings with the Philharmonia. We were in for a shock. In England we had a tradition of playing the motto figure in the opening of the Tchaikovsky *Fourth* [sings]

> and, of course, when it came to the rehearsal we played it in the traditional way.

Silvestri put his baton down and shook his head. In his heavily accented English, he exclaimed: 'Nor, nor, nor! It must be:

He wanted the tied quaver longer and the first notes of the triplet to be played faster and with a clear accent on the first one. He also wanted the last note of the triplet well separated from the next quaver; then a semi-quaver mark before going on to the next bar.

We were astonished. We just couldn't believe our ears – that was *not* how it was written. So, he kept on rehearsing us and we kept on resisting. We just wouldn't play it that way.

Eventually, he broke down our resistance, persuaded us that

was better. And that is the way we did it at the performance that week – and for ever after, because we now found it more difficult to play it the original way.

Russian conductor Kiril Kondrashin once said: 'There are conductors who direct their orchestras and there are conductors who are directed by their orchestras. You must have tremendous will-power to remain true to yourself.' Silvestri had the will-power.

But at least in Bournemouth this two-version Tchaikovsky *Fourth* syndrome had its lighter moments. James Loughran recalls:

> I was rehearsing it for an evening concert when Silvestri came in and explained he had to do something for a TV programme trailer right away. He said: 'Jimmy, do you mind if I do the opening of the Tchaikovsky *Four* for them?' I said: 'No, but don't upset it for me tonight!' because he always did it in this special way with that little rest mark. The orchestra laughed because they knew what I meant. So, I told them: 'Mr Silvestri wants to conduct Tchaikovsky *Four* for the TV. You play it as *he* does it now, and *my* way tonight!' And they did – it was a marvellous orchestra. And he was lovely – I couldn't have said that to someone who was stuffy and self-important.

When Anatol Vieru was in Russia as a young man in the mid-Fifties, he found that 'Tchaikovsky was played differently from the way Silvestri conducted it' and though he did not say whether or not the 'Silvestri way' met with approval, Costi himself told Malcolm Rayment that his treatment 'was acclaimed in Russia by the older generation who said that for the first time in years they had heard the work in the true tradition as handed down by the composer himself.'

Twenty years on, André Previn was at a performance of the Tchaikovsky *Fourth* in Leningrad conducted by Evgeny Mravinsky and, a decade later, he told his biographers that he found it 'marvellously stimulating' but 'wildly eccentric. The tempo changes were, for the most part, sudden and unprepared.' But when, on Mravinsky's advice, he managed to obtain a facsimile of the manuscript score that Tchaikovsky had written in 1878, he found that the Russian conductor had 'conducted nothing more nor less than what the composer had written.'

Can it be assumed that Silvestri and Mravinsky had arrived at the same or similar interpretations independently through studying the original Tchaikovsky manuscript or was it a case of musical intuition on Silvestri's part?

'I remember Silvestri trying to articulate, even at the risk of exaggeration, the fanfare at the beginning of Tchaikovsky *Four* which very often sounds brassy, metallic and mechanical,' said pianist and conductor Daniel Barenboim, giving his recollections of Silvestri with whom he played as a young man of 24.

> The one thing that I recall very clearly is how preoccupied he was with musical articulation – that no figure was left inarticulated. I think there is often a false idea in the minds of too many musicians – the public too –

about faithfulness to the text. When I say false idea, it means that just by playing the notes you are not necessarily being faithful to the text.

Musical articulation is the equivalent to commas, semicolons, full stops and paragraphs in writing; it is the equivalent of those things and it is not always written in the music. It comes out of the preoccupation with the balance between what is vertical and what is horizontal musically, what is melodic and what is tonal music; and it has to do with so many accoustic, physical laws. Silvestri was very much aware of it. I remember very well his phrasing, particularly the beginning of the slow movement of the Mozart *E flat Concerto*

– the K482 which he played with Silvestri and the BSO in five cities and towns in Southern England. These included Bournemouth where Barenboim himself had performed for the first time in this country, with Charles Groves at the age of 12.

Confirming a local critic's impression of 'a most satisfying feeling of partnership between the piano and orchestra,' Barenboim summarised his relationship with Silvestri as 'very professional and friendly. I got on well with him, without any problems.'

Silvestri's relations with soloists was also a matter of interpretation. Exceptionally, when the soloist held strongly to his or her interpretation which did not accord with Silvestri's the liaison was not a happy one. This never seems to have happened with young artists: each of those interviewed had only praise for his consideration.

Ashkenazy's immediate association with the name Silvestri, although he had only played with him twice, over 25 years before, was: 'We had a very good *rapport*' (Though two reviews of their performance of the Rachmaninov *Concerto No 2 in C minor* with the LPO did not give that impression: 'Ashkenazi was not always happy accompanied by Silvestri' was one opinion; and another: 'It was a case of not quite ear-to-ear between piano and orchestra' – something the other critics don't seem to have noticed and, in contrast, praised both soloist and orchestra.) The second occasion was when they performed the Prokofiev *Concerto No 3* in Antwerp.

The same 'good *rapport*' was used by John Clegg who played Max Reger's *Piano Concerto in F minor* three times in 1966 – a composer 'for whose works we were both enthusiastic'; and again by French pianist Michèle Boegner: 'Although I was very young he always respected my interpretation and we had a very good *rapport*.' Her first contact with Silvestri was in Bucharest when he

Vladimir Ashkenazi in 1967: 'Sil-
vestri was best with the Romantics'

Daniel Barenboim at 24: 'He was
preoccupied with musical articulation'

was presiding over the jury for the Enescu Competition in 1958; playing the Schumann *Piano Concerto*, she won joint second prize with a Russian. Then, based in Paris, Boegner came over to play with him seven times in the UK.

Another Parisian pianist, Eric Heidseck, knows that 'sometimes a conductor can be very unpleasant with a young soloist and, in rehearsal, stop and exclaim: "Arrr... that's no good!"' But he found Silvestri very understanding and human when they performed the Schumann *Introduction and Allegro appussionato* Op 92 and Richard Strauss' *Burleske in D minor* in BSO concerts in 1967 and repeated them over the air.

> There was no problem with rubato, in the sense of being freer at the beginning or middle of a phrase but never at the end. Silvestri understood that very well and I was very happy with the music, with the feeling I could be free. I did not feel I had to do battle with the orchestra. For a pianist it is better to play relaxed, not to feel we have somebody to fight. I was very happy with Constantin Silvestri because he had exactly the same feeling for the fluency of the Schumann theme: it wasn't stiff but all the time flowing. I was very happy with the Strauss too. Technically it is very difficult; it has to be free but also with panache. It was one of my great experiences.

And so it was with the cellists – with Paul Tortelier, 'playing at the height of his powers,' said *The Times* when Silvestri and the BSO performed the Dvorak concerto 'with complete sensitivity of response'; and with Rostropovich, with whom he 'formed a magnificent musical team' – they had performed the Dvorak concerto in Bucharest in 1950 – and who was 'clearly quite delighted with Silvestri that they were two of a kind, musically speaking,' when performing the Haydn *Cello Concerto in C* and Britten's *Cello Symphony* for the BSO's 75th anniversary in 1968 (according to Kenneth Williams.)

In the case of the English cellist Christopher Bunting, playing the Elgar concerto 'with intuitive sympathy' in Taunton with Silvestri and the BSO, it was this time 'a well-judged accompaniment,' according to a local reviewer. Bunting (whose first concerto engagement, like Barenboim's, had been with Charles Groves and the BSO and who is author of *Essay on the Craft of Cello-playing*) said he found Silvestri 'a very sympathetic colleague and tolerant, a characteristic which came in useful for the Taunton performance' and he explained why. The previous evening they had played the Elgar in Swindon and Bunting assumed it would again be an evening engagement in Taunton. 'So, I drove in a leisurely way through old haunts in northern Somerset – and arrived in Taunton at 2.40 p.m., just in time for what was, in fact, an afternoon concert starting at 3 p.m. I had no time to prepare my mind or change and played in my ordinary suit,' but evidently was able to keep his 'intuitive sympathy' for Elgar well intact. 'Silvestri was very kind and passed it off very professionally,' he remembers.

Mishaps involving Silvestri's soloist colleagues, for which he was in no way responsible, did occur as they must do with any conductor – as for instance in October 1965 when American pianist Julius Katchen played the Mozart *D minor Concerto* K466 and Ravel's *Concerto in G* with Silvestri and the BSO in the Colston Hall, Bristol. It was a civic occasion with the Lord Mayor of Bristol and the Mayor of Bournemouth sitting in the stalls wearing their gold chains of office. Halfway through the first movement of the Mozart, Katchen stopped and, turning to the astonished audience, declared:

> If it were not for the presence of Mr Constantin Silvestri, I would leave the platform in protest at the disgraceful state of the piano. I apologise for the inefficient tuning and for this ridiculous state of affairs. But we will still carry on under this intolerable burden.

Despite this little hiccup, *The Times* described Katchen's Mozart as 'inspirational' and in the Ravel he and the orchestra 'gave an irresistible performance.'

Kenneth Matchett publicly distanced the BSO from this protest; he said the Steinway was 'a first-class instrument,' but the tuning was wrong. Bristol Entertainments Committee expressed 'complete disapproval of the very unpleasant way in which the artist chose to make his announcement' and an alderman called it 'a case of artistic temperament.' (Poor Katchen, who once said that playing with Silvestri was like making love, would die in a Paris car accident in the same year as Costi.)

The 'disgraceful piano' episode was repeated nine months later in the same city, in the same hall, with the same conductor and orchestra, and almost certainly with the same piano – only the soloist was different. This time it was Denis Matthews who also stopped after playing a few bars of Alan Rawsthorne's *Second Piano Concerto* and made his protest before carrying on.

An example of a not so felicitous soloist/orchestra partnership was a Royal Festival Hall concert in 1963 at which Moura Lympany played the Beethoven *Piano Concerto No 4*, when the *Daily Telegraph* critic thought she 'was not at her most persuasive or most fluent owing, one suspects, to the emasculated support which Constantin Silvestri supplied'; and *The Times* thought 'the performance hung fire in spite of Miss Lympany's valiant efforts to inject some life into it;' while the *Daily Express* thought 'Mr Silvestri sounded erratic.'

In September 1966, Silvestri was even accused of creating chaos. In a review of Ida Haendel playing the Shostakovich *Violin Concerto No 1* with Silvestri and the LPO *The Times* remarked with heavy sarcasm: 'Great music is, of course, capable of at least two interpretations; but preferably not both at once' and maintained that while Haendel

> took a passionate, rhapsodic view of the two big slow movements, the conductor, Silvestri, appeared to favour firm, slow tempi. Perhaps Mr Silvestri's view was closer to the composer's, but his persistence in it only created chaos.

A year later, it was Ida Haendel's turn to be accused of being 'at variance with her partner [Silvestri] as regards tempi, particularly at the opening of the last movement' of the Sibelius *Violin Concerto*. 'She has always taken a more leisurely view of the concerto than most violinists,' a local critic claimed in a review of this Brighton concert with the BSO. 'But Mr Silvestri was driving with the handbrake firmly on. It was only by applying the accelerator in the last movement and asserting herself that the performance really came to life.'

Three decades later, during a Heathrow stop-over in transit between her home in Miami and Germany, the indefatigable Ms Haendel had this comment to make on these reviews:

With all due respect to critics, they always try to invent things. As a musician, Silvestri was quite different from many other conductors, in the sense
that he did some things that were unconventional musically-speaking. At
the same time, it was so artistic and so convincing that I would say to myself: this has to be the only way to interpret it. That's how magnetic he was.

He was a very individual, a very different sort of artist. Some people
might disagree with me, but I would describe him artistically as extremely
emotional. As far as I remember, the critics were generally not very keen on
Silvestri just because he was so different and if something is different and
they don't understand what it is, they always try to run it down. That's
human nature, I suppose.

I don't remember any conflict with Silvestri. Music is very complicated.
We all change sometimes – there can be a change of tempo that is so spontaneous you are not even aware you are doing it. So I would not blame him
for anything. Maybe I was to blame – who knows?

I never considered him or any other conductor as an accompanyist. We
make music and that's what it's all about. I loved playing with him and I
thought every time it was a rewarding experience, so I never paid any
attention to the words of the critics. I derived immense pleasure playing
with him.

One Bournemouth player at that time is convinced that Silvestri and the distinguished English pianist, the late Sir Clifford Curzon, 'fought tooth and
nail' during rehearsals of the Brahms *Concerto No 2 in B flat* major before a
performance on December 20 1962 (only seven months after Silvestri's
Bournemouth appointment). True, a local reviewer spoke of 'disastrous
results' but these were for the piano, not necessarily for the Curzon/ Silvestri
relationship, though he did call the two musicians somewhat cryptically 'an
unusual and formidable combination.' Curzon unleashed

all the force that lies in his slender arms with devastating, satanic fury, so
much so that in his long opening utterance before the orchestral exposi-
tion, the unfortunate instrument broke a string under the strain and the
whole concerto had to be played with a painfully recurring note one semi-
tone out.

But whatever musical differences there may have been in the rehearsal, the
personal relationship between the two men thrived on a post-concert dinner
in Silvestri's favourite Panoramic Grill, washed down with fine French wines
from the cellar of its Breton proprietor, Renée Lennoye, ex-skipper of a

merchantman which had made for the nearest English port when the Germans invaded France in 1940. In fact, so convivial did their relations become that Curzon actually returned half his fee for the concert.

Unfortunately, 14 months later, Curzon had to cancel playing the Brahms *Concerto No 1* because of influenza and, though he was scheduled to do the Brahms No 2 with Silvestri again on January 9 1968, by that time Costi was in hospital.

Peter Katin's admiration for Silvestri was not uncritical in spite of them having performed together no fewer than 25 times. This noted English interpreter of Chopin, Rachmaninov and Tchaikovsky explained why he thought Silvestri was not a very good concerto conductor:

> There have been many conductors who couldn't conduct concertos. They would have their own ideas about rubato, flexibility, which didn't happen to be those of the soloist and this would result in a musical personality clash. The soloist blamed it all on the conductor and vice versa.
>
> Silvestri wasn't like that at all. He didn't get annoyed if it didn't work – in fact, he didn't get annoyed about anything. But he was rather wayward and sometimes I did get quite exasperated, though it wasn't any good – he didn't know what he'd done wrong! He had this 'helpless child' look about him, so one just put up with it. He could always find some musical reason when he couldn't catch one up at the end of a run. I remember it happening in one of the runs in the third movement of Beethoven *No. 4*. He wanted me to slow up at the end 'to make it more musical' and added: 'We have little . . .', he hesitated, 'a little rendezvous, yes?'
>
> But on one occasion he went totally adrift. It was during a performance in Bournemouth of the Rachmaninov *No. 3* when, after the climax in the first movement, before the cadenza, he tried something I wasn't expecting. It was in a very difficult finger-passage where I couldn't look at him and he suddenly made a ritenuto just where the soloist has to keep going. He was quite happily making this rit, which we had not rehearsed, and I had to try to gradually unwind. It was a near disaster.
>
> I'm afraid Silvestri was one of those conductors unable to give and take. It wasn't that he didn't like rubato but he couldn't follow it when somebody else was doing it. I don't think he could be sufficiently neutral.

But let pianist Peter Frankl have the last word both on Curzon and on soloist/conductor relations:

> Curzon was a very classical player who had his very definite ideas and wouldn't move. I'm sure Silvestri, in his own way, was the same.

I think the ideal combination between a conductor and soloist is, how-ever definite their ideas, to be flexible enough to give and take – that's the ideal way of music-making. I don't like those soloists who impose their way of doing a piece and insist it is the only way of doing it, any more than I like conductors who take the same attitude. It is usually the soloist who has more to say in a concerto than the conductor, who is supposed to fol-low. But I like collaboration and Silvestri and I worked very well together. We would have had many more occasions to play together had he not died and, having gained confidence with experience, I wonder how it would have been in a Beethoven concerto with him?

Though Silvestri had this reputation for generally being considerate with soloists, there was an occasion when eagerness to share an anecdote with the players during a rehearsal resulted in tactless oblivion of its significance for the unfortuntunate young man at the piano. This was Peter Frankl who explained the complexities of the slow movement of the Ravel *Piano Concerto in G* which necessitates maximum concentration. But while he was actually playing the long introductory solo, Silvestri started talking to the orchestra – and this, Frankl vividly remembers, is the gist of what he was telling them:

> Be careful, because when I last conducted this piece the pianist had an in-credible memory lapse and she jumped straight into the recapitulation. So, realising what she'd done, I immediately started bringing in the orchestra to follow her. But at that moment the pianist herself realised her mistake and jumped back to the beginning. It was a total catastrophe!

At this point, the involuntary listener at the piano to this tale of woe shouted: 'That pianist was NOT me!' and the whole orchestra burst out laughing. 'But it was no laughing matter for me,' Frankl relates.

> It was a most horrifying experience to have between a rehearsal and a con-cert because I could think of nothing else but where one could go wrong in this concerto. In the event, nothing did go wrong and it was a very enjoy-able concert. It was a concerto more suited to Silvestri's temperament than, say, Brahms and he did it extraordinarily well. He was a wonderful man – but he could be very tactless.

That mild posthumous reproof by a sensitive artist prompts a string of ques-tions. First, does this isolated example of thoughtlessness bear any relation to Silvestri's *rapport* with his orchestra, which comprised some 90-plus men and women, also with varying degrees of sensitivity? Was solicitude for their feelings included in his personal code of labour relations? Or could the 'love affair' with the orchestra have been rather one-sided? How long did the Bournemouth players' first fine rapture with the guest conductor from Paris survive? With Silvestri's, at least for those days, unorthodox interpretive views, which he held with such implacable conviction, by what means was he able to mould the players to his musical will?

If, in the words of one player, 'he could be very touchy and temperamental, though in a very gentlemanly way,' he was evidently not prone to the excesses of either of the two conductors for whom he expressed admiration as a young man: he did not indulge in the fear-inducing tantrums of a Toscanini or Furtwängler's spluttering outbursts – nothing more demonstrative than, according to another player, 'mock anger when he would break a bit off his baton and at the end of a rehearsal the floor around the podium would be strewn with what looked like matchsticks.' But it was *mock* anger.

We have seen that relations with the first orchestra of which he was 'permanent' conductor, the Bucharest Philharmonic, were sometimes strained. On the other hand, the former members interviewed from the Bucharest Opera praised his patience and friendliness; the Radio Orchestra players thought his reign was the 'best they ever had;' and one encomium from a former BSO member has already been quoted. In an attempt to arrive at answers to these questions, some of Silvestri's BSO contemporaries recalled their experiences with him and gave their opinions.

First Violin Brian Johnstone said Silvestri was the only conductor in his experience for whom the orchestra would grow instantly quiet the moment he started walking through it.

We were all aware that there was something very special about him, that something unusual was about to happen. There were a lot of players like me who stayed with the orchestra because, musically, life was so interesting. He was able to galvanise players into great feats – for instance, those who had begun their careers in silent film theatres or dance bands and had come to playing in symphony orchestras rather late. I used to sit next to one of the First Violins who was well over 60 and I was amazed at the way he used to throw himself into the music. Silvestri appealed to the musical spirit in every age group.

He was remarkable, not least in the breadth of his repertoire, some of it unfortunately seldom heard nowadays. Nor are there many conductors who can turn music not of the first rank into something well worth listening to. I found César Franck's *Rédemption* for soprano, choir and orchestra very treacly and sentimental, but by the time he had finished with it, it was absolutely wonderful music. It was the same with Liszt's symphonic poem *Mazeppa* and his *Tasso, Lamento e Trionfo*' [an observation which conductor George Hurst had also made].

What also kept us going was that he worked himself as hard as he worked us. He drove himself into the ground. After three weeks with Silvestri we were feeling a bit frayed because it was really impossible to work any longer at that pitch of concentration. He did a lot more concerts in the season than principal conductors do now.

It was about six months after Silvestri's appointment and Principal Clarinet Raymond Carpenter, after initially feeling a little apprehensive at how this new, foreign conductor with strange ideas and mannerisms would react to his playing, had begun to feel a growing confidence as, so far, no serious criticisms had come his way.

Then, one morning, Costi turned up for a rehearsal in his brown suit, an ominous sign of unsettled weather ahead, as the orchestral met-prophets had come to divine. They were rehearsing Dvorak's *Third Symphony* in which there is a long clarinet solo in the slow movement. Carpenter, a hyper-conscientious player frequently singled out in concert reviews for his fine performance, had never been very happy with this solo and had tried with scant success to find a way of playing it to his own satisfaction. He takes up the story:

> We came to this solo and I felt, half way through, those eyes were on me. Silvestri stopped conducting and everyone stopped playing. I sat there feeling at last my time had come.
>
> He lit up a cigarette – a sure indication that some time was to be spent on this particular passage. Everybody then put down their instruments and some lit up. A horrible cold feeling went down my spine, especially when he began:
>
> 'Meester Carpenter,' (pause) 'your solo sounds like a first-year student's.'

The 40-year-old Carpenter thought:

> 'Oh, my God, here we go.' The maestro asked me to play it again and I did so. All the time he was shaking his head. He wiped me off the map with a single gesture and I fizzled out.
>
> And then, as if I wasn't there, he turned to the orchestra and asked:
> 'Thees Meester Carpenter – is he married?'
> Several voices: 'Yes!'

'And ees he a papa?'

'Yes, he has two children,' came the reply.

'Ah, then he must have some emotion, some feeling, yes?' was Costi's rhetorical query.

Everyone was nodding his or her agreement, thoroughly enjoying this moment as my whole history and personality was gone into, and whether I had a good instrument. I felt terrible.

After about 20 minutes of this, Silvestri wound up the discussion with:

'Meester Carpenter, maybe you will take home this early symphony of Dvorak and maybe you will concentrate on making it sound. . .' and once more he explained what he wanted.

I did take it home and worked for hours on it, looked for new reeds and tried out new fingerings.

– an echo of what Amelia Beldi had said: 'You had to prepare the score at home before coming to the rehearsal, otherwise you were not his friend;' and of the Bucharest Opera players': 'The manner in which he solicited us in rehearsal obliged us to work at home.'

By the time it came to the actual concert, which was in Portsmouth, Carpenter felt the solo was

pretty reasonable and the maestro thought I had made a big improvement, gave me a stand-up and made me take a bow. He was the severest critic, but a most generous person. He wouldn't criticise unless he thought there was hope – and in my case he obviously thought there was some. Over the years these criticisms came thick and fast, as they did for every soloist and we all improved as a result and in his last years he made a fuss of us performers.

But I always felt that embarrassing someone in front of the rest didn't come into his reckoning at all. His was a complete and utter concentration on achieving, or rather making *us* achieve, the almost impossible.

The pursuit of perfection was paramount, individual's sensibilities notwithstanding, and he expected the players to be sufficiently resilient to be able to cope with his sarcasm without getting upset. The double-bass section, for instance, were once the butt of this allegedly lowest form of wit but seem to have been more amused than hurt. The section 'was pretty awful in those days,' thinks Lyndon Thomas,

a few players plus some drop-outs from a dying jazz scene. So we were always in for a lot of stick from Silvers, as we called him. One occasion I remember was when we were asked to play a certain passage and we made a valiant attempt in our various ways to rumble through. At the end, Silvers' comment was: 'Very good. But sometimes you change ze note, yes?'

'As players we were made to face up to our weaknesses and our possibilities,' Carpenter reflects.

> We learned not to be shy or shamefaced when confronted with searching analysis of our individual contributions; we had to exceed our own limits to reach his demands and so our anxieties ended at the rostrum – whether it was in the Festival Hall or the Concertgebouw.

Silvestri himself was flexible, not only in his approach to music, but in altering his methods of getting the best out of an individual player without necessarily 'taking him apart.' There was a principal in the woodwind who had been a very fine player but who was close to retirement and losing interest. By gentle persuasion and reminding him of his great days, Silvestri succeeded in getting him, in the words of a colleague, 'to play the very big cor anglais solo in the Shostakovich *Eighth* like an absolute star.'

Carpenter himself gave two instances of a very different Silvestri from the one in the brown suit who verbally crucified him over the Dvorak solo:

> In September 1964 he wanted me to do the Mozart *Clarinet Concerto* K622 and a week or so before we were due to perform in Bournemouth, he sent a message for me to visit him in his flat for tea at three o'clock so that we could listen to records and discuss the concerto. So I went at three and the first thing he did was to give me a whisky. We sat down with his tape recorder and Mme Silvestri flitted in and out bringing me biscuits and cake while we listened to various renditions of the Mozart which he discussed with me.
>
> Before then, I had really been quite scared of the man because he just knew everything and I felt he could see right through me. But on this occasion I had warm feelings about him – and, of course, we never did have tea, only whisky the whole way through.
>
> When it came to the first rehearsal, he made it even better because he adopted a very reasonable tempo. He made me sit down with the orchestra and he sat as well – and that's the way we actually performed. I was so relaxed and enjoyed it very much. Silvestri encouraged everybody to make beautiful sounds.

And this is how it sounded to Bournemouth reviewer Kenneth Williams, evidently a Raymond Carpenter fan:

> Both conductor and soloist were seated for the performance and, with a

slightly reduced string strength, the occasion had an intimacy which was well suited to the soloist's delicate, rather introspective, approach. . .

Earlier that year, Carpenter had gone through what he called 'a bad patch' when playing the Tchaikovsky *Fifth Symphony* in the last concert before Silvestri went to Tokyo in March to keep his engagements with the NHK Orchestra. The first time he mounted the rostrum on his return to Bournemouth in May, he thanked the orchestra warmly for their last concert together and especially for the way they had played the Tchaikovsky. 'I conducted it in Japan,' he told them, 'and I realised what a good orchestra you are. But I have a special present for one player,' at which he got down from the rostrum, approached Carpenter and handed him a Japanese perfumed red silk handkerchief, saying: 'I present this to Meester Carpenter for playing so beautifully.' After more than three decades, Carpenter insists the Japanese handkerchief retains its perfume.

> I wasn't the only one that received his bouquets – in fact, he was lavish with them. If a player, despite all his criticisms, did play really well at concerts, especially if it were a big solo, he made a real fuss of him or her. He didn't do what so many conductors do: just give a player a stand-up and that would be the end of it. He would go off after the applause had started, come back and make his way to this or that player's chair and make a gesture as if to say: 'This is my oboist or my flautist or whoever. He played for me – wasn't it beautiful?' That made you feel better after all that last week of criticism. It was a very nice side of his character. So many conductors are very self-centred. They don't realise they can do a lot of damage and, if they want to, a lot of good by these little gestures.

Discounting the notional 'glamour' of being a member of a prestigious orchestra, it is a frustrating occupation for those individual members who have to conform to the conductor's interpretation and have scant opportunity for self-expression. 'As Principal Clarinet,' confirms Carpenter,

> I was expected to be able to play every note as written by the composer – also as edited by Silvestri – and only then was I allowed some freedom to use my own interpretive skills. This freedom I had to earn. Each principal player underwent a searching analysis of his contribution as a soloist and as part of an ensemble.

It is not surprising therefore that Silvestri always had to deal with some recalcitrant players whether in Bucharest, certainly in Paris where discipline

Gerry Jarvis: Tighter discipline when he became the BSO's leader

was lax – unpunctual attendance at rehearsals; resentment at his demands for what they considered were too many of them; smoking while playing – or in London during his first visits. It was remarked that some London players reacted against 'his particular brand of stick technique,' as one player put it, or against his interpretations, by a form of mickey-taking: deliberate exaggerations of his instructions even in performance. It was here that a bass clarinet player, in protest at the way Silvestri wanted something played, is alleged to have stood up and told the maestro:

> I am not paid, Mr Silvestri, to come to this rehearsal and be told exactly how to play my instrument. I spent six years in college and I've had considerable experience of better conductors than we seem to be getting these days. I absolutely refuse to play it your way. It's not the way it's written and the way I've played it in the past. . .

It would be fascinating to know the outcome of this particular contretemps but we will have to be content with the general knowledge that he did meet such opposition from the bigger orchestras and even, at the beginning, from within the BSO itself. Some principal players actually left – not necessarily solely because of Silvestri – and there was a certain amount of grumbling. (Internal discipline was tightened up with the appointment of the Canadian, the late Gerald Jarvis, as leader.)

It was in Sydney, Australia, two years before Bournemouth, that Silvestri had his most serious brush with an orchestra, which led to the only time in his career when he failed to turn up for a concert and without even giving the perfunctory 'indisposed' or any other excuse. As is usually the case, several factors were involved: he only knew a few words of English at this time and this led to a lack of effective communication and misunderstandings on both sides; and a certain rigid sticking to the letter of union rules on the part of the members of the Sydney Symphony Orchestra – already miffed by hostile press reports of Silvestri's conducting of a previous concert which they

"Sorry Silvo, you'll hafta change that last bit to allegro, fortissimo, SMOKE-OH!"

The Sydney Sunday Mirror's *cartoon treatment of the Sydney Symphony Orchestra's tea-and-smoking dispute with Silvestri in 1969*

considered reflected on their orchestra's reputation. These included headlines like 'Symphony Concert Below Par' and 'Absurd Speed – Concert Fiasco.' It had been an all-Tchaikovsky programme, including the *Fifth Symphony*.

What appears to have happened is that a rehearsal started in Sydney Town Hall at 10 a.m. one day in June 1959; at 11.30 there should have been a tea or smoking break, under an agreement between the Australian Musicians' Union and Australian Broadcasting Corporation which stated that the players were entitled to a 15-minute break after 90 minutes rehearsing. Silvestri, naturally, was engrossed in rehearsing the last movement of the Brahms *First Symphony*, but the union representative told the concertmaster that the players must have their break at 11.45. On the stroke, he did indeed tell Silvestri, through a German-speaking member of the orchestra, that it was the custom to have a break for tea or a smoke.

Silvestri's version of what then happened is that he explained to the concertmaster that he would be able to send half the orchestra home, including all the trombones, if they would play 15 minutes overtime. 'I thought I would be doing them a good turn,' he said afterwards. Instead, the orchestra walked out 18 bars or 12 seconds before the end of the symphony. So, he had no alternative but to walk out as well – and turned up neither for the rest of the rehearsal nor for the performance that evening. Another conductor substituted when it was impossible to find Silvestri.

He claimed that it was the breaking point after a number of disputes over rehearsal time with the Sydney orchestra. He told journalists he did not want Sydney to remember him as a temperamental Continental like Toscanini who used to break five batons at a rehearsal. It is the first time I have ever been insulted and the first time I have ever walked out of a rehearsal. I have given 72 concerts in the past eight months – in Warsaw, Prague, Leningrad and other great cities where I was appreciated. In Sydney I am treated as a buffoon, as an idiot. If an orchestra won't respond, a conductor can work himself silly without any effect.

He praised the musicians of other Australian cities, but did nothing to endear himself to the Sydney players or public by calling their audiences' musical appreciation 'superficial' and claiming that the Dixielanders jazz band he had listened to in a Woolloomooloo hotel had played with 'virtuosity and devotion.' So that there was no possibility of anyone missing the point he added: 'I'd rather listen to rock'n roll than a symphonic masterpiece badly played.' This was after the adverse reviews of his conducting the Sydney concerts.

But at no stage in Silvestri's conducting career has anyone accused him of malice and Kenneth Matchett vouches that he never once suggested that any player should be dismissed. 'He would talk to me about all the members of the orchestra,' said its general manager, 'and I had to read between the lines if he wasn't too happy about someone and I would then call in the player and give a sort of "don't do this or that".'

Nicholas Braithwaite remembers an occasion when the BSO manager, assistant manager, the leader, Silvestri and himself were strolling and chatting in Bournemouth's Winter Gardens and the subject came up of a certain player's conduct. Silvestri deliberately excluded himself from the topic and dropped behind. It would seem that Costi did not want to involve himself in management problems so that he could feel free to bark in rehearsal without any threat of a bite to follow. Or as Braithwaite put it:

> Although many players were terrified of him it was only because he would show up any musical shortcomings they might have, not because they were afraid of losing their jobs. If that was his policy it was good psychology.

He thought Silvestri was right to keep the players' livelihoods separate from their role as musicians.

> I think that might be why he was held in such love and affection by the orchestra even after seven years, which was a very long time to have that degree of devotion.

So the 'love affair' did last. But it was due to more positive factors than just because Costi distanced himself from a prerogative to hire and fire. His teaching of conducting in Romania for 10 years had provided him with a sound grounding in 'good psychology' and it was both the methods themselves which he employed for developing the BSO and the phenomenally successful results these achieved that produced a corporate pride and endeared the Bournemouth players to their conductor.

Even before he left Romania, to someone who was going overboard about his skill in communicating with the orchestra, he replied:

> Of course, I have the gift of transmitting to the instrumentalists my intentions, but this is a quality which every conductor must have to some degree. If you cannot make yourself understood without giving commands to the players you will only create confusion.

Although British orchestral players had the advantage over their Romanian counterparts of a decade or two headstart in experience, some of Silvestri's offbeat teaching practices he employed with the Bournemouth players had been tried out in Bucharest years before.

Nicolae Ionaşcu, the tuba player in the Bucharest Opera, remembered Silvestri working on a Beethoven symphony, section by section with his accustomed thoroughness, and then leaving the orchestra to play by itself. This bizarre experiment, Ionaşcu believed, was to demonstrate that, if sufficiently well rehearsed, the orchestra could carry on if the conductor hesitated or made an error.

It is difficult to believe that Silvestri would have used such a ploy with the BSO, but whatever the motive there was at least one occasion when he left the orchestra in mid-rehearsal. In July 1962 he was rehearsing Haydn's *'London' Symphony No 104 in D* for a Kenwood Lakeside Concert and at one point decided to go to the other side of the lake to hear the balance.

'What dynamic are the trumpets?' he called out.

'Forte' came the reply.

'They should be a little louder,' he suggested as he walked up the hill – and disappeared. The players did not see him again until the concert.

It was also by a lake, in the open-air theatre near the splendid sheet of water which is Herăstrău Lake in the spacious park of that name in Bucharest, that Silvestri had been rehearsing Enescu's *Second Romanian Rhapsody* with the Philharmonic, conductor Mircea Cristescu recalled. A viola player in the orchestra at that time, he had to do the *Rhapsody* for his conducting graduation and Silvestri said to him: 'Mircea, please come and conduct in my place. I want to listen to it from the back of the auditorium.'

This was a part of the *Rhapsody* which is particularly difficult for the orchestra and, according to Cristescu, 'they were flabbergasted. This was my baptism of fire, but I think Silvestri did it as a generous gesture to help me and not primarily for the reason he gave.'

A decade later a similar experience would befall the 21-year-old horn player Alun Francis. Before joining the BSO in 1964, he had conducted some of his own compositions with the Hallé and now decided he would like to study conducting with Silvestri. His 'strange story,' as Francis himself calls it, of what happened after making his request to the maestro, he recounts with *hwyl*, humour and graphic, sometimes comic, demonstrations of the manner- isms of the man for whom, nevertheless, he had a manifest respect, admira- tion and affection. It provides us with a cameo of Silvestri the teacher:

'So, you want to be a conductor?' he said to me. 'You think you're good enough?'

'I don't know,' I said. 'That's why I wrote to you,'

'We try. . . I try,' he said briefly.

And after a rehearsal in the Winter Gardens we walked to his apartment nearby at a snail's pace – it seemed to me as a young man that he always had this world-weary manner, everything he did was slow, such as coming on or leaving the platform. As usual, he was smoking a cigarette in a long holder which he held in a special way. Slowly we climbed the stairs to his lounge with its white piano.

He had this disconcerting trick of turning his head and speaking to someone who wasn't there:

'He wants to be a conductor,' he said to this fictitious person, shrugging his shoulders and lifting incredulous eyebrows. I wanted to look behind him to see if anyone was there.

Of course, I was terrified.

He went to a cupboard and picked out some scores: *Nights In The Gardens of Spain*, *Petrushka*, *The Marriage of Figaro* and a Rossini overture. Then he slid a bowl of sweets towards me.

'Bon-bon?'

I declined because I had just had some serious dental surgery.

'Bon-bon,' he insisted. So I took one.

He laid out on the table all these miniature scores in different colours. I said:

'You want me to play them on the piano?'

'You want to be a conductor, yes?'

'Wha . . . what am I supposed to conduct?' I stammered.

'Today, 27th of March. Me, Constantin Silvestri. You, you conduct!'

Because of his limited English he only used limited formulations. So, I had to stand up, take hold of the scores, conduct nobody, sing all the principal voices in the right keys – that meant reading in all the clefs – and eat my bon-bon as well. I got through *Figaro* OK and he nodded to his *alter ego*. Then he said: '*Nights In The Gardens of Spain*' and we went through all this laborious process. It took about an hour and a half. His glamorous wife, a Zsa-Zsa Gabor figure with a fabulous hair-do, passed through and said something, calling me 'Dearie.' But *he* said nothing. This, I thought, is the most punishing thing I've ever done.'

At last he spoke:

'I show you. I teach you.'

I said: 'But I'm not sure how I'll be able to pay.'

'I teach you, Comissiona, Cosma . . .'

He paused, thinking of these conductors he'd taught. 'You'll be better. Pay me afterwards.'

And that was the beginning. I used to go to him at all times of the day – I never knew when he would call me. His own method of conducting was not at all according to the copybook but he insisted that mine should be. It was punishing. He was merciless. The only positive thing he would ever say to me was: 'It's possible.'

But it was the right attitude.

There was one lesson when we just dealt with *fermatas* – pauses – when we went over and over again the pause in the sixth bar of the last movement of Beethoven's *First Symphony*. For some reason known only to himself he was completely obsessed with this particular *fermata*. To all my attempts he would mutter: 'No, no, *no*!' and make despairing appeals to his *alter ego*. I asked him to show me but all I got was an almost imperceptible motion of his cigarette holder which he held in lieu of a stick. Sometimes it was a nightmare trying to follow him.

Six weeks later, the orchestra was rehearsing the Beethoven *First* and we came to this very moment. . . Chaos! We repeated it. It broke down again and he became more and more sarcastic:

'If I asked an *amateur* to conduct I think it's better,' he exclaimed and pointed in my direction.

'You,' he said. 'You come and conduct it!'

Nobody knew I'd been studying with him so the players were puzzled as to whom he was referring. I got this chilling idea he was talking to me but I just sat there. He insisted:

'You come, you come!'

'I'm alright here, Mr Silvestri,' I said. But somebody muttered: 'You'd better go. We can't stay here all day.'

So, I went down and as he gave me the stick he addressed the orchestra: 'If you can't follow professionals, see if you can play with *amateurs*!'

The leader, Gerry Jarvis – he was Canadian – turned to me:

'What you goin't'do, kid?'and I replied: 'No idea!'

However, I started the last movement of the symphony and when we came to the famous moment where it had broken down at least twice, we got over it. No problem at all – not because I think I was any good but we were so fed up that we were determined to get it right, just to show him. And he walked off.

I stopped but they said: 'Go on! Conduct the whole movement, what the Hell!'

So I did – while Silvestri was having a coffee.

Six weeks before, he had laboriously gone over that bar with me and insisted: 'Don't you ever forget that!'

I'll never know whether, realising that we would soon be doing the Beethoven, he wasn't really preparing me for that moment and staged the whole show because he knew that, as a young nobody, I would never get the chance to conduct anything.

And that's how it all started,'

concluded Francis, who had recently conducted three orchestras simultaneously: the Berlin Philharmonic, the Berlin Radio and his own Berlin Symphony – a total of 480 players including 67 First Violins.

As an example of Silvestri's versatility in solving technical problems, Raymond Carpenter cites a rehearsal of Brahms *Second Symphony* where there is a passage in which the wind and the strings are supposed to play together but the wind was lagging behind.

He sent the whole of the wind section over to the far corner of the hall so that we were as far away from the strings as possible. Then he ordered: 'Now, you play in time with the strings!' And after we'd been through it three or four times we went back and felt it was quite easy. He sometimes tried to make something more difficult for the players so that, when they actually had to perform, it seemed easy.

He had a fabulous knowledge of instruments and what they were capable of doing. If I had a problem he would come right up to my desk and discuss it with me. Whether it was fingering or articulation he would make suggestions.

Principal Bassoon Eric Butt also remembers how Silvestri, not satisfied with the way he was playing the solo 'that growls low down at the beginning of the Tchaikovsky *Sixth*,' left the rostrum and stood in front of him while he repeated it time and time again. 'That was good training,' Butt is convinced. 'I was never afraid again of doing a solo.'

We have already seen how impressed Ioan Maxim was with Silvestri's ideas about how the percussion should sound in *Oedipus*. In the scherzo of the Tchaikovsky *Fourth Symphony* he would insist on the timpani playing with their hands. In Mussorgsky's *Pictures at an Exhibition* he would tell the first trumpet how to play the *Shmuyle* theme, giving it a new incisive character, and so on. Fabulous perhaps, but not unique – if we are to believe G.B. Shaw, 'Elgar takes the whole orchestra in his hand and raises every separate instrument in it to its highest efficiency until its strength is as the strength of ten. One was not surprised to learn he could play them all, and was actually something of a virtuoso on instruments as different as the violin and trombone'; while Glazunov is supposed to have quashed an incipient revolt when conducting a British orchestra: provocatively a French-horn player had stood up and declared he couldn't play a certain note, whereupon Glazunov took the man's instrument and played the note himself. Applause from the orchestra and collapse of 'revolt' – a story also attributed to Hans Richter.

These days, when conductors' tricks of the profession are fairly common knowledge and it has been largely demystified by media and biographical exposure, Silvestri's methods may not sound at all extreme. However, they had sufficient impact on players 30 years ago for them to be recalled with something of the same wonderment with which they were greeted at the time. How, for instance, if there was a difficult phrase which had to be repeated on various instruments, he would choose the one on which he considered it sounded best and ask the most talented player, maybe a flautist, to work on the phrase until he or she got it exactly as he wanted it: the right technical finesse, all the subtle shades of meaning, colour, dynamics or tone that he required. That accomplished, he would get the whole orchestra to listen while, in this example the principal flautist, played it. He might then turn to the oboe for the phrase to be repeated as it had been played on the flute – and so on, section by section. In this way each department improved its technique, fluency and style to the point where the orchestra as a whole could do instinctively what he wanted.

Alun Francis remembers when he first joined the BSO how impressed he was with Silvestri taking 'infinite pains over the first four bars of Schubert's *'Great' C major Symphony'*; how, in a work of Debussy or Ravel, he would spend half an hour over five bars.

> He would stop, then have the second clarinet playing on its own; add the second horn very, very slowly and put those two together. (Meanwhile, of course, the whole orchestra was sitting there, waiting.) Then he would add the second bassoon and, finally, the first and second oboe. The end effect was that, when the moment came in the concert, those five bars were just perfect.
>
> This method of building very slowly, like a painter putting colours to canvas from his palette – getting the first colour absolutely right before adding the next one – produced marvellous results. But, naturally, there was an element in the orchestra that couldn't stand just sitting around while he worked with only a few players. The era has gone when Silvestri would labour, with great skill and knowledge, over four bars in Ravel's *Daphnis and Chloë* – nowadays the players wouldn't put up with it. There are all sorts of union rules that came in in the Seventies that prevent a conductor doing that.

One observer, not herself a professional musician, sat-in on one of his rehearsals and watched him spend two hours on one work. 'At the end I felt that even I could have fitted in with his wishes, so clear had they become. He was so relaxed and so swept away by the music that he drew it out of each player,' she remarked.

Silvestri always emphasised that talent was no substitute for rehearsing and that it was essential

> to allow for a little flexibility and spontaneity in the concert itself, a consistent work pattern in rehearsal as well as in-depth treatment of the music.

Players to this day remember in detail the time he would spend rehearsing sections, even passages, of a work: threequarters of an hour with the oboes, double-basses and cellos on the first few bars of the *Pathétique*; hours spent rehearsing the long *Prélude à l'unison* first movement of Enescu's *Suite No 1* in order to achieve the quintessence of unanimity in the strings accompanied by timpani rolls of varying dynamics (for a Festival Hall concert in May 1965.) A total of 21 hours was spent rehearsing the BSO for its first performance of *Manfred* in November 1962 – 90 minutes on the percussion alone for the bachanale in the last movement; another 90 minutes with the harps who have an important duet solo and, to get the exact flexibility he wanted, Silvestri sat down with them until it was achieved.

He would be particularly keen to impress soloists with the excellence of his orchestra and even before they had arrived – perhaps days before – he would rehearse the tuttis in a concerto.

In a broadcast, he once recounted how in Leningrad he had spent three hours rehearsing Debussy's symphonic triptych, *Nocturnes*, and because he had been able to spend that amount of time they had sounded better than when he conducted the *Nocturnes* again in Brussels in 1958 with a Belgian orchestra with whom there had been a strictly limited amount of rehearsing. Nevertheless, the leader of the orchestra – who had actually been to Debussy's home and played his *Violin Sonata* with the composer and subsequently the *String Quartet* and other chamber works – said that, although he had played the *Nocturnes* hundreds of times, he had 'never understood them' until they were played with Silvestri.

Reminiscent of Toscanini's oft-repeated dictum: '*Cantando, sempre cantando*,' Silvestri was a keen advocate of singing to demonstrate the basis for one of his ideas of melodic form. Brian Johnstone remembers the whole of his violin section singing 'the great melody at the end of Brahms *First Symphony* to teach them how to arch a phrase; and the celli would sing the opening of the *1812 Overture*.' Once Silvestri got the Principal Oboe into a corner when the rest of the orchestra were having a tea break and he went over a passage with him and made him sing it.

Even in the early days when Silvestri's English was limited, explained James Loughran,

> he succeeded in getting the orchestra to be so pliable that they could watch his every movement, every nuance, and respond to it. So it became by far the freest and most virtuoso orchestra in the country. It was quite extraordinary. It came to Edinburgh or London to play something like the *Manfred Symphony* and it was like nothing the British had ever heard because it was absolutely free – it would vary from performance to performance, the hallmark of every good musician. There was nothing static about it; communication had always to be fresh, had to be rebaked at every performance.

Actually Silvestri brought the *Manfred* to London rather late. It was not until September 1967 that Ronald Crichton in the *Financial Times* could refer to its inclusion in 'a refreshingly unusual programme' as a 'courageous act' and praise the BSO for an expressive style reflecting its conductor's volatile temperament, his elegance of phrasing a4nd his keen ear for instrumental colour. . . In the fantastically difficult scherzo, Silvestri and his players produced some of the most delicate playing of the evening.

Three other examples of Silvestri's teaching methods were provided by Nicholas Braithwaite:

I remember him rehearsing the Rachmaninov *Symphony No 3* which has a little phrase with three quavers leading to a bar line in the four horns and the flute. He stopped the orchestra and they did it again. But again he stopped them and repeated: 'No, we'll do it again.' And they did it several times without him telling them why.

Eventually, the First Flute said: 'Just tell us what you want and we'll do it' and yet again he replied: 'No!' and made them repeat it – until suddenly, about the tenth time, something clicked and it sounded right. Everybody knew it sounded right, but nobody knew exactly what had happened.

I think his principle was that if he had said: 'OK, Third Horn, you've got to play the second note a little bit longer and the Fourth Horn the third note a little bit shorter' and so on, all that would have happened would have been that those players would have concentrated on doing that little instruction rather than trying to work as a group and make it function as a whole. So, quite often he would not say what he wanted; instead he would make the players become aware of the possibilities themselves.

Another thing he used to do in rehearsal was to take a musical phrasing, a *rubato* or *rallentando* for instance, out beyond the limits of good taste so it was really plainly not something one would do. But in the process he would discover where was the edge between what could and should not be done. And that was also a great lesson because so often we'd try to get it right and, in doing so, never really find the border between getting it right and getting it wrong.

On a third occasion, he was rehearsing a full orchestral chord and it just didn't sound as he wanted it to. So he treated it like erecting a flagpole: he played just the bass notes in each section – the double-bass, the tuba, the contrabassoon and so on – and made them pause on each note for ages. Then he made the second note in the chord – the cellos, the bass trombones – play as well, also pausing. In this way he gradually built up the chord from the bottom note upwards.

Then he did it again, without pausing, one after the other – like that [and Braithwaite snapped his fingers]. Gradually he tilted the chord upright from being horizontal. Then, in the performance he didn't do anything in particular with his hands at that moment, but the chord had a weight and gravity which it just didn't have before – a fascinating technique!

It was only through thousands of hours of employing methods such as these that mutual confidence could be built up between conductor and players – 'obtaining from them the sound image in the conductor's mind through sheer force of personality, through his temperament and character,' as Riccardo Chailly has succinctly put it – to a point where 'a magic word' from Silvestri could have an electric effect on the orchestra.

This was the English equivalent of the term used by Hungarian-born pianist Livia Rev who spoke about her 'marvellous memory' of a rehearsal with Silvestri in Bournemouth in June 1965 when she was playing the Beethoven *Concerto No 1*:

> In the *tutti* at the beginning of the concerto I could hear that many things needed to be put right. Silvestri simply said to them: 'You are not happy enough in your playing,' and at that moment the orchestra was completely transformed. It was fantastic! It was what we call *le mot clef* [literally the key word]. It was so characteristic of Silvestri.

Peter Katin remembers an occasion in October 1964 when the BSO was rehearsing the Mendelssohn Italian *Symphony*:

> Silvestri wanted beautiful colours in the third movement. They started and he stopped them – about six times altogether – until he finally threw up his hands in despair and implored: 'Roses, think of roses!' Which actually was a very good description of that movement.

So much for the various methods Silvestri employed for getting the sound he wanted from an orchestra. But what was that sound? What was the goal to which all these efforts were directed: the training of individual departments of the orchestra, of individual sections and individual instrumentalists?

The reason Anatol Vieru thinks Silvestri was 'a revolutionary in conducting as far as Romanian orchestras were concerned' is because 'he wanted to produce more refined sounds such as those produced by a chamber orchestra. To achieve this he was trying out ideas as in a musical laboratory.'

Silvestri's Hungarian contemporary, the violinist Josef Szigeti thought it was possible for a large orchestra to play with the precision of a quartet. Twelve years after Silvestri died, Riccardo Muti was expanding on the same theme: '. . . players must listen to each other while playing in the same way that a string quartet listen to one another. . . It makes for a better, more precise ensemble.'

In the meantime, Silvestri had achieved just that; not only in Romania but in the Britain of the Sixties this aim – let alone his methods of achieving it – was also revolutionary.

Among those convinced of this is Roger Winfield, the BSO's Principal Oboe in Silvestri's time who, it will be recalled, had played under Barbirolli and Karajan and, since Silvestri, under other conductors of world repute: 'What Silvestri did was to make an orchestra sound like a solo instrument,' he maintained.

> In the Tchaikovsky *Violin Concerto*, for example, even with a good orchestra, because the flute who has to play a solo passage does not have the advantage of being near the soloist, they will play in different styles. But when Silvestri conducted, both played in the same style.
>
> There are now several players in London who will play like that and will convince conductors that that is the way it should be played. But, at that time, Silvestri was the only conductor able to make an orchestra play like a soloist. Now, the style has evolved from the Bournemouth tradition he initiated because people realise its validity after all these years.
>
> The conductor has the music in front of him and it says *rallentando*, *accelerando* and they are so terrified of it coming to pieces that they won't take any chances. But Silvestri did take chances and he was able to make 90 people play with the same *rubato* as an individual. It was terribly difficult to do, but he did it – and the records are there to prove it.
>
> There are today in London orchestras who are direct descendants of the Silvestri style of playing. People hear it and it gets passed on. He was ahead of his time. People are starting to do it now, but in the Sixties for a section to attempt to play rubato it was a pretty tricky affair. This seldom enters into Classical music because it is very rare you get this requirement but in, say, Liszt or Tchaikovsky it's an essential element; otherwise, if an individual player has rubato, flexibility, and everyone else in the orchestra is playing without it, he has to get back into the box again. Silvestri was the first person to break away from that. Barbirolli had the ability to make orchestras blossom, but not in the same way Silvestri did.

So far we have been able to form a fairly comprehensive impression of the orchestra's and soloist's view of Silvestri, of their mutual interaction, particularly in the casual-dress atmosphere of rehearsal, free from public attention;

and of his methods of preparation for a performance.* But what was the view of him from the auditorium? Was his own personal 'performance' on the podium sufficiently consistent for a hypothetical regular attender at his concerts over the years to be able to form a general impression?

Toscanini was supposed to have had a profound unawareness of the audience and one keen orchestral observer of conductors was of the opinion that there was 'nothing of the showman in his constitution.' Lorin Maazel has inveighed against conductors who bring 'a lot of unfocussed energy on stage like some kind of raging sea lion'; Leonard Bernstein, according to a fellow conductor, had 'crazy movements'; while in contrast there are those who conduct like Sir Adrian Boult used to, whose communication with the orchestra is confined to a glance or a flick of the wrist.

At Silvestri's first London appearance a reviewer referred to his economy of gesture; in Rotterdam the same year, the Concertgebouw 'reacted with extreme precision to his particularly sober gestures'; in Australia it was noted he conducted the Brahms *First Symphony* with 'a minimum of movement until building up to great climaxes'; and in Nottingham after a concert in March 1965 it was noted:

> Silvestri, who sometimes stands impassively on the rostrum with his baton limp in one hand while the other is flicking over the pages of a racing score, is always ready to pounce into action to get the effects he wants.

The Times reviewer of a BSO Festival Hall concert in June 1966 found Silvestri's conducting of Dvorak's *Slavonic Dances* 'marvellous to behold' and with gentle irony described his 'more spectacular strokes: the backhand swipe, the blackboard wiper, the orator's promise, the cranium scratcher, and even the military "shun". . .' Yet whoever wrote his obituary in *The Times* concluded 'he was not a showman conductor.'

An even more detailed description of his conducting from the critic's viewpoint was given in a review of a BSO concert in the Fairfield Hall, Croydon in November 1963:

> The players interpret Mr Silvestri's gestures to the letter – and his gestures are not of a textbook pattern, either. His predilection for hand-to-hand baton changing, his somewhat ostentatious twirls of the wrist (charmingly done in the fleet-footed finale of Schubert's *'Tragic' Symphony*) and his thrusting forearm motions, apparently achieve the desired results.

---

* A tape has survived of Silvestri actually rehearsing the BSO, surreptitiously recorded by a player, probably more in fun than with an eye to posterity. A transcription is in Appendix 3.

Pianist Michèle Boegner remembers an embarrassing moment during one of the three performances of d'Indy's *Symphonie sur un Chant Montagnard*, written for piano and orchestra, which she played with the BSO during her third English tour in 1967.

> Silvestri evidently liked this piece very much. Personally, I thought it was bad music and there was one ugly passage which I could see particularly delighted him. His gestures at this point struck me as so funny that I couldn't help smiling and I had to turn my head away from the audience to hide it.

Without disputing the tenor of *The Times* obituary conclusion or the genuineness of his emotional reactions, could there not also have been an element of the showman in the Silvestri who, in Bucharest, turned towards the audience and stepped off the podium 'in a drooping way' at the end of Corelli's *Badinerie*? Or stretched wide his arms at a dramatic moment in the Resurrection in Mozart's *Great Mass*? Or when he would 'carry' an imaginary cross over his shoulder in the first movement of the Tchaikovsky *Fifth Symphony* – a gesture he repeated in Reginald Smith Brindle's *Via Crucis* – holding back the tempo and creating immense tension? Or at the climax of the *Daphnis and Chloë Suite No 2* (where Chloë falls into Daphnis's arms) when Silvestri would fold his arms like a couple embracing?

These gestures were quite uninhibited in rehearsal and no doubt were intended to accentuate the drama of the music and infect the players with his own intense feeling – and, though modified and more subtly, he would repeat them even in performance.

Once when rehearsing the *March to the Scaffold* in the *Symphonie Fantastique* his miming was so dramatic that fellow conductor Rudolph Schwarz, who happened to be looking on from the wings, was heard to mutter: 'I can't stand it!' – for him the drama diminished by what he apparently regarded as excessive histrionics.

First Violin Brian Johnstone:

> Sometimes he would have his baton down by his side and he would almost conduct by hand; at times he would love not to conduct at all, but let the orchestra have its head, like a racehorse. But in climaxes he was the master of the grand gesture.
>
> He was very aware of the visual potential of a lot of music-making – something conductors don't often think about. For instance, he always wanted the percussion to hold their instruments at head level, up in the air where they could be seen by the audience. In the *Overture to Die Meister-*

singer he would have the harps on the outside of the First Violins, about the second or third desk. It looked grand and they could be heard more clearly.

He would stimulate the imaginations of the players with his own mental images of programme music: to the talented Cor Anglais Judy Bass he would suggest before she played the poignant theme at the end of *The Pines of the Appian Way*, the last of the impressions in Respighi's *The Pines of Rome*, that it represented, amidst the pomp of the Roman legions marching to the Capitol, the pathos of an unknown soldier who did not return; or he would stoke up the Trumpets with: 'It's very hot in Hell, you know!' in Tchaikovsky's symphonic fantasy, *Francesca da Rimini* inspired by Gustave Doré's illustrations for Dante's *Inferno*; or in the triumphal finale of the *Fifth Symphony* he would exclaim: 'The Tsar is here!'

(Judy Bass's playing was singled out in a review in *Record and Recordings* of a record made by Silvestri and the BSO which included Borodin's *In The Steppes of Central Asia*: 'When we reach the oriental melody the BSO provide an absolutely superb cor anglais player and, with much emphasis on the grace notes, the tune sounds convincingly Eastern.')

Players and Kenneth Matchett are agreed that, though the quality of the music-making was his paramount priority, Silvestri was certainly aware of the audience: in his selection of programmes, in their presentation, in his acknowledgement of applause (which he was assiduous in sharing with the orchestra, giving precedence to the principals before taking his own bow) and in his choice of encores.

There is little doubt that he had a sense of theatre and planned for certain contingencies, knowing from long experience the effect on audiences of the results of his interpretations, of his diligent rehearsing and of his conducting, combined with the technical excellence and musicianship of the orchestra. It needed, then, only his sense of the dramatic to tell him when to put a pre-planned action into operation. A graphic illustration of this is afforded by the triumph of Silvestri and the BSO at the Edinburgh Festival of 1963.

The run-up to this event is a fascinating example of the behind-the-scenes wrangles in concertbiz to which the public are seldom privy. At this time, only two years since the appointment of Silvestri, the BSO was still struggling to get its refurbished reputation recognised in the top echelons of the British musical hierarchy. Because of the prestige value of appearing in the Edin-burgh Festival, Matchett was determined that the orchestra should be there. He, therefore, seized the opportunity when George Lascelles, Earl of Hare-wood, its artistic director since 1961, phoned him to ask if the BSO would

Peter Frankl: 'Silvestri and I worked well together'

Peter Katin: 'He was not a very good concerto conductor'

accompany the Stuttgart State Theatre Ballet in eight performances in the pit of the Empire Theatre – all the other British orchestras were unavailable at this short notice. Only on condition, stipulated Matchett, that the BSO was given a proper concert in the Usher Hall where the other orchestras – of the Royal Opera House, the LSO, the BBC Symphony, the BBC Scottish, the Scottish National and the Concertgebouw – were booked to perform and he stressed the Festival administration's moral obligation to compensate for the cancellations the BSO would have to make of its own engagements.

The administration hedged: they were fully booked (Matchett learned afterwards that there were protests from the Scottish National Orchestra who could not understand why this Sassenach end-of-the-pier band should be put on a par with these other famous orchestras); but he insisted and the BSO was offered a matinée engagement. Not good enough for my orchestra, replied Matchett, knowing he had the administration over a barrel. Eventually, the BSO was fitted into the Usher Hall programme on August 31, right at the end of the Festival.

The first half of their programme was the same as the one that had been greeted with such enthusiasm in Amsterdam: the *Manfred Symphony*, never played before in Scotland, and Stravinsky's *Le Chant du Rossignol*. The applause at the end of each piece was thunderous. Because of the circumstances in which the concert had been fixed and the behind-the-scenes backbiting, the BSO manager had insisted on an undertaking from Silvestri that he would be on his best behaviour – 'no shinanigins, no milking of the audience,' in Matchett's colourful idiom – more prosaically, no encores. The two of them had arranged that the programme would end with Enescu's *Romanian Rhapsody No. 1* – 'a bit of froth after the "heavy" *Manfred*.'

By the end of the *Rhapsody*, the response was almost frenzied, the whole audience rising to its feet as Silvestri, keeping to his word, left the platform. Matchett continues:

> The Usher Hall has about four tiers and when the audience started to stamp in unison, it was dangerous, like soldiers crossing a bridge without breaking step. It went on and on, but there were no signs of the maestro returning. George Lascelles who was sitting next to me said: 'What's gone wrong? Why isn't he coming back?' So I ran backstage where Silvestri said to me: 'You say no encore', and, with a shrug, 'so, no encore!'
>
> The place was still erupting and the major-domo [the Usher Hall manager] rushes up very agitated: 'For God's sake give 'em an encore or the balcony will collapse!' So I said to Silvestri: 'Take a couple of calls, then bring the boys [*sic**] off.' I stayed in the wings because I knew what was going to happen – so did he!

This was one of the contingencies for which Costi had planned.

Raymond Carpenter takes up the tale:

> Silvestri had an arrangement with me: when it came to doing the *Romanian Rhapsody* he would give me a signal and I was to start whether he was on the rostrum or not. He had taken several bows and was waiting on the side, but we remained in our places on the platform. The storm calmed down to an expectant silence – they were wondering what was going to happen. I had my eyes on him and, sure enough, he suddenly turned to me and raised his eyebrows. So, I started: terrara-ra-pom-pom-pom – as he walked slowly up to the rostrum. The duet between the clarinet and oboe which we had practised came off beautifully and just as he reached the rostrum the string entry came in – and he started conducting us. The whole repeat performance was so fantastic that the audience went mad again and we had to be fetched off.

This kind of reception in Edinburgh is what is occasionally referred to as the glamourous side of an orchestra player's life. Audience appreciation is indeed some reward for what a Principal Viola once described as 'one of incessant strain and backbreaking work in which minutes of pleasure are paid for by hours and hours of slogging.' For both conductor and players there is also

* Exactly a quarter of the BSO at this time were women.

little glamour in playing to half-empty halls in provincial towns, which was also part of Silvestri's and the BSO's work pattern. In the early Sixties they did a 12-day tour in Northern England consisting of 16 performances, including some for children. Silvestri was not too keen on these tours because they were so demanding physically and some of the venues were depressing.

But even these vicissitudes could have their droll side – as when the BSO was trying to rehearse the *Pathétique* in the King George Hall in the Lancashire town of Blackburn simultaneously with a military band playing directly outside the windows in an open-air Remembrance Day service. It was an unequal contest and Silvestri and his troops had to beat a retreat.

In another northern town, there were only a couple of hundred people in a hall that held 2,000 and when Silvestri was told before he came on stage that there were almost more players than audience, he asked: 'Where's the next stop?' Leeds, he was told. 'OK, let's get to Leeds as quickly as possible' – and again it was the aptly-named *Pathétique* that suffered, driven along in places at a breakneck tempo that broke all records.

Peter Frankl maintains that Silvestri's programme planning came in for some criticism and Matchett disclosed he had 'arguments with him over programming when he became more confident.'

'He wanted so much to create the maximum effect,' said Frankl,

and this was sometimes overdone. It was typical of him that he went in for the big fireworks. For example, after I had played in the second half of a programme we did in April 1965 Bartók's *Piano Concerto No 2* which has a fantastically loud ending, he felt he had to go one step beyond that; so he finished with the incredibly loud *Sensemayá* by the Mexican composer Silvestre Revueltas. [This is a musical picture of the bloodthirsty rituals of the pre-Spanish Mayan empire. Kenneth Williams claimed Silvestri conducted it 'with the fervour of a high priest'.]

Frankl's second example was when they included two concertos: Britten's and Liszt's *E flat major*, in the same programme in a series of three concerts in 1967.

I thought the Liszt was better for the second half. But, of course, he had to choose as the last item what must be the loudest piece in the repertoire: Respighi's *Feste Romane*!

Some of the most experienced and renowned soloists are chronic sufferers of pre-performance 'nerves'; there must surely be occasions when even the maestros feel less confident than normally. Despite the 'glamour,' the best of them certainly make mistakes and have memory lapses.

Players claim that Silvestri was always the maestro in every sense, in total command and never showing signs of nervousness. However, they do recall an occasion in April 1965 before a concert in Wolverhampton when the orchestra was on tour and there had only been time for one rehearsal of a programme which included Bartók's *Music for Strings, Percussion and Celesta*, a very complex work. Evidently Silvestri was unable to master it to his satisfaction in the time, the rehearsal did not go at all well (it was the one where the leader asked him to clarify his beat) and everyone was petrified – no one less so than the maestro himself though he concealed it on stage. The woodwind, waiting in the wings to come on for the next piece, heard him admit as he came off: 'I have never had such a terrifying experience in my life!'

It was Bartók again who caused problems for Silvestri and Peter Frankl, two months later in Southampton – this time in his *Second Piano Concerto*:

> I appreciated very much that on this and other occasions he was giving me, a young artist, maximum exposure by playing two concertos in one concert. The first one was Mozart *K459 in F* which itself is a very difficult concerto needing a lot of concentration and involvement. But I remember that the only thing I was able to think about while playing was the Bartók – even now that I have played it in about 50 performances I find it difficult memory-wise and at that time it seemed really almost impossible.
>
> Unfortunately, Silvestri had a concentration lapse at the very beginning of the prestissimo section of the second movement – where it is always a problem for the conductor – and he was one bar behind. Although he had the score, he started it wrong and it was impossible to correct because my part was a perpetuum mobile. We both realised it immediately, but he had to continue to beat it, so the orchestra went on, both of us knowing that he was one bar behind and I was one bar ahead.
>
> Fortunately, about one-third of the way through this middle section there is a short solo passage for the piano when the whole thing settles. I don't suppose anybody noticed in the audience – but what a fright I had! We are all human and can make mistakes like that. Apart from that little slip I thought he did it exceptionally well.

Usually, if the conductor has a lapse a well-trained orchestra will help him out. It was a choir which saved the situation for Silvestri once in Romania. He was conducting the Mozart *Mass in C minor* with the Radio choir in the Athenaeum when, at one point, he was so carried away, his eyes closed, that he forgot to give the entry to the tenors. A few bars later he suddenly remembered, opened his eyes and looked so mortified that all the tenors came in together at precisely the right point for the music – and on the very syllable of a word the beginning of which they had had no chance to enunciate. Opera conductor Constantin Petrovici who told the story gave it as an illustration of what he called 'Silvestri's power of suggestion.'

Gwen French, a member of the Bournemouth Municipal Choir (now the Bournemouth Symphony Choir) recalls how its 200 members, together with the BSO, would fill the Winter Gardens stage.

> Yet Silvestri's control and magnetism was such that at times he would conduct us with just his little finger. We knew exactly what was wanted during the performance.

But slippage can occur in the most ideal liaisons. Rehearsing the wordless choral part in Ravel's *Daphnis et Chloë*, the choir missed an entry. 'Silvestri stopped the orchestra and mimed some breast strokes to show that we were out of our depth and with wonderful good humour went over it again.'

But once the maestro paid forfeit for having taken liberties with the score: in this case Rachmaninov's *Third Symphony*. It had been performed by the BSO a few times, but in the rehearsal for the last concert of a Welsh tour, in the Glamorgan seaport of Barry, he decided he would cut one or two bars in the coda at the end of the last movement. The players were in the dark as to the reason for these cuts and when it came to the performance itself he completely forgot he had made them. The orchestra finished, but Silvestri went on conducting a further couple of beats before holding his baton hand down with the left – his chest heaving with his characteristic laughter.

Finally, an example of near disaster ending in a triumph.

In July 1964, the Inland Waterways Association held a National Festival of Boats and Arts, a highlight of which was a concert by the BSO conducted by Silvestri on the banks of the River Avon at Stratford. The programme was given a fluvial element with the inclusion of Delius's *Summer Night on the River* and Shakespeare was well represented with Tchaikovsky's *Fantasy Overture, Romeo and Juliet*, and his *Symphonic Fantasia, The Tempest*.

Not so appropriate to a pleasant English summer evening was music evocative of French soldiers freezing to death in a Russian winter; nevertheless, Silvestri and the concert organisers decided to exploit to the full the dramatic potential of an open-air performance of the *1812 Overture* by calling upon the services of the Royal Artillery.

The meticulous preparations for this item must have appealed to the histrionic streak in Costi. The audience would be on one of the grassy banks of the Avon, while the orchestra would play from a pontoon moored to the side. In position on the opposite bank would be gunners from the Junior Leaders Regiment of the Royal Artillery with three 25-pounder field guns, ready to fire salvoes of blanks at the appropriate places in the *Overture*. Maximum co-ordination to achieve split-second timing was of the essence: the guns had to start firing in the right place in the music and finish before the last chord – the dramatic effect would be ruined if they went on firing after the music had stopped.

So Silvestri devised a plan: Alfred Jupp, one of the Second Violins, would stand on the bank with a white handkerchief and wave it to the gunners on the other side of the river as a signal when to start firing and when to finish. Silvestri's instructions were that the guns should cease firing about six bars before the end so that the orchestra could be heard in the climax. But Robert Burns was never so canny as when he coined the aphorism about the 'best laid schemes o' mice an' men. . .'

The bank filled up with the audience, the distinguished visitors in the front, including Peter (later Sir Peter) Hall, director of the Royal Shakespeare Company. The concert duly opened with the *Meistersinger* overture and the orchestra played through the programme with arcadian inspiration.

The *1812* was the last item and, thanks to Jupp's white handkerchief, perfect synchronisation was achieved between the orchestra, the simulated peals of cathedral bells and the first salvoes of the 25-pounders.

But what neither the Army nor the musicians had taken into account was the wind direction and that smoke from the guns would drift across the narrow river completely concealing from the gunners' view Jupp's anticipated signal. That the players started choking on the burned cordite fumes was a minor inconvenience in comparison with the impending catastrophe. When it came to the last six bars, the 25-pounders were still joining in with gusto – vwoomph . . . vwoomph . . . vwoomph – and the orchestra went pa-pa-pa-paaaa . . . with Silvestri holding on to that last chord as if his whole reputation, if not his life, were at stake.

But there are limits even to final chords and it was impossible to hold on to this one any longer. In despair, he brought his baton down – and the last salvo went VWOOMPH right on the beat.

The effect could not have been more climactic. Hall leapt to his feet, cheered and clapped as did the whole audience, no doubt convinced that it was a splendid piece of stage management. In fact, a kindly zephyr had wafted away the smoke, revealing that frantically waved hankie just in the nick of time.

CHAPTER 8

'THE WORLD HAS LOST
A GREAT MUSICIAN'

November 1968 was half-way through the Bournemouth Symphony Orchestra's 75th anniversary commemoration. For Silvestri personally, the concert on Saturday, November 23 in the Royal Festival Hall (a repeat of the one in Bournemouth two evenings before) was a triumph for the 'unknown' Romanian who nearly a dozen years earlier in this same hall had conducted the first concert of another anniversary series: the LPO's centenary.

Even then, as we have seen, he was praised by the critics although he had expressed privately the fear that, due to what he considered insufficient rehearsing, it would be 'one of the worst concerts of my life.'

Neither he nor the critics could have foreseen that in four years he would have his own British orchestra with, if not unlimited, certainly considerably more rehearsal time than he had been able to obtain with any other orchestra since leaving Romania. The development of the BSO over the years now won for them and himself bouquets such as this one after the November 23 concert: 'In Prokofiev's *Scythian Suite* the spitfire brilliance and glinting colours that Mr Silvestri extracted from his players with the minimum of effort came as another reminder of the benefits of regular training under a resident conductor.' That was from the sapient Joan Chissell who earlier in her *Times* review praised the BSO and its conductor for their courage in tackling Panufnik's *Sinfonia Sacra*.

But if for the BSO it was half-way through their birthday celebrations, for Costi it was near the end of the road: this would be his last concert in London.

It had been a triumphant year, with a galaxy of world-famous artists paying tribute to the orchestra and its conductor – sometimes performing in their seaside hometown in advance of doing a repeat performance in the metropolis.

It had begun in May with pianist Victoria Postnikova (wife of the Russian conductor Gennady Rozhdestvensky) winning such plaudits for her Mozart *K488* as: 'Her playing was as brilliant as it was disciplined' or: 'The most satisfying concerto performance I have yet heard from this magnetic pianist.' This last was from *The Guardian's* Edward Greenfield who also praised Silvestri's 'striking degree of identity with the composer' in Elgar's *Symphony No 1*:

Only an orchestra at the very peak of its form could have produced such tender, hushed playing in the slow movement. . . In Mozart's *A major Piano Concerto* the accompaniment to Victoria Postnikova was a model of style and delicacy.

Alan Blyth in *The Times* wrote: 'It was most interesting to get a new Romanian slant' on 'Elgar's mammoth *First Symphony*' and noted Silvestri had 'emphasised a host of omissions, undercurrents and dissonant challenges.'

In July, before Polish-born Mexican violinist Henryk Szeryng played the whole of the Bach *Chaconne* as an encore, he announced: 'I would like to dedicate this to maestro Silvestri and the orchestra.' The visit of Mstislav Rostropovich in September has already been mentioned; David Oistrakh played the Prokofiev *Violin Concerto No 1* also in September; Svyatoslav Richter the Grieg Concerto and Joan Dickson the William Walton *Cello Concerto* in October. 'I remember approaching the first rehearsal with some apprehension,' she recalled,

> because he had wanted me to play the Saint-Saëns *Cello Concerto No 2 in D minor* and not *No 1 in A minor* as my agents had told me. I had only found this out one week before the performance – too late for me to learn it. Although he was rather unwilling at first, nevertheless I persuaded him to agree to me playing the Walton, which he didn't know. But when I got to Bournemouth he had clearly studied the score thoroughly, we had a marvellous rehearsal and he said he was delighted with the work. We played in Plymouth and then in Bournemouth.
>
> I thought he was a marvellous musician with whom I had real communion. I loved him from the first moment – but, of course, I never saw him again.

Concerts apart, Silvestri also received high praise in the August *Gramophone* for his recording with the BSO in Winchester Cathedral of Vaughan Williams' *The Wasps* and *Fantasia on a Theme of Thomas Tallis* and Elgar's *In The South*:

> The Bournemouth orchestra has made impressive strides under their dedicated conductor and were I in HMV, I would make sure that he was contracted to record some Enescu with them,

wrote the anonymous reviewer; while the November *Records and Recordings* called the Bournemouth orchestra 'one of the most exciting in these Isles' and in two records of a Mussorgsky, Rimsky-Korsakov, Ravel, Saint-Saëns, Sibelius, Borodin and Dukas assortment the orchestra 'surpassed themselves.'

On Friday, November 22 – the day before his final Festival Hall concert – he was heard over BBC Radio 4 conducting Stravinsky's *The Firebird* (the revised 1945 version in 10 movements) and Elgar's *First Symphony*.

Then, on three successive nights in the last week of November, a terminally ill Costi conducted the same programme: *Discourse for Orchestra* by Bliss, the Tchaikovsky *Violin Concerto* and the *New World* – first, in the Devon naval town of Plymouth; back to Bournemouth for the second concert and finally south-west to Devon again to the cathedral city of Exeter. This involved over 400 miles of travelling by road as well as the strain of at least one 'seating and balance' rehearsal (to test the accoustics of an unfamiliar hall) as well as the actual performances.

These would be his last concerts.

Two years before, in December 1965, the *Bournemouth Times* had announced in 72-point bold headlines: ILLNESS HITS BSO CHIEF, followed by:

> A statement, which originated in Paris, that the Bournemouth Symphony Orchestra's world-famous conductor Constantin Silvestri may retire due to ill-health, has caused consternation in music circles.

Kenneth Matchett was quick to jump in with a denial and, in fact, it turned out to be a false alarm, ostensibly nothing worse than 'flu.

But less than two years later, in the summer of 1967, there was another scare – and this time with justification: Costi was haemorrhaging very badly and had to have massive transfusions.

By October, the doctor recommended by Matchett had noted that X-rays showed 'varices of the lower end of the oesophagus' (a dilation of the veins in the gullet) and that he was having frequent high fevers – something, it will be recalled, he suffered from even as an adolescent in Târgu Mureș.

Far graver, was that cirrhosis of the liver had been diagnosed. 'After examination,' says Matchett,

> the doctor was placed in a difficult position because of patient confidentiality and I was actually the representative of the employers. He was very loyal to his patient and tried to hide the truth of Costi's illness by saying he had 'an ulcerated liver.' But I gathered enough to realise that, unless Costi completely stopped drinking, he was going to be in a bad way. He did stop eventually – I don't think he drank during the last nine months – but it was too late.

Costi went to Switzerland to recuperate and on August 8 from the little town of Montana high up in the Berner Alps he wrote to Ana, his mother:

I didn't write you for a month because I went to rest in a completely remote place, cutting every link with the outside world. I feel a little more revitalised now, but not completely. I will try to benefit from this a little longer because I still have two weeks of vacation before I am again in harness.

Being back in harness actually meant that in the next 13 months this desperately ill man conducted no less that 47 concerts, 38 of them with his own orchestra and another four with the Royal Liverpool Philharmonic, the LPO and the Ulster Orchestra, as well as four in Sweden and one in Finland, with Claudio Arrau playing the Beethoven *Piano Concerto No 1*.

By mid-1968, the toll Costi's wasting disease was exacting on a frame that had never been robust was sufficiently obvious to cause alarm even to those unaware of what was ailing him. In July, in a letter addressing him as 'Dear Maestro,' the chairman of the BSO's management committee conveyed the 'hope that you will take care of yourself, for we realise that a continual giving-out is ever present in your work.' In the BSO's 75th anniversary year the letter expressed gratitude to him for giving new life to, and increasing the prestige and reputation of, what had become an orchestra 'internationally renowned and acclaimed. . . We know that there will be many more triumphs as the result of your genius. . .'

In October, Alun Francis (who had left the BSO and become second conductor with the Ulster Orchestra) met Silvestri when he came over to Belfast with John Ogdon for a concert that included the Beethoven *Piano Concerto No 3*. During a painfully slow stroll, Francis remembers

he was convinced that there was something very wrong with his blood. 'It's very hot,' he said and I thought he meant some kind of fever. He was frustrated because he thought the doctors either were not taking any notice of this or didn't know what was causing it.

Silvestri was a staunch champion of British music, thus carrying on the tradition begun by the BSO's founder, Dan Godfrey, whose record of presenting British works was unequalled even by Sir Henry Wood. By 1911, the orchestra had played works by 130 different British composers and that year gave its first London concert with an all-British programme in the Festival of Empire at the Crystal Palace. Sir Dan was knighted in 1922 for his 'services to British music.'

It was a significant reflection of Silvestri's consistent adherence to this tradition that in the programme for what would be his last three concerts he included the *Discourse for Orchestra* by Master of the Queen's Musick, Sir Arthur Bliss (who was, incidentally, president of the Western Orchestral Society.)

In a radio interview in Paris in December 1966, Silvestri had said he was returning to Bournemouth to make records, including the Vaughan Williams and Elgar mentioned above. 'We must make English music better known,' he told French listeners.

In Bournemouth we are trying to introduce the music of Italy, France, Germany and America and, in France, to introduce English works which audiences on the Continent have probably never heard before. This is our international policy.

His and the BSO's performance of Vaughan Williams' *Fantasia* had already come in for special praise during their European tour in 1965 – 'The applause nearly brought the house down,' it was reported after one concert in Holland. Likewise, Britten's *Sinfonia da Requiem* and *Four Sea Interludes* from *Peter Grimes*, Arnold Bax's *Tintagel* and George Butterworth's *A Shropshire Lad* 'captivated the audience' (to use a Czech reviewer's expression) whether in the Leipzig Gewandhaus, Warsaw's Philharmonic Hall or Prague's Dum Umelcu.

In posthumous appreciations of his over seven years with the BSO, British critics invariably referred to his promotion of English music. *The Guardian* said he shed new light on Elgar's *In The South* and Vaughan Williams' *Fantasia*; while *The Times* referred to his 'sympathetic performances of music by Elgar and Delius as well as later works by Britten, Tippett and Malcolm Williamson among other living English composers.'

His own orchestral colleagues were among the most ardent admirers of his Elgar interpretations – Brian Johnstone: 'He is an unsung Elgarian of the first order, from the *First Symphony* to the miniature *Sospiri*'; Raymond Carpenter: '*Sospiri* for harp and strings was one of Silvestri's favourite encores. He invariably gave a most beautiful account of it which created a wonderful atmosphere bringing the house down'; Roger Winfield: 'If Elgar had heard *In The South* the way Silvestri did it, with a Latin flair instead of the incredibly ponderous way we often hear it, there is no doubt he would have loved it,' a view heartily endorsed by conductor Nicholas Braithwaite: 'His recording of *In The South* is the most wonderful performance I know.'

Silvestri used to declare with conviction that there was a lot more lyricism and emotion in Elgar than was revealed in the way it was traditionally performed in Britain. At the same time he was aware that to interpret Elgar so as to bring out these aspects of his music might upset English susceptibilities and he felt that to some extent he had to compromise.

For all his Romanian background, there is no doubt Silvestri loved this quintessential Edwardian English composer. 'Elgar was fond of the term *nobilmente* and nobody was more *nobilmente* than Silvestri,' in Carpenter's opinion.

> *The First Symphony* is a very nationalistic piece of music. Adrian Boult was a famous conductor of Elgar but he didn't do the *First* as well as Silvestri did it with us. He could really be martial – *grandioso* – when he was supposed to be. About nine months later we did Elgar's *Second Symphony* with Boult and it was just a run-of-the-mill performance.

There have been conductors who seldom ventured to promote new compositions by less well-known composers, either from an Olympian élitism which precluded such experimentation or because they feared their own reputations might suffer from adverse criticism of these works. Silvestri had the magnanimity, enterprise and courage to conduct first performances of British composers irrespective of their previous exposure. Apart from Malcolm Rayment's *Sinfonia Concertante* and Malcolm Lipkin's *Second Violin Concerto*, among British premières he conducted was a symphony in 1962 by Derek Bourgeois, when he was still a Cambridge student; and among works he introduced to Bournemouth, apart from Britten's *The Building of the House** and *Scottish Ballad* and Alan Rawsthorne's *Second (Pastoral) Symphony*, were: Cornishman George Lloyd's *Scapegoat*; Londoner Peter Fricker's piano concerto, *Toccata*; Glaswegian Eric Chisholm's *Celtic Wonder Tale*, which he conducted only months before the composer died in South Africa in 1965; and, in Bristol, the *Symphony No. 1 (Elegy)* of Merseyside's John McCabe and the *Concerto for Piano and Orchestra* of Leamington's Robert Simpson, played by John Ogdon to whom it was dedicated.

When Ida Haendel came on stage in the Great Hall of Exeter University on the evening of November 29 1968 to play the Tchaikovsky *Violin Concerto* it would be the twelfth time she had performed with Costi. For him, though he was not conscious of it, it would be the last concert he would conduct.

> I remember the way he conducted it. There were certain phrases that were so melancholy and there were very, very few people who were able to bring that to the fore. So, I was impressed by that and it had a very special meaning for me because I knew how ill he had been. I tried to deny to myself how seriously ill he was. Nobody wants to accept terminal illness, partic-

---

* Composed December 1966/January 1967, inspired by his excitement at the planning and building of The Maltings at Snape. Silvestri conducted the Bournemouth performance on November 23 1967.

*Ida Haendel: 'He was desperately ill
. . . but within himself he was strong
enough to rise above it'*

*Nicholas Braithwaite: 'When he took
his bow, a real pride came into him and
he stood up, inches taller'*

ularly when it concerns somebody for whom you have so much affection, as I had for Silvestri. I did not know what was wrong with him but I could see he was desperately ill and, by the look on his face and by his colour, that he was suffering terribly. But within himself he was strong enough to rise above it and he conducted wonderfully – with so much feeling and emotion. But it was a very, very sad occasion.

Perhaps when he chose *From The New World* as the final work in what would be his last programme, Silvestri recalled for an instant those boyhood moments when he used to listen to Dvorak's pupil, the old Hungarian professor, Laszlo Arpad in Târgu Mureş, telling him about the symphony. One can imagine him with a hint of a quizzical smile as he may have recalled his satisfaction at discovering that more people were buying his version of the *New World* made with the ORTF than any of the other 10 recordings available; or he may have had a mental echo of the acclaim he received when it was awarded the coveted Charles Cross prize.

Or again we can conjecture whether this creation of the homesick Dvorak in Iowa, pining for his Bohemian forests and rivers, struck a nostalgic chord in the expatriate Romanian: a fleeting yen for the beech and pine-clad mountains of Transylvania.

From The New World was Silvestri's swan song, the last piece of music he would conduct, as indeed it was Dvorak's farewell to symphonic writing. Its multiple sudden changes of mood, from martial grandeur to bucolic serenity, blazing outbursts of brass punctuating haunting themes on woodwind and strings, were a fitting valediction to a life that had also been subject to radical change: the struggle against ill health and for recognition as a conductor; many triumphs, at first tempered by ideologically-induced frustrations; the stimuli of repeated audience acclaim; and oases of tranquility when he stood in waders with rod and line in the shallow waters of Transylvania's mountain streams or by the Hampshire Avon or Dorset Stour.

Braithwaite remembers the penultimate concert in the Winter Gardens:

> I think most people felt that this might be his last concert in Bournemouth. I was standing in the wings. It was a marvellous performance of the *New World* – there was so much emotion around. Silvestri was standing sideways to me but I could see his eyes were almost closed – he was on a lot of pain-killers – but when he went out to take his bow at the end, a real pride came into him and he stood up, inches taller. It was quite incredible.

Did he have a presentiment that he had reached the end? Consciously, it would seem most unlikely. Despite the painkilling drugs, his mental capacity was evidently as keen as ever and he must have been imbued with the conviction that he had a lot more to give those who thirsted for superb performances of classical music. The will to live, sustained by the goodwill of his Bournemouth comrades-in-musicmaking and the warmth of audience approbation almost certainly outweighed any pain-induced fatalism at this stage.

About his very last concert in Exeter one thing stands out for Brian Johnstone, obscuring every other memory of it:

> At the end of the *New World* there is a big chord, a tenuto in the wind. The strings stopped playing and the wind held on to the chord. He looked desperately ill. Probably Ida Haendel and the management knew more than we did, but I am sure we all thought this would probably be the last time he would conduct us. He held this chord . . . and held it. He wouldn't let go and, on reflection, I think he didn't want to let go. The wind players were gasping for air, coming in again after having taken another breath. It was abnormally long – and there was a curious moment's silence at the end, before the applause burst out.

After the concert, Silvestri, Haendel and Matchett went for supper in a hotel on the outskirts of Exeter. Ida remembers clearly him ordering a raw steak with a raw egg on top – a Steak Tartar:

Although I knew he had difficulty in eating, this was the one thing he still liked and he seemed able to digest it.

Afterwards, in spite of being so ill and weak he insisted on carrying my violin. We all pretended that everything was all right and we'd all be seeing each other again. Costi even said to me: 'What would you like to play next time?' But I knew somewhere in my mind it was not going to be. Yet one always hopes – we were always trying to be optimistic.

All his concerts were cancelled for the rest of the 1968–69 season and he went into a private ward of the Royal Free Hospital, Hampstead, attended by Professor Sheila Sherlock, an eminent specialist on diseases of the gastro-intestinal tract. But after an exploratory operation he occupied a bed in a public ward with about 30 other patients. When she heard about this, Haendel, who by then was in the US, was very disturbed.

I could not believe that such a great maestro would not have all the privacy that he was entitled to. I kept enquiring about him and each time was told he was getting worse. I hoped they would say he was recovering . . . he was so young.

Another who was shocked, especially by the unplastered, bare brick walls of the public ward, was conductor James Loughran:

I looked down this grim-looking ward and couldn't see him. Then I spotted a man sitting up in bed with a transistor radio and I thought the chances are that's him, listening to the radio as usual. I walked up to him and, despite a very sunken face, I could see by his eyes it was Silvestri. I stood for a moment looking at him and he came alive. 'Jimmy,' he said

– and Loughran imitated the feeble tone of the emaciated man in the bed. Then, much louder, in the authoritative voice of Constantin Silvestri, principal conductor and artistic director since the age of 32 of, successively, four orchestras:

'Why did you use horns in Haydn *27*?' He had evidently listened to this symphony which I had conducted but had completely forgotten about. He had seen the original score which had no horns in it and chided me for using them. I had the latest Robbins Landon edition on Haydn in which there are both oboes and horns.

As early as 1946, somebody stumbled upon a manuscript of Haydn's *Symphony No 27 in G*, composed in about 1760, in the Bruckenthal Museum in

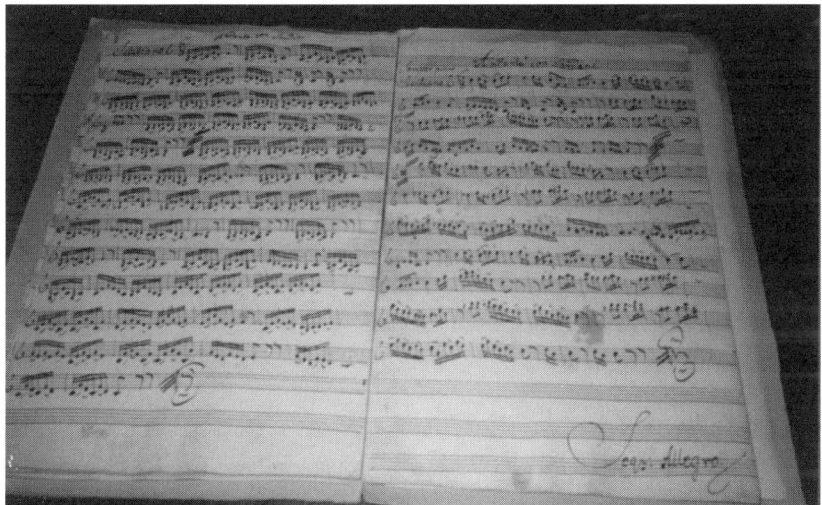

Visited in hospital by James Loughran, his erstwhile assistant BSO conductor, the emaciated Silvestri demanded: 'Why did you use horns in Haydn 27?' The score displayed in the Bruckenthal Museum, Sibiu, in Romania vindicated his contention that they should not have been

James Loughran

Sibiu, Transylvania. (This was not far from the sanatorium of the same name in Avrig in which Silvestri had convalesced in 1940 after one of his bouts of pleurisy.) This manuscript is on view in the Bruckenthal Museum today but it bears its original number: 70. (What is now known as *Symphony No. 70 in D* was composed 19 years later.) The Bruckenthal symphony is clearly marked for strings and two oboes – no horns – and this is no doubt how Silvestri conducted it with the Bucharest Philharmonic in a concert for young people in January 1950. He also conducted it in Sibiu itself and in Belgium; recorded it with the Radio Symphony Orchestra in Bucharest and with Supraphon in Prague in June 1953. He conducted it again in concerts in 1955 in Prague, Bratislava and Brno.

Presumably he had no prior view of the programme notes for *Symphony No. 27* printed for his first conducting of the Hallé Orchestra, in the Free Trade Hall, Manchester in February 1959. He would have taken exception to them if he had. These stated: 'No authentic manuscript of this symphony has survived; it is believed to have been scored for two oboes, two horns and strings. (The horn parts were printed for the first time in an appendix to H.C. Robbins Landon's book *The Symphonies of Joseph Haydn*, published in 1955.)'

Silvestri evidently preferred the evidence of his own eyes, which had actually seen the Bruckenthal no-horns version, to the claim in Robbins Landon's appendix – hence his querulous censure of Loughran's use of them. It was characteristic of the man who thought primarily in musical terms that this is how he immediatley greeted his erstwhile assistant conductor whom he had not seen for years.

On one of his many visits to the Royal Free, Kenneth Matchett brought Silvestri the manuscript of a symphony dedicated to him and the BSO. Its composer was Australian-born Malcolm Williamson, who is also a pianist, organist and conductor. Now, a genial and intellectually vigorous sexagenarian, Williamson's style has been described as individualistic and he combines a fluent Latinity with acknowledgement of such latterday influences as jazz, Messiaen and Britten. In his early days in London he played in a night club ('to support myself'). The successor to Sir Arthur Bliss as Master of the Queen's Music is probably the most atypical incumbent of that exalted post and it is not surprising that he felt an affinity with the unorthodox Silvestri.

Although the two men had never actually met, Williamson was commissioned by the Western Orchestral Society to compose a symphony for the BSO's 75th anniversary and as a tribute to the maestro's conducting prowess. This was Williamson's *Symphony No 2* which he entitled *Pilgrim On The Ocean*. He has explained that the 20th century had written the word 'refugee' (and in a sense Silvestri was a refugee from the country of his birth)

> in immense letters across the world, and the word shows no indication of being eradicated. The refugee is a compelled pilgrim and, through his rejection, he shines with dignity.
>
> Rather than write an extrovert work in jubilant vein I wanted to take as a starting point the particular virtues of the orchestra and of Silvestri which had deeply impressed me in the past and to write a more personal work. The Bournemouth strings, for example, had great plasticity, the wind at least as much warmth as brilliance.
>
> Silvestri's ability – by no means common among conductors – to sustain both tension and serenity in very slow music always dazzled me.

The score was headed: *'For Constantin Silvestri and the Bournemouth Symphony Orchestra'* and Costi's musical initials, C and S (E flat), were embedded in it. Williamson recalls:

> I wrote it night and day to catch him before he left this world. I wanted to dedicate it to him while he was still alive, not to his memory. I finished it two days after Christmas and was told that the manuscript was held up to him in hospital so that he could see the dedication.

The programme for all the 12 months of concerts for the BSO's anniversary up to mid-April 1969 had of course been planned, fixed and printed many months before Costi went into the Royal Free. According to this programme, he himself was due to conduct the Williamson symphony in the Royal Festival Hall on February 22 in a programme which included Paul Tortelier playing *Tchaikovsky's Variations on a Rococo Theme* and Strauss's *Don Quixote*. In the event the symphony was not played and the *Daily Telegraph* reviewer rather unkindly drew attention to 'displeasing band-leader prancings and forced grunts' which Silvestri's substitute, who had come from abroad and was making his London début, 'seemed to aim at the audience rather than to the orchestra.' Even Joan Chissell felt some gentle advice would not be amiss: 'On the rostrum his movements are almost as dramatic as Nureyev's. Perhaps he should be aware of getting too intoxicated by high powered virtuosity.'

On the other hand, Chissell noted, Tortelier 'gave one of the most gracious, tingling and lyrical performances' of the *Rococo* 'that anyone would ever want to hear – adding innumerable inches to its stature.' Could it have been that such a sensitive artist as Tortelier was so affected by the absence of his dying friend – they had done the *Don Quixote* together 19 months before at the Chester Festival and the Dvorak *Cello Concerto* in Bournemouth the previous February – that the poignancy of the occasion gave an added dimension to his playing?

The next day, Sunday February 23 1969, Silvestri died. He was three months and six days short of his 56th birthday.

He was the second distinguished conductor to die that week; four days before, Ernest Ansermet, founder of the Orchestre de la Suisse Romande had died in Geneva, but at least he had had a good innings: he was 86. Enescu had played Brahms's *Violin Concerto* with him in 1920. Silvestri had been proud to include the Suisse Romande among 'the world's most famous orchestras' he had conducted.

Five days later, Professor (subsequently Dame) Sheila Sherlock wrote to Costi's Bournemouth doctor:

> I know you will be sorry to learn of the death of Mr Constantin Silvestri. He went steadily downhill and died a few days ago. An autopsy has been done and this has confirmed our earlier suspicion. There was a primary liver cancer in the upper part of the right lobe, a very difficult position for diagnosis. There was also a very grossly cirrhotic liver. I think this explains his deterioration over the last few months, and the swinging temperatures. Even if it had been diagnosed *ante mortem*, nothing could have been done.

The letter was typewritten but the professor added in her own hand: 'The World has lost a great musician.'

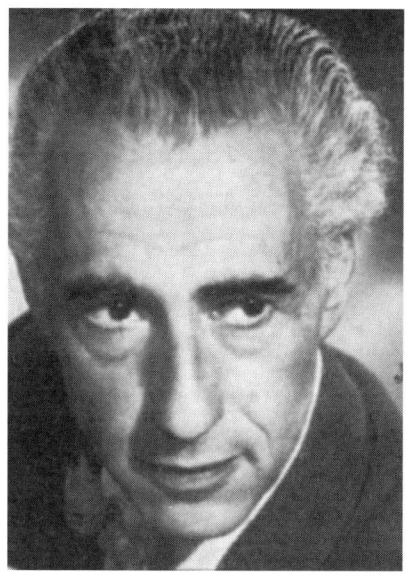

*George Hurst conducted the postponed
first performance of Malcolm
Williamson's* Second Symphony
dedicated to Silvestri and the BSO

*It was Silvestri's express wish that
Rudolf Schwarz should conduct the
Mahler Seventh at his memorial
concert*

At the funeral service in the parish church of St Peter, Bournemouth, the orchestra's brass and timpani ensemble played Purcell's *Queen Mary's Funeral Music* and a group of over 20 members of the Bournemouth Municipal Choir sang *How Lovely Are Thy Dwellings Fair* from Brahms' *Requiem*. In the course of his address, Kenneth Matchett observed:

> In an age of technology and materialism he tried to remind his audiences, through his music-making, of deeper and more lasting values. Nobody who has listened to his concerts will ever forget the sense of involvement which he created, the pathos, excitement and sheer beauty that appealed irresistably to our emotions. . . We have all been deprived of a great personality and a remarkable man.

Matchett supported the twice-widowed Pupa in the cortège behind the coffin as it left the church to the strains of Elgar's *Nimrod*. Members of the orchestra wept, as did those former members who had come from afar to pay their last respects.

In the same week as the funeral, Costi's immediate successor, George Hurst, conducted in the Winter Gardens the BSO's first concert since his death in a programme that included the *Prelude and Liebestod*, the Wagner which had so moved Costi in Winchester Cathedral that he had admitted to not being able to control his baton hand; and *Sospiri* which for him had encapsulated the lyricism of Elgar.

It was Hurst who conducted in Bristol, Bournemouth and finally in the Royal Festival Hall in the last three days of October 1969 the postponed first performances of Malcolm Williamson's *Second Symphony*. From William Mann it received the tribute:

> This is one of Williamson's serious, thoughtful pieces, beautiful to listen to . . . a long arduous journey through luxuriant jungle foliage (very rapid figurations in voluptuous, subtle colours), where wild beasts lurk and huge birds screech violently. . .

The Daily Telegraph called it 'a most impressive piece of work, containing perhaps the most personal and singleminded music the composer has given us.'

Williamson says it had another 14 performances in various countries up to the time he himself attended the symphony for its first performance in Bucharest, conducted by Petre Sbârcea, at the final concert – televised and broadcast on all Romanian channels – of the 1992 Silvestri International Festival. Silvestri's widow was there too.

When Costi eventually admitted, in the last days in hospital, that he was approaching the finale of his own symphony, he had expressed the wish that Rudolph Schwarz should conduct the Mahler *Seventh* at a memorial concert. Schwarz had been the Bournemouth Municipal Orchestra's conductor from 1946 to 1951 and was currently Chief Conductor of the BBC Symphony Orchestra.

In fact, there were three memorial concerts: in Bristol, Bournemouth and in Exeter, venue of Costi's last concert, on three consecutive nights in December 1969, with Schwarz directing the full BSO, augmented by the Sinfonietta – more than twice the number of players for this mammoth, 80-minute work than when he had conducted the postwar Bournemouth orchestra.

Just as there had been controversy over Costi in life, so it persisted immediately afterwards over where the urn containing his ashes should have its final resting place. The Western Orchestral Society wanted it to be in a specially laid-out Garden of Remembrance in St Peter's churchyard where Sir Dan Godfrey is buried (and also the heart of the poet Shelley.) This would, at least in part, fulfil Costi's own wish that his remains should lie within sight of the

His memorial stone in the churchyard at St Peter's near the burial place of the Bournemouth Symphony Orchestra's founder Sir Dan Godfrey and the heart of Percy Bysshe Shelley

sea in which he had so enjoyed his pier-end fishing – though a view of the Winter Gardens, his other wish, would be obscured.

The first hitch in this project was that the churchyard had been declared closed to further burials. Matchett attempted to get special dispensation from the Bishop of Winchester, in whose diocese St Peter's lay, in view of the outstanding contribution Silvestri had made to the fame of the town to which he became so attached. But at some point in the negotiations Bournemouth Corporation stepped in, took over maintenance of the churchyard and rejected the idea of a Garden of Remembrance. Even the specious objection that Silvestri had been 'Jewish' and therefore should not be in Christian hallowed ground had to be refuted.

The vicar of St Peter's, Canon Dick Jones, a frequent attender of BSO concerts, was very supportive and, years later, a memorial stone was erected inscribed with the epitaph:

CONSTANTIN SILVESTRI

1913–1969

'THE MAESTRO'

OF THE

BOURNEMOUTH

SYMPHONY ORCHESTRA

1961–1969

AN OUTSTANDING MUSICIAN

AND A REMARKABLE MAN

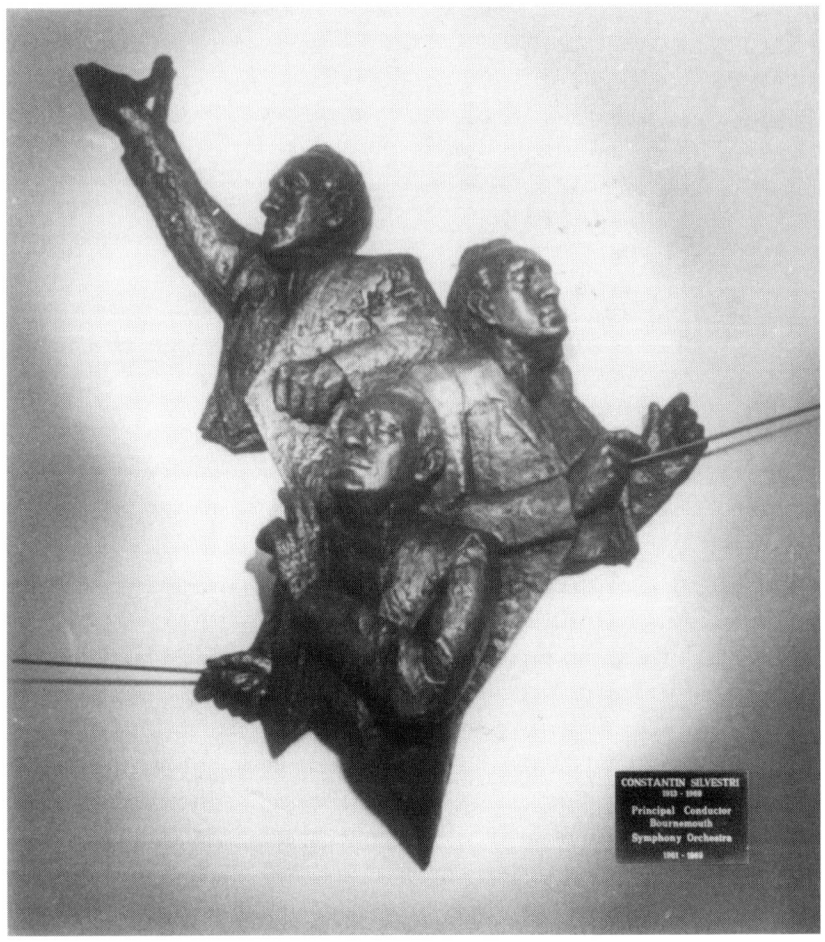

Diane Garvin's bronze plaque of Silvestri in the BSO's headquarters

Diane Gorvin, a Bournemouth College art student, was commissioned to sculpt a bronze plaque of Silvestri for the BSO's headquarters. She had previously made sketches of and produced a plaster relief of sections of the orchestra which also grace the building. She sculpted the Silvestri bas-relief in bronze from press photographs of the maestro in three conducting attitudes – the same photographs from which double-bass Lyndon Thomas had made a pencil, four-figure composition of the maestro in action, much admired by his colleagues. Thomas paid this tribute to the sculptress:

I think her solution to the form, though similar to mine, is much better and

The sketch by double-bass Lyndon Thomas shows Silvestri's
'predilection for hand-to-hand baton changing'

her realisation of the man, in three dimensions – she must have been a toddler when he died – is nothing short of miraculous.

There is one significant aspect of Thomas's sketch: two of his four Silvestri figures are holding the baton in the left hand, demonstrating the maestro's 'predilection for hand-to-hand baton-changing,' previously noted.

In April 1981, Pupa Silvestri came over from Paris and unveiled the plaque at a ceremony attended by contemporary and former members of the BSO, the local Member of Parliament and other dignitaries. In August 1992, a bronze plaque of the maestro was unveiled in the Palace of Culture in Târgu

Mureş during the Silvestri International Festival. At the commemorative ceremony, which included a performance of two of his works – the *Sonata for Oboe and Piano* and *Nacht und Träume* for mixed choir, were the mayor, a Secretary of State from the Ministry of Culture in Bucharest and former members of the Bournemouth Symphony Orchestra. And, in 1998, a delegation consisting of the mayor and other civic functionaries of Târgu Mureş visiting the twinned Bournemouth laid a wreath on the Silvestri memorial stone in St Peter's churchyard.

In Romania (where Gheorghe Gheorghiu-Dej had died and been succeeded by Nicolae Ceauşescu in 1965) there had been a virtual blackout on Silvestri's activities in the West for over a decade. There was now a bare news announcement of his death in London.

However, as early as two months after this, one of his Elgar overture recordings was played over the radio and Mircea Cristescu was conducting the George Enescu Philharmonic Chamber Orchestra from Cluj in a programme which included Costi's *Three Pieces for Strings*. In May, first, the Radio Orchestra played his *Prelude and Fugue* over the air and on TV and, in a programme called *An Anthology of Records*, the Bournemouth Symphony Orchestra's recording of him conducting Rimsky-Korsakov's *Sheherazade* was broadcast.

His elderly and lonely mother, Ana, heard both of these and in a letter to Pupa in Paris told her that when she heard the *Sheherazade* she had embraced the radio.

The Three Pieces were again played over the air in September. In October, the first item in another concert of the Philharmonic, this time conducted by Mircea Basarab, was Silvestri's *Prelude and Fugue* and the programme contained a four-page potted biography of the composer, with an analysis of the work by V. Pop Băleni.

It would seem, therefore, that even if the official attitude was to ignore the man the state had honoured with the title Artist of the People as if he had never existed, his old musician friends were doing their best to keep his works and his name alive – apparently without official interference. In fact, in February 1972 a talk on him was given over the radio in which he was called Romania's 'second composer and musician after Enescu.' The speaker announced that in the next broadcast he would quote from conversations he had had with Silvestri and 'on Monday at 10.20 his own voice will be heard.' This was greeted by Ana Cariade, by now 80-years-old and who had not seen her son for the last 10 years of his life, with: 'Can you imagine – I'll be able to hear his voice on Monday!' The old lady was also able to hear 'his' *Sheherazade* again two months later.

The Bucharest Philharmonic played his *Prelude and Fugue* during their tour of the Soviet Union in November 1972; in the same month his *String Quartet No 2* was included in a chamber music concert in the Sala Mica a Palatului performed by the Philharmonic's Quartet. Principal music critic Alfred Hoffman wrote: 'It made us remember how passionate and fantastic a musician he was, how skilfully he handled instrumental timbres and ingeniously interwove them.'

In 1977 his *Piano Sonata No 3* was on TV and on the air and throughout the Eighties either his own works or records of him conducting were occasionally played over the radio. In April 1984, leading critic and radio and TV personality Iosif Sava, in a series of talks on Romanian musicians, devoted one to Silvestri.

However, *The Concise Encyclopaedic Dictionary*, published in Ceauşescu's time became almost laconic in its conciseness when dealing with:

> Constantin Silvestri (born 1913 Bucharest, died 1969). Romanian conductor and composer. Symphonic works: *Dances from Bihor*; *Pieces for String Orchestra*; works for piano (suites, sonatas, études); chamber music.

The Calendar of Universal Music, published in the Sixties by the Union of Composers, an otherwise informative book about Romanian musicians, did not even mention him. It was thought at the time that his name had been removed.

One can imagine Silvestri making a sardonic comment on these examples of his official ostracism, perhaps comparing them with his inclusion, despite not having lived in Paris for five years, in the 1966 edition of *Le Livre d'Or*, the fifth volume of the *New National Dictionary of Contemporaries*, a kind of French Who's Who. This Golden Book only contained a selection of *la crème de la crème*. To Costi's amusement he was in it – Brigitte Bardot was not.

PATIENCE, THE ESSENCE OF GENIUS

Concertgoers were fascinated by Silvestri the young pianist improvising on given themes or by Silvestri the virtuoso concert soloist; they reacted in their individual ways to the music of Silvestri the composer; most were deeply affected by the sounds the little figure on the rostrum conjured from an orchestra.

But about Silvestri, the person behind the performer, they had no opportunity to observe or make an assessment – at least, not during the years he was in the West. They knew nothing about his life outside of his profession: he did not grab the headlines by piloting his own jet, driving high-powered cars, racing a king-size yacht; nor did he cohabit with, marry and divorce a Hollywood film star. He did not die leaving a multimillion estate.

To borrow the words on his epitaph, he was 'a remarkable man' *because* he was 'an outstanding musician,' not on account of anything sensational outside of his music.

So far, we have learned something about his methods of music-making and the opinions of critics and players concerning these; about his attitude to orchestral colleagues and soloists and theirs to him; and we have attempted to portray Silvestri the conductor as audiences saw him. From these vignettes certain impressions may have been formed.

There remain a few details to flesh out a likeness of the whole man. They have a consistency, whether provided by those who knew him in Romania, in Paris or Britain, as a young man or in later years, which give substance and authenticity to the portrait.

Although formulated very differently, there is a consensus among those who knew him that music was his mainstay: an intellectual stimulant, spiritual balm and a refuge from mundane irritations, complexities and involvements.

When Judith Vancea was asked for her impressions of the young man who frequently stayed as a guest on her Târgu Mureş estate, she said: 'He read a lot and did have other interests, but music came first.' Anatol Vieru thought he had many personal problems and was 'a complex figure, not a happy soul. His happiness was in music'; and each time composer Marius Constant met him in Paris 'it was a musical pleasure because the only subject of discussion was music.' Ken Matchett conjectured that, being an only child and rather frail, he

About Silvestri, the person behind the performer on the rostrum, Western audiences knew next to nothing. His private life did not grab the headlines

probably spent a lot of time away from school, ill in bed where he used to fantasise.

> He was not a practical man and in some respects he lived in a fantasy world – not the real world which was a bloody nuisance, but which he had to live with. Music is all that he lived for.

There was nothing conjectural about the amusing impression this aspect of Costi left on Jane Judd, the Silvestris' groundfloor neighbour in Cranborne Road, Bournemouth:

> He was not very sociable. If I went up for a chat he would say: 'Every minute I am with you keeps me away from my music,' so he would come and kiss your hand and hope you would go!

This was not, however, at variance with another impression Jane Judd had of him: his 'kindness in lots of things,' such as bringing back from the restaurant at the bottom of the road, where he and Pupa had supped, little snacks 'for the girls, like profiterolles or something he thought we might enjoy and putting them outside the window for us. The Silvestris loved the years they were here – happy years the whole time.'

Regina 'Pupa' Silvestri:
happy years in Bournemouth

One happy occasion was a party they threw, for which Pupa asked Jane to make a Romanian flag, otherwise unobtainable. 'I got three ribbons – the right colours: blue, yellow and red – and sewed them together and made a beautiful flag. She was delighted and put them in a gorgeous arrangement of flowers.' The party went on until the early hours. One of the Silvestris' guests was Prince Carol, half-brother of ex-King Michael of Romania, who lived in Upton House, a few miles away. As he took his leave, Jane remembered, he said: 'It was a lovely party, darling, but the stripes on our flag are going the wrong way: they should be down instead of across!'

Because of Costi's 'impracticality,' he entrusted Jane Judd with the task of paying their bills, for which he would give her a lump sum that more than covered them. When she returned the surplus cash after paying the bills, he is reputed to have enquired: 'What is change?' Thenceforth, Jane meticulously accounted for everything in a cash book and would leave this and the bills on his piano.

> He wouldn't even look at them and, once, when he saw them on the piano he swept them all off on to the floor. He really hadn't a clue about anything English.

But it was not clear whether Silvestri was clueless about specifically English money matters or whether he had an ambivalent attitude to money in general.

His predilection as a young man for gambling at cards (mentioned *en passant* by Vieru and others) does not seem to have become obsessional and was probably no more than a temporary and not very successful attempt to augment his limited resources. Even so, it did lead to an unfortunate temporary break with his old friend Zeno Vancea whose widow related this curious story:

> Through his passion for playing poker he once owed one of the players quite a large sum. It so happened that he was himself owed money at this time by the Union of Composers, so he asked Zeno, who was vice-president of the Union, if he could get the money immediately so that he could pay off the debt. Zeno explained that for technical reasons this would not be possible for eight days. Though Silvestri was not normally quick-tempered or quarrelsome, on this occasion he immediately flew into a temper and kept demanding the sum immediately while Zeno insisted: 'Just wait eight days and I can get it for you.' After that episode, Costi became very cool and distant and it was only after some years, when both of them went to the Bartók Festival in Budapest, that they became friends again.

His impecuniosity as a young man, accentuated by ill health and having to pay doctor's fees, and the embarrassment of being dependent at one time on Jora's 'begging bowl,' could have resulted in an overcompensatory combination of parsimony and avarice when his fortunes changed. Neither seems to have been the case.

Whereas in Bucharest he is said to have confronted the central committee of the party with an ultimatum: 'Either you multiply my salary several times over or I cease to conduct,' there is no hint of dissatisfaction with what his employers in Bournemouth were paying him, despite Matchett's regret that it was never commensurate with his worth.

It was fortunate for his reputation that he lived prior to the big concertbiz and megadollar recording era and was therefore never tempted to amass an astronomical fortune like certain of his contemporaries and successors.

Ostentation does not seem to have been a significant factor in his collecting enthusiasms in Bucharest – other reasons have already been suggested – and it would be churlish to think it played any part in the hospitality with which it evidently gave him great pleasure to wine and dine colleagues and visitors

*Edgar Cosma: 'Silvestri was never
envious of anybody and admired
others in the profession'*

*Michèle Boegner: 'Silvestri always
respected my interpretations'*

within – and sometimes beyond – the comparatively modest limits of his income and taxable expenses allowance.

The labyrinthine complexities of the British tax system were beyond his comprehension. 'He was very generous with his hospitality,' Matchett recalls.

> Artists used to enjoy coming to us because they were always assured of a good meal. We'd either go to the Panoramic Grill owned by the Breton André Lennoye, a marvellous cook, or an Italian restaurant, the St Marco, where we could also get excellent food equal to any first-class hotel. They even started stocking wines Silvestri enjoyed.
>
> So he would keep all the bills and when I would say 'No, I'll pay for it,' he would lower his voice and say: 'No, I'll get it off the tax!' But when he put the bills in, they came to 50 per cent more than his total earnings in a year!

(One of the artists invited to the Lennoye establishment was Peter Frankl who particularly remembers Silvestri introducing him to frog's legs and was apparently grateful for the experience. Another pianist, John Clegg, remembers him as a 'real gourmet.' Less appreciative was a member of the orchestra and his wife whom Silvestri treated at the St Marco, having previously arranged with the proprietor that there would be only two dishes on the menu presented to them – both Romanian specialities. The first was *mămăligă* (polenta), which his guest described, 30 years later, as 'savoury porridge,' followed by the main dish, *creier* or *cervelle d'agneau* (sheep's brains), regarded as a great delicacy in Romania, but to his guest it was 'a warm greyish stew and when I learned from him what it was, I went absolutely green.')

Conductor Edgar Cosma made the point that 'Silvestri was a very generous artist who I felt was never envious of anybody. He actually admired others in the profession.'

Attestations to Silvestri's generosity were sometimes accompanied by allusions to some other (not necessarily musical) attribute. Ida Haendel:

> As a person he was extremely generous – he never thought of tomorrow. I felt he thought there could never be a rainy day. So, in fact, he behaved as if there were no tomorrow – that was charming and impressive.
>
> We had some wonderful times together that had nothing to do with music. As a personality he was warm, interesting – what more can one say about a human being? It's true I didn't have many intellectual discussions with him because when we met it was briefly at the rehearsal, at the concert, then we went to dinner, to which he loved to invite everybody. That was the man Silvestri.

Pianist Michèle Boegner also found him

> a marvellously warmhearted man, very loyal in his friendships, musically extremely lyrical and with a big human dimension.

Another pianist, Livia Rev, thought

> he was such an intelligent and marvellous musician. He could make immediate contact with everybody. He was very human, able to give you everything immediately, even his heart!

And to BSO Principal Oboe, Roger Winfield

> Silvestri wasn't élitist, like some conductors who behave like royalty with their coterie of sycophants. He would sit down to a meal with anyone. Conductors get so dependent on praise; they will sit down with the crowd because they want to talk about themselves and they feel they've got to sit with someone who is prepared to listen. They have no interests except themselves. But Silvestri wouldn't always rabbit-on about what a great conductor he was or how many records he'd done. He could talk about scenery or cooking or fishing. . .

Silvestri, to be sure, would have been pleased to learn that he shared this characteristic with Elgar, who (if one is to believe G.B. Shaw) 'could talk about every unmusical subject on earth, from pigs to Elizabethan literature.' John Clegg found him 'a great conversationalist . . . a really cultured man.'

There were two contrasting Silvestris: the *bon viveur*, the Bucharest party-goer, poker-player, *pronosport* (pools) punter; the passionate, delicate young man with soulful eyes whose alleged *affaire* with composer Hilda Jerea and, reputedly, with several others, were grist to the gossips' mill. And there was the solitary Silvestri who, all his life, would sit up half the night listening to records and making notes; the avid reader of Goethe and Eugene O'Neill; the philatelist meticulously mounting stamps in albums; the Silvestri who was never happier than when fishing, one of the most away-from-it-all of pastimes.

There was the Silvestri who naturally appreciated audiences enthusiastically demonstrating that they shared with him the love of the music he had helped recreate, yet who, far from controlling and driving (conducting, the Romans called it) vehicles at speed, found it essential, every so often, to relax far from the crowd – on the banks of the River Mare, for instance, a remote spot at the foot of Mt. Retezat in the Western Carpathians, or at Giureni, a primitive hide-out where only special friends were permitted to visit him. The solitude of the Lapland hut appealed to him and, after the shock of the haemorrhage, like a wounded animal he chose (as he explained in the letter to Ana from Switzerland in August 1967) 'a completely remote place cutting every link with the outside world.'

For all his sarcastic goading and patient persistence in willing an orchestra to play the way he wanted it to play, it is hard to believe that this man had a compulsion to dominate. He is surely the exception to the hypothesis that many conductors are impelled by some Adlerian power-asserting drive. Can one imagine Herbert von Karajan sitting for hours on end on a river bank or at the end of a pier with a rod and line?

Tales about Costi the fisherman are still recalled even in Romania; and in Bournemouth with a kind of affectionate amusement.

Dr Emilian Bancu in Târgu Mureş remembers him coming every summer from Bucharest to fish in the mountain rivers that flow into the Mureş

> because of his nostalgia for the places familiar to him since childhood. His favourite spot on the Deda Bistra, the most beautiful of these rivers, was a

A snap taken by the composer Paul Constantinescu: Costi watching
village priest Father Crăciun baiting a hook. Note the ever-present
radio which he took even on fishing expeditions

bridge at the end of the village. Because of the heavy poaching, our rivers in these parts are poor for trout and Silvestri used to catch what we call *clean* [carp]. I only went fishing with him once, in 1958. I had a hut up there in the mountains and we barbecued our catch by dropping it into sizzling sheep's butter – only the King and Ceauşescu used to have it like that!

But the next year he didn't turn up. . .

That was because he was on the Australian tour; yet even in the Antipodes he was thinking of his Transylvanian mountain streams. He sent a letter to one of his old fishing companions, a village priest called Father Ionel Crăciun (Romanian for Christmas). 'Dear Nelu,' he wrote,

I regret not being in Deda Bistra, but I am in Melbourne. I'm sorry I'm not fishing for carp but, instead, I'm 'catching' a lot of applause.

He was also entertaining Australians with some fishermen's stories: in Brisbane, for instance, where he said he was president of the Romanian Fishermen's Association and had once caught a catfish in the Danube weighing 200 lb. In another postcard to Father Crăciun, postmarked Sydney June 10 1959 – he had already been in Australia for six weeks – there is an almost pathetic expression of his nostalgia:

My dear brother fisherman,

These days I am among the sharks and hundreds of fishes which would be as strange to you as they are to me. When I see and taste them in the restaurants, I start missing you very much, envying you your tranquil pastime which you are able to enjoy to the full. It's such a long time since I've been able to. How I long to see you and our favourite spots, the river bank, even the cart ruts. . . Oh, how very far away it all is!

With loving thoughts for your family,

C. Silvestri

Nearly 40 years later, Father Crăciun relished recalling his fishing days with Costi and especially – this village priest being something of a piscine gourmet – the meticulously prepared meals that followed.

Members of the Bucharest Philharmonic used to come to our village for holidays. One of them was Viorica's brother, the violinist Mircea Vasilescu, and it was through him I met Silvestri. That was when our many long talks about fishing began.

He was a skilful fisherman and had an impressive arsenal of tackle. On one memorable occasion he came to a dinner which we had specially prepared after he had brought me a carp which weighed two kilos – exceptional for the River Mureş. First, I served the carp together with some crunchy little fish – that was just for starters; then with smoked trout; then with grilled trout with haricot beans and mayonaise. But when I asked him which of these combinations he had most enjoyed, his answer shocked me: 'The one we had for starters.'

On another occasion I invited him to a fishing party in the valley of the Răstolița, 19 kilometres from our village. But we didn't go far up the valley, we stayed instead in the spot where there are no trout, but the *lipan* [grayling] are plentiful. Costi was essentially a fisherman of the slower-flowing rivers of the plains where he didn't have to do much moving about. So, on this particular day, he was very put out because he wasn't having much success. He complained to his wife:

'Dear Viorica, I'm an idiot.'

'Why Costi?'

'Well, we were both fishing in exactly the same place, but while I was catching only *clean* and *mreană*, [barbel – a fish of the carp family] my pal here was catching *lipan* all the time.'

That was a fish dinner to remember too! It went on for a long time. At midnight we went into the garden and sat around a flower bed, in the middle of which we placed a paraffin lamp, and savoured the last stories of the evening – and the last glasses as well.'

No wonder that this Father Christmas got a picture postcard from London in January 1958 (that is, some 18 months before the Australian tour) 'from your far-distant fishing colleague and soul-mate' wishing him, his wife and daughters a happy and prosperous New Year.

> That was all of three decades ago, but I remember when he gave me his impressions of the musicality of different nations he said the English were the most musical, in the sense of amateur connoisseurs, basing this opinion on the large number of radio broadcasts of religious music such as the Bach *Passion* and Handel's *Messiah*, compared with other countries.
>
> I was left with the impression of a strange and fascinating personality.

The conductor considered by the more orthodox to be something of a maverick was no conformist either when he started fishing in southern England's gentler Avon and Stour. Told before he tossed a line that he must put back anything he caught into the river on pain of being fined, he would wade into mid-stream without any attempt at concealment and, if he made a worthwhile catch, take it down to the Panoramic Grill and tell André or Renée Lennoye with pride: 'We will come down tonight to eat my fish!'

Later, he did get a permit to fish the Avon on the Royalty Estate near Christchurch where salmon and trout were plentiful. Whether or not he thought going legitimate was responsible, his luck now ran out. Having bought a very expensive Japanese rod and a plethora of tackle, some of it inappropriate for his kind of fishing, and rigged himself out in all the gear of the compleat angler, he was naturally frustrated that the fish were no longer biting.

As a companion on some of these expeditions he would take along with him one of the BSO's cellists, Douglas Morris – he and Costi enjoyed their long mutual silences. It was Douggie who solved the mystery of the fish's allergy to Costi's bait: in the process of being put on the hook it was being seasoned by his particularly pungent hand cream which was not at all to their taste.

But let Ken Matchett himself tell the story to cap all Costi fishing yarns:

> I used to do a lot of sailing in my 33-foot motor ketch and I thought it would be good for Silvestri's health if he came on a trip. He wasn't terribly interested in sailing, but at last he agreed to come, provided he could fish from the boat. So, one weekend, four of us set out from Poole Harbour: myself, my youngest son, Richard, then 14 years-old, a solicitor friend and

Displaying a 16 lb pike he caught
in the Dorset Stour

Fishing on the Răstolița
in Transylvania

Silvestri with all his fishing gear – totally unsuitable for sea fishing of course.

It was a bit choppy as we crossed the bay and Silvestri looked pale and started to slump. After a while he wanted to fish, but as he wasn't feeling very well, he thought he would have a little drink 'to settle my stomach.' We always stocked the boat with plenty to drink and Silvestri brought his own supply of red wine, which he always used to dilute, Continental fashion. So we set him up in the stern in all his gear – sou'wester, oilskins, waders and with this enormous bag he had with about 10,000 baits and a million hooks and very beautiful rod and line. (Richard just had a hand line with a spinner at the end. We used to be very successful catching mackerel with this.) He had his bottle of wine with him and a glass and he came back to us and said he wanted some water. I explained it was below in a screw-top bottle so it wouldn't slop over in heavy weather.

After a couple of hours, Richard came to me and said: 'I don't think Mr Silvestri is very well. He's in the cockpit, not in the stern where we put him.' So, I went down – and there he was as happy as the day is long, out for six.

I don't know how it had happened, but he'd picked up the wrong bottle. I sniffed at his booze and he'd been 'diluting' it with gin or vodka from a bottle with a transparent liquid that he must have mistaken for water.

We got him into the cabin and strapped him into a berth so he could sleep it off.

When we got to Yarmouth, Isle of Wight, he eventually came round but said he didn't want to eat and would be perfectly alright on his own. So we went ashore in a dinghy, leaving him with his line out over the side because I told him he was bound to catch something in the harbour.

Towards the end of our dinner in a hotel I said to the others that, whereas we'd caught more mackerel than we knew what to do with, Silvestri had caught nothing and would be terribly disappointed. So I bought a couple of plaice from the chef and sneaked them aboard. Silvestri had evidently gone on to his 'special' again and was flat out on the bunk. I was very glad because he needed a rest after the lot of touring he'd just done. His line was still out so I stuck the plaice on the end of it.

The next morning while we were having our breakfast on board, Silvestri was only drinking a cup of tea, so I said: 'You'd better pull in your line and see what you've got.' So he pulled it in and announced triumphantly: 'Two lovely big plaice!' I replied: 'I told you so!'

Later, when we were in the stern I explained to him that all his precious tackle was useless for sea fishing – and he threw the whole lot overboard.'

Among all those interviewed and in other sources concerning Silvestri that have been consulted, it is only in this story of the trip in Kenneth Matchett's ketch that there is any mention of Silvestri being inebriate – and that was plainly an accident. Alun Francis, who both as a pupil as well as being a member of the orchestra, had a dual opportunity to observe him over the years, stated: 'I have no knowledge that he drank larger quantities of alcohol than most people. I never got the impression that he was a heavy drinker.' Yet those who knew he had a liver complaint have assumed that, as one of them put it: 'Unfortunately, he had a few drinks too many and died far too young' – a glib oversimplification.

There is certainly the indisputable evidence of the autopsy. Professor Sherlock said it revealed 'a primary liver cancer in part of the right lobe.' If it had been in the left lobe there might have been a possibility of removing it since it is a quarter of the size of the right one. But even then it would have left the 'grossly cirrhotic liver' about which nothing could have been done at that stage.

Cirrhosis has many causes and there may even be a hereditary cirrhosis which predetermines the possible development of the diseased liver. After all, Queen Marie of Romania, who died in 1938, had an extremely rare type of cirrhosis of the liver not caused by alcohol. But the most common cause is related to chronic alcohol consumption and it is this, insofar as it had significance in the case of Costi, that concerns us here.

Whether or not the actual cause of his death reached Romania and how widespread it was known among his old friends, Judith Vancea – talking about his health as a young man and certainly with no prior reference in our conversation having been made to his death – volunteered the following:

> He drank enormously. When he came to visit us he drank enough to put a fire out. I never saw anyone drink so much wine, but I never saw him drunk. That was his misfortune because if he had got drunk he might have stopped drinking. But he never drank when conducting – not a drop passed his lips.

That was a very shrewd judgement. Whether as early as this he had incipient cirrhosis – possibly hereditary (it is not known what his heavy-drinking father died of) – no one will now know. But what is indisputable is that absolute teetotalism is vital for anyone with the disease. Even the hereditary variety can be dealt with if the person rejects alcohol permanently.

Silvestri's social drinking had the East European hallmark of an almost coercive hospitality, summed up in Peter Katin's impression after seeing 'everyone getting sloshed' at Costi's dinner parties in the Panoramic Grill:

> It was very difficult to be with him and not drink a lot because he insisted that everyone should. It wasn't that he wanted to see you get drunk, but if you weren't drinking he thought you were unhappy about something.

Judith Vancea was in all probability quite correct in suggesting that, had Silvestri not had this capacity to drink in excess without showing any signs of inebriation, he would have done something about it. He was obviously a man with a strong will, with no manifest suicidal tendencies, who would have cut down on his alcohol intake, perhaps cut it out altogether (as he did belatedly) if he had realised what it was doing to him.

The tragedy is that he did have this ability to remain sober at will, compounded by his ignorance – shared by large sections of humanity – of the dangers of alcohol poisoning.

Added to this is the further tragedy that no one diagnosed the cirrhosis at an early enough stage for him to be told that by drinking he was radically cutting short his life span. Stopping only nine months before the end was obviously too late. It may be that whenever he felt unwell and consulted a doctor he drew attention to his early trouble with his lungs and this diverted attention away from symptoms which would have given an indication of his liver complaint. (Some Romanians, unaware of the cause of his death and with the conventional Dickensian image of England, believed it was due to his chronic lung debility accentuated by London fogs!)

As to whether at any stage of his illness a liver transplant could have been attempted on Silvestri, this is largely academic since, though the first liver graft on man was carried out in the US in 1963, the invaluable collaborative work in this domain at the Addenbrooke Hospital, Cambridge, and King's College Hospital, London was, as far as human grafts were concerned, at a very early stage in 1968.

There remains the more complex, psychological question as to why Silvestri drank as much as he did. We don't know to what extent it was obsessional, if at all. It could only be called such if he had persisted, for probably deep-seated reasons, in drinking when told it was fatal to do so. But since no one apparently did tell him, and since he was able to control its visible effects, there is no evidence that he was a compulsive drinker.

Although his father was a heavy drinker, the medical profession does not seem to have come up with any evidence that alcoholism is hereditary. Nor, in the circumstances, is it likely that the young Constantin was influenced by his father's example in this respect if it is recalled that he virtually never saw Aloysius until he was five and then only knew him briefly before he had a second 'father' who seems to have been a sober enough character.

We have mentioned elsewhere the early traumas, including his parents' separation and the deaths of both his father and step-father when he was still in his teens – which may have contributed to buried anxieties in the young Costi and accounted for why he sometimes seemed to his friends withdrawn and, in maturer years, what Ida Haendel described as introverted. The close contact of the only child with a mother who must have had many anxieties living without a supportive partner during wartime deprivations could have resulted in a prolonged mother-dependence; and continuing to live with the widowed Ana as a young man may have had some influence on his subsequent relationships with women.

These can only be hypotheses, mere suggestions that deepseated unconscious anxieties needed relieving – even though he seemed to find maximum solace in his work – by recourse to the odd bottle or two of wine during his lonely night vigils or when being convivial with friends.

To fill in our picture of the whole man, warts and all, there is a curious aspect of the 'fantasy world' in which Kenneth Matchett as well as friends in Costi's youth thought he lived to some extent. These are the various harmless little fictions about himself which either he personally propagated or which he failed to correct if they were put about by others.

Mention has already been made of his alleged breast-stroke championship and other examples of his sporting prowess which he tried out on the Australians; and the 'fishermen's stories' for which a Romanian friend presented him with a symbolic fishing rod. These were probably little inventions to compensate for his embarrassment at being round-shouldered and narrowchested, as described by those who knew him.

If some of the expressions he used in his letters as a young man verge on the melodramatic, seem overly self-pitying or to protest too much over man's ingratitude, nevertheless he obviously did not enjoy robust health and he did have to fight in a competitive profession for recognition of his talents, especially as a conductor. One can almost admire the boldness of mustering Lotte Lehmann or Toscanini as promoters of his works when he was inveighing against the tardiness of his recognition at home.

But for a biographer his exaggerations do create problems.

For instance, why in his letter to Zeno Vancea of March 8 1940 (already quoted) did he specifically say that he had burned all his own compositions 'except for a few early *lieder* and Romanian dances up to Op. 10' when, for example, these would have included *Nacht und Träume* for choir and piano (Op. 2 No. 1); his piano suites such as *Jeux d'enfants* Nos 1, 2 and 3 (Op. 3 and 6); his *Sonatina* (Op. 3 No. 3); as well as his *Three Pieces for Strings* (Op. 4 No. 2) which have often been and are still being played? Either the *auto da fé* he kindled was not very effective or these works bore the charmed life of a Phoenix – and the world of music is the richer for it.

The most persistent piece of misinformation after he came to the West (in PR hand-outs, programme notes and appreciations of him) was that 'he began his activities as a conductor when only 17 with the Radio Symphony Orchestra,' and one is left with the impression that his conducting career took off thenceforth. Evidence to support this, as we have seen, has proved elusive and his own correspondence reveals he had a hard and frustrating struggle in Romania to win recognition as a conductor.

Programme notes for his concerts in Britain used to maintain that 'between 1935' (that is when he was 22) 'and 1956 he was Musical Director and Manager of both the Philharmonic Orchestra and State Opera in Bucharest,' when we now know it was October 1945 when he became principal conductor of the Philharmonic and 1947 (when he was 34) that he became its director; and that he was dismissed from one of these positions and resigned from the other in December 1953. It was only subsequently that he became director of the Opera (and principal conductor of the Radio Symphony Orchestra.) In no way was he director of the Philharmonic and the Opera at the same time.

One can hazard guesses as to why these claims were made on his behalf. They could be due to faulty communication between Silvestri and the writers of the hand-outs or programme notes or a sloppy, irresponsible attitude on their part. In that case, would not Silvestri himself have seen them at some stage and corrected them? In fact, they were repeated year after year.

It is more probable that Silvestri was no different from many other artists who feel, in order to survive in a very competitive profession, they are justified in massaging the truth ever so gently if it enhances their reputation; especially if they happen to be building it either in their youth or in a foreign country where they are relatively unknown and it is therefore all the more important to impress audiences, most of whom may be attending their concerts for the first time. If the world is impressed by young prodigies, then knock off a couple of years or more as to when you first conducted *Le Sacre du Printemps* or whatever. Who is going to check? And no one will be hurt by it anyway. Such is probably the reasoning behind these inexactitudes, no worse than knocking a few years off a birth date, dyeing hair or other generally accepted deceptions.

But if one takes the risk of misinforming, the misinformation does have to be credible.

In programmes over a four-year period (July 1962-October 1967) the following claim was made repeatedly on Silvestri's behalf: 'During his last visit to Russia [1958] he conducted the first performance of Shostakovich's *Eighth Symphony* in Moscow.'

The *Eighth Symphony* was composed in 1943 (in Moscow) and for the first time Shostakovich dedicated it to an individual: Yevgeni Mravinsky, principal conductor of the Leningrad Philharmonic. It was Mravinsky who conducted its first performance, on November 4 of that year, during a Festival of Soviet Music in Moscow. When Shostakovich was 'in disgrace' the *Eighth* was dropped from the Soviet repertoire for 15 years after the war. So, only in 1960, in order to survive did he join the Communist Party, pay lip service to 'Soviet realism' and attack Schoenberg's 12-tone system for which, as a *quid pro quo* the ban on the *Eighth* was lifted.

So Silvestri certainly did not conduct its première in Moscow and since his 'last visit' to the Russian capital was in 1958, it is unlikely he conducted it two years before the ban was lifted. (As we have already noted, he did play it in Bucharest in 1956, according to Bălan.)

Whoever was responsible for this solecism in these programmes would have served Silvestri better by drawing attention to the compliment the composer paid him when he conducted the Shostakovich *First Symphony* in Moscow. Another of these potted biographies had him leaving Bucharest in 1956 'and he made his home in Paris,' that is two years before he settled in the West.

His sense of humour would have been tickled by some other examples, if ever he saw them. For instance, by what sounds like an outback journal, the *Murwillumbah Daily* in New South Wales describing him as 'a visiting Hungarian celebrity'; while visitors to the Dublin International Festival of Music and the Arts in June 1961 must have knotted their brows on reading in the festival programme: 'Constantin Silvestri, Rumanian conductor, composer and pianist, who comes to Dublin to sing. . .'

If some got the impression Silvestri was 'introverted,' none thought of him as a dour character. On the contrary, he was easily amused and his own humour was a cocktail of the ingenuous, the Puckish, with at times a dash of acetic acid.

The story is told in Bucharest of how, when he was working in a recording studio at the Radio, he was puffing away as usual at a cigarette, when a security guard came in, drew Costi's attention to the NO SMOKING notice and said:

'You'll have to pay a fine.'

'How much?' asked Costi and when told 20 lei, paid on the spot and the guard gave him a ticket by way of receipt. But this did not deter Silvestri from smoking and the guard 'caught' him umpteen times that day and each time the offender paid up. At length Costi's patience wore thin and the next time the guard appeared he enquired caustically: 'Do you still have tickets? Because I assure you I still have money!'

Nina Cassian recalled that in Romania 'he used to tell a lot of jokes. He had wonderful laughter and, like the portrayal of Mozart in the film *Amadeus*, Silvestri had a histrionic side.' So, it is not surprising that occasionally he would play jokes on his Romanian audiences. Once, when he conducted Respighi's suite *The Birds* and the public clamoured for an encore, they had to be content with no more than the trumpet 'cackle' in the Hen movement. Similarly, when the audience demanded an encore after *L'Apprenti Sorcier*, he gave them just the final two bars (which in Disney's animated cartoon *Fantasia* accompany the magician's dismissive kick in the pants to the naughty apprentice.)

In his Bournemouth phase he was still using the same jocular device for escaping exigent audiences. In Nottingham, for instance, after returning to the platform four or five times at the end of a concert which had included *Manfred*, *Pictures at an Exhibition* and the *Romanian Rhapsody No 1*, he turned to the orchestra and silence fell immediately as everyone anticipated an encore. But all they got was a single resounding chord – and he made his final exit followed by the players.

Nor was he averse to a little Hoffnungery. Before the BSO left for its 1964–65 European tour, he decided to show his Winter Gardens clientèle another, lighter side of the Silvestri *persona* not hitherto revealed. Not only did he choose Mozart's *Musical Joke* K522 as the opening piece in an *au revoir* concert, but accompanied it with a bit of clowning on his own part, ably assisted by carefully rehearsed players and Winter Gardens staff. The initially bewildered audience were treated to the spectacle of the orchestra starting to play without a conductor; the cellos playing when Silvestri was turned towards and conducting the First Violins; of him giving a clinical inspection of the horns that were blatantly producing 'wrong' notes; having an altercation with a dissident Gerald Jarvis, the leader; and glaring melodramatically at the piano-shifters who twice brought the *Joke* to a halt, first by removing the stool, then the instrument itself from the stage.

On another occasion his hamming relieved a situation which was becoming tense. A visually perfect recording had been made of Ravel's *Daphnis and Chloë*, with the BSO and choir, for transmission as part of Southern Television's inaugural programme in November 1968. But unfortunately the sound had not been recorded. It had to be done all over again the following day and Geoffrey Hughes, a member of the Bournemouth Municipal Choir (and subsequently its chorus master) recalls how 'on a very wet Sunday morning we trudged through the streets of Bournemouth at 9 a.m. looking very out of place in our evening dress.' In the empty, cold Winter Gardens hall, the re-recording was continually interrupted while the engineers checked each part. The orchestra's commitment and professionalism was being severely tested; up to the point when, during one of these breaks, Silvestri, in his tails, put a handkerchief over his arm and took a few steps pretending to be a waiter. There was a huge laugh and good humour was restored. 'He was a great mimic,' says Hughes.

When the lights were blazing during a rehearsal for this recording, he did a wonderful mime of someone wiping the sweat from his brow and putting up a sunshade. But it was a very different Silvestri who rounded on the producer who had been unwise enough to tell him not to worry about balance, that it would be done in the control room. A furious Silvestri pointed out in no uncertain terms that that was the conductor's job, not some pip-squeak twiddling knobs!

There was an entirely unrehearsed interruption and more mirth in 1968, this time in Brighton's Dome. The Queen's punctiliously loyal subjects who were regular attenders of the Brighton Philharmonic Society's concerts knew from hallowed custom that these invariably started with the National Anthem, which itself began with a drum roll to bring them to their feet. Sure enough, the Sunday matinée concert on April 7 started with a drum roll and, if it sounded different from what they had been used to, the audience no doubt attributed it to the conductor's Romanian origins (he was a British citizen by then) or his reputed eccentricity. They duly rose to their feet. But to their astonishment and growing unease, not the first bars of *God Save The Queen* met their ears, but of Tchaikovsky's *Fantasy-Overture*, *Hamlet*, the first item on the programme. Silvestri was equally astonished at the noise behind him and brought the *Overture* to an abrupt stop. He looked around at an audience trying to make up its mind whether to stand or sit and, as comprehension dawned, he started to heave with laughter – in which he was joined by players and audience. When it subsided, *Hamlet* began again.

In rehearsals, too, merriment that in the early years was occasioned by a combination of Silvestri's unfamiliarity with English vocabulary, syntax and vowel inflexion was later, as his knowledge of English idiom grew, more often sparked off by his deliberate witticisms. Some of these would have shocked the primmer among the old school of English conductors, but the players, especially the male members with sexist hang-ups, loved them.

A bassoonist remembers the BSO rehearsing the *Habanera* movement of Ravel's *Spanish Rhapsody* when Silvestri was trying to get a certain character of sound, playing and especially rhythm:

> It was very free and very tight at the same time, but it was never good enough for him. Finally, he came over to the woodwind, and speaking particularly to the flute section very conspiratorially, with his forefinger to his lips making a shush sign, he lowered his voice and said: 'I have a word that will help you with this rhythm. Always remember this word,' and as he said it he accented the syllables: '*Sper* . . . mato . . . *zoa* . . . *Sper* . . . mato . . . *zoa*. . .' And he repeated: 'Always remember this and you'll get the rhythm right.' Of course, everybody fell about laughing.

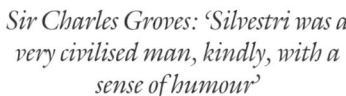

Sir Charles Groves: 'Silvestri was a very civilised man, kindly, with a sense of humour'

Livia Rev: 'He was more human than George Georgescu'

Sir Charles Groves mentioned two qualities in Silvestri which impressed him:

He was a very civilised man. In his ordinary contacts with one, which had nothing to do with music, he was very kindly and had a sense of humour.

These were the qualities one would expect Silvestri's predecessor to have admired since he was himself amply endowed with both. It was the Rabelaisian side of Costi's humour which particularly appealed to Groves, who it was that christened Silvestri's special padded and carpetted rostrum 'The Whore's Bedroom.'

But some would say that Costi's kindness was conditional on whether he was on or off this or any other rostrum – in rehearsal he was capable of reducing a more sensitive player to tears. Yet everyone from Groves to Katin ('One always forgave him things because he was such a nice person'); to Silvestri's driver ('The most gentle conductor I ever had to deal with'); from young soloists like Michèle Boegner ('When I was rather nervous before doing a BBC broadcast he advised: "Drink a large glass of warm milk!"') or Livia Rev ('He was more human and kinder than George Georgescu'); not to mention his colleagues in Romania – all vouched for his gentleness and humanity in their off-stage contacts with him.

John Clegg: 'He was a great conversationalist'

The 'magnificent birthday cake' Silvestri ordered for her eighth birthday is vividly remembered by Tanya, daughter of the late Malcolm Rayment, the composer and music critic whose 'discovery' of Costi in Bucharest had led to his London début. Her birthday had coincided with Costi's conducting of the première in Bournemouth of her father's *Sinfonia Concertante*. From her own memories of Costi over a four-year period and from what her parents told her, Tanya's impression of him was 'of a very warm, gentle and generous man.'

Kenneth Matchett said it for them all in his valedictory tribute to the maestro:

> He was a modest man with a tremendous sense of humour, generosity, sincerity and a warmth of personality that endeared him to all those who had had the pleasure of meeting him.

Rounding off his assessment of Silvestri, Groves (shortly before his own last illness) said: 'It's sad he died so young. He was odd, not a usual man at all. When I say "odd" I don't mean peculiar. I mean he was not in the common run at all. He might well have been a genius.'

The epithet genius was applied by so many sources to Silvestri that, by looking at the context in which it was used in each case, we may find some common denominator, a litmus paper that may reveal how far it was justified.

Further evidence that his music-making, like the man himself, was 'not in the common run' was provided in Paris by composer Marius Constant:

> Silvestri had this genius for giving to each piece a very special interpretation. He was the only one who did it. His conception and analysis of the score was better, or at least different, from Karajan's.
>
> I once conducted at the Opera, here in Paris, a ballet based on Tchaikovsky's Manfred Symphony and I remembered when I was a youngster in Bucharest Silvestri conducting it. It was an amazing performance and it was still in my mind when I did it for the ballet. I told Rudolf Nureyev all about this man in Bucharest and how he did it and Nureyev agreed with all his interpretations.
>
> Each of Silvestri's interpetations of a work – whether it was well-known, not so well-known or a new one – was an event because his musical conception and the colours he wanted to give to each piece was something really extraordinary. When I now listen to his records, I realise no one did those pieces like he did. You may or may not like his interpetations, but they were an event.

Referring to the 'marvellous improvisations he gave on the piano,' Judith Vancea said:

> He could play anything – all music flowed from his fingers. He was very close to being a genius. If conditions had been different, he might have become a great pianist. His destiny might have been different.

But it was Silvestri's own choice to pursue a career as a conductor rather than as a pianist; 'conditions' had little to do with that choice. Whether by confining his talents to the keyboard he would have become a great pianist, there is insufficient evidence to make a credible conjecture – only a few years of brilliant improvisation and a few concert performances with negligible reviewing material on which to make an assessment.

His 'destiny' if he had stayed within Romania might have been different only if the regime had become more liberal. If he had stayed under conditions as they then were he would have basked in the acclamations of the public at home and of audiences in other East European countries, continued to be honoured by the state, and his wealth and social security would have been assured – for a while. It was his own instinct of intellectual self-preservation that made him aware of the objective limitations the system put on his conducting potential. That is why he took the first opportunity to get away from them.

Furthermore, if he had stayed another seven years in Romania he would have been overtaken by the Ceauşescu era and one can well imagine that mutual tolerance would have worn thin very quickly. Silvestri was anything but conformist by temperament and it is more than likely that dissidence on his part would have led at least to his official ostracism and increasing isolation, if not to more direct punitive measures. He would then have had to attempt what he actually did seven years before: seek involuntary exile.

In any case, the George Georgescu factor, though it played its part, was not of paramount significance in restricting his development within Romania.

For Silvestri the 'conditions' did change by his decision to go where he had more freedom to conduct the kind of music he wanted in the way he wanted.

Nina Cassian thought there was no comparison between George Georgescu, 'a good professional,' and 'the genius Silvestri,' but the former was 'much more acceptable to the authorities than Silvestri who was a rebellious type, an individualist and much more original.' Conductor, composer and musicologist Constantin Bugeanu called him 'a fantastic musician.' For Anatol Vieru, Silvestri was also

> an outstanding musician who left a stronger impression on me than did Celibidache. I was an impressionable young man, of course, but for me at that time he was a musical god. . . He died too early.

Radio Symphony Orchestra violinist Radu Zvorişteanu thought Silvestri was the only Romanian musician who could be compared with Enescu since he was 'a brilliant instrumentalist, a wonderful conductor, a composer of genius and an excellent teacher.' To which Radu's colleague of those days, Amelia Beldi, added: 'In our generation Silvestri was the one from whom we learnt most and I believe our musical development was due to him.'

For Iosif Conta, who became principal conductor of the Radio Symphony Orchestra after Silvestri left, he was also the great teacher responsible for a whole new generation of Romanian conductors, including himself, and many living abroad.

> He introduced a school of conducting which superseded the diletante methods and was modern in outlook. He deserves immortality because he was a genius.

In Britain, a London critic claimed: 'As an orchestral trainer, Silvestri is among the world's best' and Malcolm Rayment, the composer/critic who set in motion the process which eventually resulted in Silvestri taking up the

Bournemouth post, was convinced he was 'one of the greatest conductors of our time'. This view is endorsed by those who played under him: by the BSO's then manager and secretary and by today's managing director, Anthony Woodcock, in whose opinion

> Silvestri was not only a major conductor in the British and international music scene, he was also a fine composer of major stature.

Kenneth Matchett believes:

> There is no doubt that up to the time of his death, the BSO was one of the best orchestras in the country. It could stand comparison with any of the others. But I think there was a lot of jealousy on the part of the musical Establishment in London. Every time we appeared at the Festival Hall at our own-promoted concerts, every critic in the business was there. Occasionally we got marvellous notices, but usually they would hold back a little bit, almost as though they were frightened to say what they thought: how dare this Bournemouth orchestra come up here! I am quite convinced that, had Silvestri not been taken ill, given another two or three years he would have broken down this barrier by the sheer standard we were producing. It was a tragedy that ill health caught up with him when he was so close to the summit of his career.

Violinist Brian Johnstone thinks

> Silvestri had just reached the point where people really sat up and listened to what the BSO was doing. Had he lived he would have been just as famous as Barbirolli or Karajan.

In the view of Principal Oboe Roger Winfield:

> One of the greatest tragedies for music is not only that Silvestri died so young, but that somehow he was just a bit too ahead of his time. When he first arrived on the London scene, they were not quite ready for him. His technique was absolute clarity but so understated that people had to have the eyes, the youth and the intelligence and general sense of humour to appreciate it. The London players were used to the Beecham/Boult approach which is less humour, more laid-back, British *sang froid*, less emotional. Now, styles have changed and Silvestri made a big contribution to that.
>
> Before he came, Bournemouth had some very fine players; there was nothing provincial about it. But he got that orchestra to rival anything I have ever heard – and we've got the records to prove it.

Eight years before I knew Silvestri, I had had the opportunity of going on an American tour with Karajan and the Philharmonia – the greatest orchestra in the world in the Fifties – and had also been playing for 13 years with Barbirolli and the Hallé. So I knew what a fine orchestra should sound like. I knew what results Karajan could get and I was always comparing him with Barbirolli, and the Philharmonia with the Hallé. As far as making a comparison is concerned, there was quite a gap between my personal experience of Karajan and Silvestri, but I remember when the BSO did Ravel's *Rapsodie espagnole* it sounded like magic. I had done it 15 years before with Karajan and it's probably the only time I've ever made a comparison between these two conductors. I thought: 'Where have I heard that played so beautifully before? Ah, yes! It was with Karajan with the Philharmonia.'

The Philharmonia had 16 First Violins, 13 were leaders and three were soloists – and yet I remember believing that the Silvestri performance was every bit as beautiful. They both achieved their results, but Silvestri must be the greater conductor because he could do it without calling on the best players in the world – and that's not to denigrate the BSO who had very fine players (many of whom left to go to very good jobs.)

Attempts to define genius have been legion; what proves elusive is the qualitative difference between genius and brilliance. To a few mortals the term genius can be applied without fear of challenge – the spark that needs no defining is communicated through their work and sensed intuitively. But in less evident cases it is sometimes too glibly applied and as a consequence a reputation can be diminished when the intention is to enhance it. In one 24-page appraisal of a certain conductor, he is referred to five times as a genius. This is the word choice of the author and others, a word the conductor himself, a shy and self-deprecating man with several of Costi's gifts and characteristics, would no doubt eschew.

Of the dozen people whose tributes to Silvestri have been quoted here, five of them explicitly referred to one or other of his attributes as the inspiration of genius: whether it was his interpretative skill as a conductor, improvising on the piano, or teaching; many implied as much among the over 40 who contributed their recollections of him. That Silvestri had the spark that galvanised concert audiences is indisputable.

Advice he used to give his students of conducting in Bucharest is evidence for the belief that his own concept of genius would have approximated to de Bouffon's: '*Le génie n'est qu'une grande aptitude à la patience*'; for he used to tell them: 'If you appear to be a genius it is because, among other things, you have done ample rehearsing with the orchestra. Perfection is only attained through hard work.' Silvestri's own rehearsals meant infinite patience on his part (and his players needed it in good measure as well). So at least he qualified for de Bouffon's definition of *le génie*.

His homily for the students was also intended to deflate any incipient arrogance by pointing out to them that an individual 'genius' burgeoning in the course of orchestral musicmaking was dependent on working with and having the support of the ensemble. In all humility and gratitude to his orchestral colleagues, he would have been the first to apply the same proviso to himself.

At the thought of posterity attaching the label genius to any of his talents, the mature Silvestri (who as a lad had liked praise but was suspicious of those who gave it) may well have been amused – and left us with another sample of his banter delivered with that infectious laugh.

SALA SOCIETĂŢII PENTRU RĂSPÂNDIREA ŞTIINŢEI ŞI CULTURII

ATENEUL R. P. R.

JOI 20 NOEMBRIE 1952, orele 19⁴⁵ precis

CONCERT

AL ORCHESTREI SIMFONICE

Dirijor : CONSTANTIN SILVESTRI

PROGRAM

GOLĂNIN	: Poem epic pe teme populare ruse
SCHUBERT—LISZT	: Fantezia pentru pian şi orchestră
	Solistă : ELVIRA LOEBE

PAUZĂ

BRAHMS	: Simfonia II-a

Concertul fiind radiodifuzat, uşile se închid la orele 19³⁵ iar accesul publicului în sală după începerea concertului va fi permis numai în pauză.

The four programmes on this and the following pages span Silvestri's conducting career. Above: November 1952: conducting the Bucharest Radio Symphony Orchestra

Music

of a

Century

(1857— 1957)

AN ILLUSTRATED HANDBOOK

Issued in connection with the London Philharmonic Orchestra's

Anthology of nine concerts at the Royal Festival Hall

January — May 1957

PRICE ONE SHILLING AND SIXPENCE

His first concerts in Britain were part of the London Philharmonic Orchestra's
Music of a Century *series*

ST. CECILIA'S FESTIVAL

Under the Patronage of Her Majesty The Queen

Royal Concert 1966

Tuesday, November 22nd at 8 p.m.

in the presence of

HER MAJESTY THE QUEEN

and

HIS ROYAL HIGHNESS THE DUKE OF EDINBURGH

*November 1966: The Bournemouth Symphony Orchestra's
Royal Concert in London's Royal Albert Hall*

75th Anniversary Year
1968/1969

BOURNEMOUTH
SYMPHONY
ORCHESTRA
1893-1968

The Orchestra of the West

PROGRAMME

WINTER GARDENS, BOURNEMOUTH
Thursday, 28th November, 1968, at 7.45 p.m.

ONE SHILLING

November 1968: His last concert in Bournemouth

A SILVESTRI CALENDAR

(Age in brackets)

1848		Maternal grandparents, the Havliceks, flee Bohemia to Bucharest. Paternal forebears living in valley of the Piave, north of Venice. Grandfather Constantin moves to Bucharest (date unknown); later to Vienna.
1874		His father, Aloysius, born in Vienna.
1891		His mother, Ana, born in Bucharest.
1913		(May 31) Constantin born in Bucharest but given his father's official nationality, Austrian.
1918	(5)	Sees father for the first time. First music lessons.
1920–22	(7–9)	Bucharest primary school.
1922	(9)	Parents divorce. Ana remarries and becomes Mrs Cariade. Moves to Târgu Mureş, Transylvania.
1925	(12)	Zeno Vancea starts teaching Costi composition etc. at the Târgu Mureş Conservatoire.
1928	(15)	Passes with honours one of the advanced courses at the Conservatoire. His Opus 1 published.
1929	(16)	Stepfather dies. Returns to Bucharest.
1930	(17)	Enters Bucharest Conservatoire and becomes a pupil of Florica Musicescu. Dinu Lipatti, four years his junior, is a fellow pupil.
1930s–1945		Concert pianist
1932	(19)	First recorded intimation of ambition to become a conductor. First Mention in Enescu Prize for his *Bihor Dances*.
1934	(21)	Wins joint second Enescu Prize for his *Five Capriccios* Op.10. (Lipatti got First Prize).
1935	(22)	Obtains Romanian citizenship. Répétiteur at the Romanian State Opera. Conducts Bucharest Radio

Symphony Orchestra in his *Five Capriccios* for the first time.

1936 (23) Second Enescu Prize for his *String Quartet* (Op.16)

1937 (24) First Enescu Prize for his *Cello and Piano Sonata* (Op.12)

1939 (25) Conducts full programme with Radio Symphony Orchestra

1940 (27) Conducts Bucharest Philharmonic for the first time, ending programme with his own *Prelude and Fugue (Toccata)*.

1942 (29) Marries Viorica Vasilescu. Conducts the Berlin Philharmonic.

1944 Ban imposed on George Georgescu conducting.

1945 (32) Appointed 'Permanent Conductor' of the Bucharest Philharmonic.

1947 (34) Appointed Director of the Bucharest Philharmonic. Carried shoulder-high by audience after first concerts in Budapest. Ban lifted on George Georgescu conducting.

1948 (35) Starts teaching at the Conservatoire. In private, condemns Zhdanov's resolution *On Music*.

1953 (40) Dismissed as Director of Bucharest Philharmonic and Georgescu appointed in his place. Silvestri resigns as its principal conductor and Georgescu resumes former position. Silvestri appointed artistic director of the State Opera and of the Radio Symphony Orchestra. *Three Songs* (Op.28), his last composition, published.

1956 (43) Honoured with title of People's Artist.

1957 (44) London début with LPO in January and invited again in June. First concerts in France and his recording of *From The New World* with the ORTF wins the Charles Cross Academy first prize and that of Enescu's *Dixtuor* the Grand Prix du Disque. Conducts in five more countries before returning behind the Iron Curtain.

1958 (45) Returns to UK to conduct seven concerts with the LPO, records with the Philharmonia and conducts concerts in Paris before again returning to Romania.

Conducts Enescu's Chamber Symphony twice in the same concert at the Enescu International Festival in Bucharest and, six times, the first full performances in Romania of Enescu's *Oedipe*. Leaves Romania for the last time. Concerts in the USSR.

1959 (46) Makes Paris his domicile; concerts in Brussels; in UK conducts nine concerts with the LPO, four with the Hallé and more recordings with the Philharmonia. Australian tour.

1960 (47) First American visit: conducts Chicago S.O. South African tour.

1961 (48) Second US visit: conducts Philadelphia S.O. First concert September 26 as Principal Conductor of the Bournemouth S.O.

1963 (50) Conducts *Khovanschina* at Covent Garden and BSO at Edinburgh Festival.

1964 (51) In Tokyo conducts NHK S.O. and guest conducts in five European countries.

1965 (52) BSO's first European tour.

1967 (54) Silvestri and his second wife, Regina ('Pupa'), granted British citizenship. Bournemouth SO at the Proms for first time in 12 years.

1968 (55) BSO's 75th anniversary year. November 23, commemorative concert in the Royal Festival Hall is Silvestri's last in London. Last concerts before going into the Royal Free Hospital, London, were in Plymouth, Bournemouth and Exeter at the end of November.

1969 (55) Manuscript of Malcolm Williamson's Symphony No 2, *Pilgrim On The Ocean,* dedicated to Silvestri and the BSO, shown to him in hospital. Dies February 23.

Years later Memorial stone erected in St Peter's churchyard, Bournemouth.

SILVESTRI'S WORKS

Op. 1 Part 1	*Lieder* (set to Heine). Published in Timisoara in 1928. Revised 1934.
Op. 1 Part 2	*Lieder* (set to verses by Heinrich Heine)
Op. 1 Nos. 7–24	*Lieder* (Heine) 1928. Ms.
Op. 2 No. 1	*Nacht und Träume*. 1929. Choir and piano.
Op. 3 No. 1	Suite 1 *Jeux d'enfants*. Piano. 1931. Dedicated to H.M. the Voivod of Alba-Julia. Salabert.
Op. 3 No. 2	Suite 2 *Jeux d'enfants*. Piano. 1931–33. Salabert.
Op. 3 No. 3	*Sonatina for Piano*. 1931. Salabert.
Op. 4 No. 1	*Romanian Dances from Transylvania (Bihor Dances)*. For piano four hands. Orchestrated in Prague. Piano Salabert. Orch. – Novello. Distinction in 1932 Enescu Competition.
Op. 4 No. 2	*Three Pieces for Strings*. 1932 or 1933. Revised 1950. Novello.
Op. 5	No information.
Op. 6 No. 1	Suite 3 *Jeux d'enfants*. Piano 1933. Salabert.
Op. 6 No. 2	*Piano Bachanale* (Suite No. 3). Salabert.
Op. 7–9	No information.
Op. 10	*Five Capriccios* (Orchestra and voice) 1934. Dedicated to Jora. Second Prize in 1934 Enescu Competition. Ms.
Op. 11	No information
Op. 12	*Sonata for Cello and Piano*. 1935. Won Enescu First Prize 1937. Ms lost, possibly destroyed.
Op. 13 No. 1	*Woodwind Quartet*. 1935. Ms.
Op. 13 No. 2	*Sonata Breve A Due Voci*. Written for clarinet and bassoon (cello); viola (violin) and cello; piano. 1938, revised 1957. Dedicated to Zeno Vancea. Salabert.
Op .14 No. 1	*Concerto Grosso*. 1934–36. Ms.

Op. 14 No. 2	*Concerto Grosso.* 1934–35. Ms.
Op. 15	No information.
Op. 16	*String Quartet No. 1.* 1936. Second Enescu Prize 1936. Published 1939. First performed 1940. Ms.
Op. 17	*Metamorphoses (Prelude and Fugue).* Piano and Orchestra. 1939. Ms.
Op. 17a No. 2	*Prelude and Fugue (Toccata).* Composed for piano 1938. Orchestrated 1939. Revised 1956. Salabert.
Op. 18	No information.
Op. 19 No. 1	*Sonata No. 1 for Violin (Oboe, Clarinet or Flute) and Piano.* 1939. Salabert.
Op. 19 No. 2	*Sonata for Piano.* In two parts. 1940, revised 1957. Salabert.
Op. 19 No. 3	*Sonata No. 2 for Violin and Piano.* 1940.
Op. 20 No. 1	*Quartet for Violin, Oboe, Clarinet and Cello.* 1940. Ms.
Op. 21 No. 1	*Sonata for Harp.* 1940. Schott. First performed in England, by Nicanor Zabaleta, Wigmore Hall, November 1965
Op. 22	*Sonata for Bassoon and Piano.* 1941. Ms.
Op. 23 No. 1	*Sonata No. 2 for Clarinet and Piano.* 1941
Op. 23 No. 2	*Sonata for Flute and Piano.* 1942. Ms.
Op. 24	*Sonata No. 3 for Piano.* 1943. Ms.
Op. 25	*Pièces de Concert Nos. 1–3.* Piano. 1944. Salabert.
Op. 26 No. 1	*Variations: Liebe ein Lustiges Thema.* 1944. Ms
Op. 27 No. 1	*Chants Nostalgiques.* Piano. 1944. Salabert.
Op. 27 No. 2	*Music for Strings (Quartet No. 2).* 1944. Salabert.
Op. 27 No. 3	*Quartet No. 3 for Strings* (parts 3 and 4) 1948. Ms.
Op. 28 No. 1	*Sonata No. 4 for Piano. Rapsodia in Tre Episodi.*
Op. 28 No. 2	*Three Songs* (to verses by Reiner Maria Rilke) 1953. Ms.

In his letter of March 8 1940 to Zeno Vancea, Silvestri mentioned works not on this list such as a Trio for Winds and Quintet. Vancea himself (*Appendix 2*) also mentions a Quintet.

ZENO VANCEA'S ANALYSIS

Silvestri was one of the most complex and interesting figures after Enescu. Because of his conducting commitments he wrote a relatively small number of songs, piano pieces, chamber and orchestral music.

His first compositions were written between 1924 and 1927. His piano & theory teacher at the Târgu Mureş Conservatoire, Rudolf Zsizsmann, did not pay much attention to Silvestri's attempts at composition; I was a teacher of harmony and counterpoint at the same Conservatoire and when I was shown some of his compositions by the director, Max Costin, I was very impressed by their sense of 'form' which demonstrated to me that he had a precocious talent.

Ten *Lieder*, Op.1 on verses by Heine (revised in 1934) were written after a three-year course with Mihail Jora; they showed a good compositional technique and to some extent the influence of Reger, Hindemith and Honegger, composers who were becoming better known in Romania at that time. Silvestri wrote them with the emphasis on harmony rather than on melody, unlike in his later works, especially in his chamber music. These *lieder* are influenced by the great German Romantics, especially by Schumann, but in some, like in *'Sterne mit den goldenen Füsschen'* (Stars in Little Golden Shoes) from the first book, and in *'Sie floh von mir'* (She Was Fleeing From Me) from the second book, the young composer uses new harmonic means and with a more personal touch:

The very next work, a five-part choir (1929), *Nacht und Träume* (Night and Dreams), Op 2, on verses by Matheus de Collin, represents a considerable change in the harmonic complexities and in the free treatment of the dissonances; he combines impressionistic effects with a sure expressionistic character:

By temperament, Silvestri was inclined to Expressionism, to an intense demonstration of his own feelings – as in the slow movement of the *String Quartet No 2* or in the piano pieces, *Chants Nostalgiques*. From then onwards throughout the remainder of his composing years, this characteristic was tempered by the demands of the compositional forms which balanced his urge to improvise. His approach of combining free improvisation with more rigorous writing often resulted in themes in the same work being written in different styles, as in his two suites for piano, Op 3, Nos 1 and 2 *[Jeux d'enfants]*, both composed in 1931. Some themes sound as if they were the spontaneous, almost accidental, creations of his fingers while others seem to be thoughtfully selected.

One could be misled into believing from the title of these two works that they are pieces written for beginners, when in fact they present considerable difficulties of execution and interpretation and the pianist must possess an advanced technique.

One of the characteristics of Silvestri's style, present in all his works, appears very early on when he was trying to find a personal mode of expression: the presence of diatonic as well as of intensely chromatic tunes within the same piece. Another aspect of his style is the use of bi-tonal chords, not very common in the Romanian music of that time, and which Silvestri used systematically in later works. Here are two examples: the first one is a fragment from *The Lead Soldiers* from *Suite No 1* and *The Clown* from *Suite No 2*:

In the same year he also wrote the *Sonatina for Piano Op.3 No 3* which is not essentially different from the two Suites, with the exception of the following theme from the final rondo:

in which the diatonic structure is predominant in both melody and harmony. Embodying as it does a certain reserve in its expressiveness, the work gains a more emphatically neo-classic style and has certain similarities to the piano works of the same period written by Dinu Lipatti.

Under the influence of Mihail Jora and of the national current in music which was asserting itself very vigorously in the Thirties, folklore attracted Silvestri's interest for a short period. He composed the *Romanian Folk Dances from Transylvania* [*Bihor Dances*], which, although bearing the number Op 4 No 1, had been sketched out way back in 1929. These dances have a version written for piano four hands, presenting some harmonic differences from the orchestral version and containing an additional dance. It is believed that at the time he wrote these dances Silvestri had studied the adaptations of Romanian folk dances by Bela Bartók, yet he did not adopt the same methods as the great composer but, instead, used a more traditional harmonic treatment, with the exception of the sixth dance, *Joc din Drîmboaie*, in which the harmonic support is a combination between a pedal chord and a continuous succession of two chords of juxtaposed fourths:

After this first incursion into the domain of orchestral music, Silvestri resumed writing piano music in the same year, 1933, with the *Suite Op.6 No 3*, which contains six pieces: *Prelude, Duet, Capriccio, Nocturne, Sacred Dance* and *Bacchanalia*. Here he returns to the espressivo of Romantic essence, characteristic of the other two Suites. At the same time he expresses himself with the help of an intensely chromatised melodic line which now performs more autonomously, supported by harmonies with mainly colouristic functions:

The last two pieces, *Sacred Dance* and *Bacchanalia*, assert themselves by their sheer virtuosity, anticipating Silvestri's later piano pieces which he composed for his own performances. At the time they were written, Romanian pianists avoided tackling Silvestri's pieces because of their novel style; it is also true that Romanian pianists in general failed to show much interest in works by their Romanian contemporaries.

In 1934, he composed the *Five Capriccios for Orchestra Op.10*, on folksongs collected from Bartók's collection; the work bears evidence of an incompatibility between the essentially diatonic structure of the folk songs and their harmonic and polyphonic integument which is intensely chromatic. Judging from the manuscript of the *Third Capriccio*, the whole work was initially composed for voice and piano and was only later orchestrated. It is based on *Melody No 44* from the Bartók collection: *Romanian Folk Songs from Bihor*, published by the Romanian Academy in 1913:

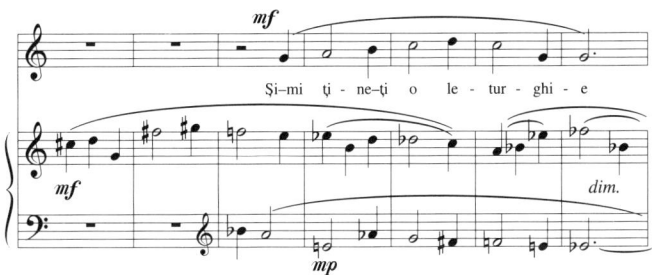

The third *Capriccio* is a rather curious case: although the ms, in the composer's handwriting, bears the indication Op. 10 No. 3, virtually the same accompaniment which sustained its folk melody appears again without it in the first section of the third movement of the *Sonata a due voci per Clarinetto e Violoncello* (Fagotto) Op. 13:

Between 1934 and 1938, Silvestri was very productive. He composed two *Concertos for String Orchestra*, a *Woodwind Quartet*, a *String Quartet* and a *Sonata for Cello Op. 12* (for which he won First Prize in the 1937 Enescu Competition). These show a continuous evolution of his compositional technique and at the same time the diversity of influences on his work. It was a period when his musical identity gained more definition.

Written in 1938, the *Sonata for Clarinet and Cello*, marks the beginning of Silvestri's chamber music period with works of a neo-classic character *par excellence*. This would last until 1944, when he composed *Chants Nostalgiques for Piano* and the *String Quartet No 2*, works which express a deeper emotional content. I am using the term neo-classic in the broad sense, that of the aesthetic conceptions of the 20th century trend, born as a reaction to Expressionism, and seeking a method of expression less charged with the emotional tensions of post-Romantic music.

His two works with eminently polyphonic structure are the *Sonata for Clarinet and Cello*, mentioned above, and *Metamorphoses Op 17 for Piano* which have an *Introduction, Three Preludes and Fugues* and an *Intermezzo*. The *Sonata* is in four movements, each a two-part invention set in a contemporary context.

In both the *Sonata* and the *Metamorphoses*, Silvestri's chromatic writing reaches its apogee and, at the same time, in conformity with the linear character of this music, a completely free mode of treating the dissonances. Later he transcribed for full orchestra one of the *Preludes and Fugues* from the *Metamorphoses* cycle.

For reasons unknown to us, Silvestri replaced the original *Prelude* anticipating the Fugue with another one.*

Obviously, the orchestral version is of much greater complexity than the one composed for the piano. Silvestri introduced additional parts and used specifically orchestral colouristic effects (as in pp. 18 and 19 of the score), generally not used in works of polyphonic writing. One interesting particular of the *Prelude* from the metrico-rhythmic point of view is the constant succession of bars with different time signatures 4/4, 3/4, 2/4, 1/4, lasting until the end of the piece without, though, giving it a sketchy character

* Probably in 1955 or 1956.

The *Fugue* does not take the traditional form. Apart from the fact that it is not constructed on the tonal basis of a classical fugue, many sections have an essentially homophonic setting which confers on it the character of a toccata. Silvestri obviously noted this when giving it the additional name: *Toccata*.

In between the statements of the theme which appear throughout in the mode of *re*, the tonality is in fact suspended, because of the permanent juxtaposition of polytonal lines and chords.

The toccata character is also due to the procedures used in the development section, which are not based on real polyphony but, with the exceptions of a few contrasting moments, on rhythm and conglomerations of accords plaqués played with the participation of the whole orchestra:

In my opinion, the third *Fugue* from the original piano cycle is more interesting from the point of view of construction and counterpoint, with a polyphony of great complexity built on three themes.

The following example is the climax of the *fugue* in which the three themes are juxtaposed:

The sonata form was Silvestri's favourite. He distanced himself from the classical type through his avoidance of a precise tonality and by using a larger number of themes.

In chronological order, the first of the 1939 sonatas was written for Oboe/Flute/Clarinet /Violin and Piano Op. 19 No. 1:

followed by the other two: *Sonata for Piano* Op.19 No. 2:

and *Sonata for Violin and Piano* Op.19 No. 3:

Characteristic of the style of these three works is the coincidental presence of themes with varied melodic structures (some chromatic, some diatonic) and containing leaping intervals.

Silvestri's harmony can only be described with great difficulty because it cannot be categorised within any system. In general, it is neither bi-tonal nor polytonal, nor is it organised by serial principles and it has more the function of a 'neutral' sonorous support. The melody detaches itself from it in a most independent way.

The *Sonata for Piano No 4*, subtitled *Rhapsody*, (without any date as to when it was composed) is different from the previous ones by its freer shape and by the greater technical difficulties which it presents for the pianist. Here are two themes from these works:

As an ending for the *Sonata-Rhapsody*, Silvestri uses the adaptation of the last of the folk dances from the piano suite for four hands, a dance which in the *Rhapsody,* differs quite considerably from the one in the Suite.

Related to it by their pianistic writing and technical difficulties are the *Six Concert Pieces* Op.25 (two volumes with three works in each), with the character of concert studies.

The feeling of the second study anticipates the atmosphere of a later piano work, *Chants Nostalgiques*, Op.27 No 1. In these three pieces, Silvestri returns to eminently expressive writing. The work bears the sub-title '*Studies for Dynamics*,' which corresponds to over 20 dynamic indications from *pp* to *fff*:

which gives the impression that Silvestri mostly had in mind the colouristic effects of the piano. In reality the diversity of sonorities contributes to deepening the expression and to diffuse the atmosphere of profound depression by which the composer was sometimes overwhelmed. Their inner content remind us of some piano pieces by Bartók (*Naenia, The Voice of the Night* etc).

During the same year, 1944, Silvestri wrote another most representative work, the *String Quartet* Op.27 No 2 which shows the composer at the fully mature stage of his creativity. Having passed through the *sturm und drang* period in which experimentation and the seeking of new harmonies and tone colours were basic to his compositions, the *Quartet* constitutes the testimony of a musician of great sensitivity and of a rich inner life, who also had the gift of moulding his music in forms of impeccable logic.

The harmony is simpler and clearer than in previous works, the melodic line more defined, the polyphony subtler and less adorned. Although Silvestri was not a string player, his longstanding contact with the orchestra helped him to use the various specific effects of string instruments, without any ostentation and only in the service of expression. Here is the beginning of the first movement – Allegro:

and the beginning of the *Third Movement – Adagio*, a beautiful nostalgic song:

Although the *Scherzo* (Second Movement):

and the *Finale* differ in a way from the other two movements by their melodic structure being more diatonic, this does not interfere with the stylistic unity of the *Quartet*, considered to be one of the most valuable works of this genre in Romanian music.

There is another *Quartet*, written in one movement, with a scherzo character which was commissioned by the Union of Composers and which, from Silvestri's own indication, appears as Op. 27 No 3 composed in 1948. The style of the two *Quartets* differs considerably. In the Op. 27 No. 3, for the first time in Silvestri's compositions one can feel Bartók's influence in the melodic, harmonic and rhythmical structure:

In the years following 1944, when the majority of Romanian composers drew on folklore for a rich source of inspiration, Silvestri was in a way an isolated example in the Romanian musical scene, manifesting only sporadically an interest in folk music. His *Three Pieces for String Orchestra* (revised in 1950) prove that he could indeed create very valuable works based on folk material and they are acknowledged as among the best written in Romania. This was also a work which owes its existence to a commission from the Union of Composers.

The first of the *Three Pieces* (the first and third of which have a dance character and the middle one that of a *doina*) is preceded by a short introduction with a melody in the spirit of folk tunes from the Bihor district. The piece then develops as an authentic folk dance from the same district and returns several times in varied forms, similar to a rondo. The composer obtains an interesting harmonic effect through the frequent usage of bi-tonal juxtaposition.

The second piece, of a slower tempo and written in the form of a *lied*, contains an outstanding cantabile melody which, for all its folk character, does not seem to derive at all from folk but more from the composer's own imagination:

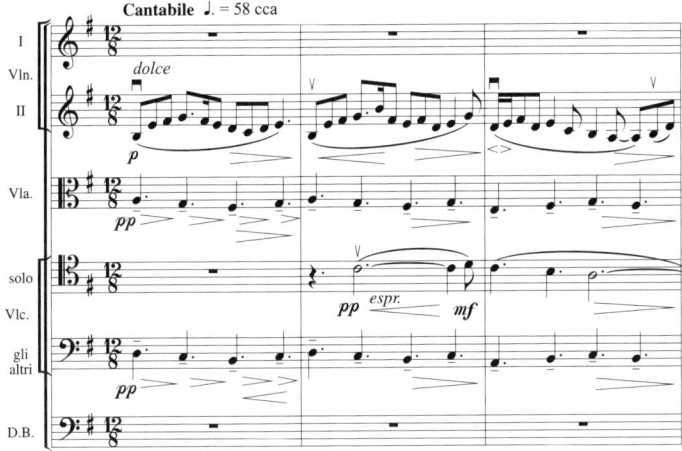

Very interesting from the harmonic point of view is the beginning of the third piece, a dance with bi-tonal structure:

At a time when Paul Constantinescu was working on the same melody for the *Finale* of his *Concerto for String Orchestra*, keeping to the structure of the folk melody without altering its modal element, Silvestri was using it in the Third Piece with bitonal harmony as well as with several other harmonic inventions, not hitherto used by anybody in adaptations of Romanian folk tunes. The exception was Theodor Rogalski with the second of his *Three Symphonic Dances*.

Also most impressive is the mastery with which Silvestri highlights all the colouristic resources and the diversity of sound combinations of a string orchestra.

SILVESTRI REHEARSING ELGAR'S 'IN THE SOUTH' (ALASSIO) CONCERT OVERTURE WITH THE BSO

While on holiday in Italy at the end of 1903 and beginning of 1904, Elgar wrote back to England: 'We are both riotously well and shall never come home.' This overture reflects 'thoughts and sensations of one beautiful afternoon' in the Vale of Andora close to the seaside town of Alassio between San Remo and Savona on the Italian Riviera – very far from Campanian Naples where Silvestri seems to have thought it was!

On the front page of the manuscript are two quotations: one from Tennyson's *The Daisy*:

O love, what hours were thine and mine,
In lands of palm and southern pine,
In lands of palm, of orange-blossom,
Of olive, aloe, and maize and vine.

The second is from *Childe Harold* where Byron contrasts ancient Rome's military might with the present glories of the countryside:

. . . the land
Which was the mightiest in its old command
And is the loveliest. . .
Wherein were cast. . .
. . . the men of Rome!
Thou art the garden of the world

Below is a transcription from a tape of a rehearsal in the Winter Gardens concert hall. Some words are inaudible or so distorted as to be unrecognisable. We do not know the date when it was made, but judging by Silvestri's English it was probably fairly soon after he came to Bournemouth. It should be remembered that he had been based in Paris for over three years, hence his occasional lapses into French. One has got to imagine the East European pronunciation – all the 'th' sounds are 'z' (zer and wiz) and all the 'i' sounds are long ('ee'.)

(Movements and subdued talking in the background.)

SILVESTRI: 'Very fast bows here. *Nobilmente*. Very fast for the viola, too. But, suddenly, after a lot of – tee-da-tee,' (this is almost shouted, then he sings lyrically) 'tee-raa – there is nothing then. The *nobilmente* is not here. . .'

(Pause during which there is a twittering of voices; a single note from a string; submerged tuning of the tympany and a *sotto voce* – etee-raa-ra. Upon this there suddenly bursts from Silvestri:)

' – Yum-tee, da-dai-yum pum – yes! – Yum-ta-dee, dai-yampa' (then an ascending) 'Ta-ree-rai-yam-pum-ta-rum' (and at a still higher pitch, but descending) '-Tee-ra-ra-yom-pa. Every time I've got, before the *legato* . . .' [Inaudible mutter from a player.] 'No, the first bit is faster, a little faster than the *diminuendo* – yum-tee-da-da-dee-dum. This come from the fast bow. For the fast bows the sound is killed, no? Slaughtered. The last bowing connection. . .' (His voice drops.) 'One bar before 6, please,' (repeats) 'one bar before 6. Four bars before 6, to bring the [inaudible] bow.'

(Orchestra plays.)

SILVESTRI: 'Suddenly . . . I think Elgar was a very big sarcast. I feel from all his music he was a very big – what can I say? – ironic in all that he made, apart from his symphonies. Even in the *Enigma* if you think, *Enigma* – and nobody know what the theme is.' (Pause.) 'No, *I* discovered what the theme is, and then. . .' (A roar of laughter from the orchestra as they catch the significance of the remark) '. . .and then . . . and if you see *Cockaigne*, if you analyse *Cockaigne* it is the *Meistersinger* in mirror, exactly, exactly all contrary: Tee-ra-ree-ra is raree-ra-tee – *exactly* contrary. He made a joke; he may be serious, I don't know, but probably a joke. And so a lot of things in Elgar are sometimes cheap, sometimes *schmaltz*.

'So here is a trumpet solo. In this, *Don Juan*, he turns on Alassio. Can you hear *Till Eulenspiegel*?' (Sings – then sorts out which trumpets should play. A player calls out: 'All of them.')

SILVESTRI: 'All three? Much better! Then the double bass, very nice. I like to see your big effort . . . but the effort must not ruin the music. Make the break like you make – with intensivity, *vibrato*.

'Now, another thing: and here I ask you again, careful with your kind of sound in a low instruments between the double bass, again trombones, even cello. It is sometimes coarse, the sound. It was again in Tchaikovsky last night and before last night, and again in Brahms and so and so. The control about the sound – don't give more than the instrument can give.' (With a slight pause between each word for emphasis) 'A good . . . nice . . . soft quality.

Fortissimo or not *fortissimo*, don't overtake the possibility of the instrument.' (He follows up this little homily with a quick-fire vocal demonstration – *staccato*, raucous and spluttering – like a duck having its neck wrung. A titter from the players.)

'You must be *nobilmente* every time, even in Tchaikovsky with his vodka and his youth and other things. And, especially, later in Bruckner. Next year we start with Bruckner, we come back with this nice soft quality. It is very pity you probably don't heard so, after our last concert was . . . the Bruckner Ninth Symphony with Vienna Philharmonic with Karajan. It will be in our programme after two months. What a nice quality, the fortissimo! The trombone, the double . . . never with. . .' (and he gives an exaggerated ejaculation to illustrate straining.) 'Every time torcht, tought.' [Taut or tough?].

(A player speaks.)

SILVESTRI: 'So . . . pardon?'

PLAYER: 'They've got about six players I don't think you realise what that means.' (Some stamping and good-humoured vocal approbation from the other players.)

SILVESTRI: 'Don't want excuse. All the possibility in your hands so make this quite soon. . . So, 7 . . . 7 and I want some colours in the First Violins. . . I say nothing, Mr Jarvis.' (BSO leader Gerald Jarvis says something inaudible.) 'No, make a small [inaudible], Mr Jarvis.'

(Laughter and further remarks by the players. Then Silvestri's rapid:) 'No, no, no! I know how nice you . . . (laughter) . . . 'Now, listen to the First Violins to see if you're satisfied.'

(They play.)

SILVESTRI (shouting): 'Bravo! Bravo!' (and enthusiastically) 'This is the sound. This is warm, this is music. Thank you. Second Violins, please the same!'

(*They* play.)

SILVESTRI: 'Yes, that last beat must come a little bit more warm, but not very warm, that last beat. You know what? (Presumably turning to the First Violins.) They played lower than you. Much more force than the First Violins. Much better position in a violin to use the colours. Thank you very much. . .'

(A few moments later he turns to the woodwind.)

'I have some small details in the flutes and first oboe: – La-re-rum-perum-tee-da-re-rum. Can I hear this? This is some bars before 10. I think eight bars or something, so you vou . . . vous avez trouvez?' (Player says something) 'Ah, ca n'est pas la deuxieme flute. Two, four, six, huit, er . . . eight, ten. It's First Flute . . . First Flute and First Oboe.'

JARVIS: 'First of all, let's get it straight. One, two, three, four, five, six and *seven* .'

SILVESTRI: 'Eight' (rapidly) eight, eight. Or I'm wrong – rumti-ra-ti-ra-rum – this is ideal!'

(Flutes and oboe start playing, but Silvestri interrupts.)

'No, no, no! You are not in order. First, first, first, first.'

(They resume playing.)

'So, so, so – a little *mandolinata*. We're in Italy, Alassio is a town in Italy, no? Cam . . . Neapolitan. Again, please. One, two, three.'

(They play.)

'That's fine. So don't, er lose this with, er. This is eight bars before 10. I show when the moment is here, when the oboe and the flute is playing this. And all your enthusiasity – Tatee- (rising) Tar-tiddy-dum-ta-da – you listen what you play it and the other ear is for the First Violin, yes?'

(A player says something.)

'Fine. You must have three ears. Nine ears. . .' (Ripple of laughter) 'Nine er . . . Figure 9.'

(Later.)

'It was a word: espressivo here and you can play this much more vibrato and much nicer sound. Please, First Violin and Second . . . Seconds. . .' (Inaudible remark by the leader.) 'What is here? Four bars . . . Yes, Seconds, Second Violins not First Violins.' (Sings and they play.) 'No, no, no, no, I like the eye-Be sounds, (repeats) the eye-Be sounds:' (Sings)

'*Piangendo*'.

(They play again. Pause.)

'Look at the score and play exact what is there.'

(Passage repeated.)

'So, bring in the Norwegian . . . [?] – La-di-da-dee, ya-dee. . . (fading away).

(Playing resumed.)

'Ah, ha, ha, ha yes. Yes, thank you, thanks . . . 10 . . . 10. . .'

[Indistinct] . . . 'No, no, no. . . maestro . . . bridge . . . marvellous. If you play it so marvellous you must continue hearing his idea. Now this pianissimo of Viola and First Violin . . . pianissimo. One, two. . .'

(They play.)

'No, no! Was very good technical, very good. I need to play the quaver in the right place, but not . . . (sings, first demonstrating the distortion, then how he wants it played) and so on, with all nostalgical, a little leaven if you like. One, two.'

(They play again.)

'More sort of. . . A little better, not exactly. Twelfth then, and Mr [Inaudible]'

(While they are still playing, he exclaims:)

'Marvellous, the clarinet!'

(Orchestra playing.)

'Something not . . . the cellos and viola. It is 14 bars before. Fourteen, four bars before. . . Yes, it's a small dot here. One, two' (and as they resume playing) 'One tee. . . Here is the second bit and then you come after – Yee-aa. Yum-pa. Ta-ree-dum – so!'

(Playing.)

'No, no! Be a nice good cellist, no – the cello, I mean. Speculate the sea breeze.'

(Passage repeated. Silvestri hums).

'You must be a. . .' [word unintelligible. Phonetically: rees] Cassado. [Or reescassado, perhaps? Gaspar Cassado was a Spanish cellist – a clue?]

(Playing resumed.)

'Tchaa. . .' (Sings with cellos). 'But come in tempo – yeear-dada-da. You know what I mean: it is so typical cello to speak with all the cello possible.' (Again sings with cellos.) 'This is . . . so, small things here. Once more here, (repeats) once more here, all together bring a nice colour. Thirteen, four bars before. OK, 14.'

(Playing.)

'Thirteen. Viola and First Violin. (Playing) And First Cello. (Playing) Please, four bars before. Mr Carpenter, [word unclear – clarinet?] two bars before and the sound was Mr. . . the two clarinets finished. You must continue to bring this back. Four before 13.'

(As orchestra plays, Silvestri sings with it.)

'One . . . and two. . . Yes, the first time you come in [a word that sounds like maxralia?] note – Ya-ra-dee. Ya-ree (rising) – like a flower in the spring. Mr Carpenter finish so marvellous, he prepared you the sound and then' (a disparaging) 'er-rer. It's clear now in ears, the sound, eh?' [Inaudible reply.] 'So. Thank you. Forty-one.'

(They play and as the sound swells, Silvestri shouts:)

'Yes, thank you!. . . You must see here the convulsion what was in the last, 19th, century: the quietness, the tranquility and in some time . . . um . . . his hysterical [*sic*] ideas about social life and all the things, no? They disappeared when the revolution started, Socialist new ideas, Marx and so and so. All the world, no? It is something in the air. This is here: love mixed with all the things together. Now, from 17 to 19 you come back in this hysterical enthusiasm one time, tragedy in another time – this all involved one in another, no? This is a bridge. So this *crescendo* in the two bars before 17 (sings) *la dolce vita, la dolcezza della vita. Alora*, all this was here and 17 slowly, slowly starts to be more and more involved in the negative world. Seventeen. . .'

(They play until he stops them. Pause.)

JARVIS: 'It's absolutely right.'

SILVESTRI: 'No, there is a mistake.' (Sings)

JARVIS: 'There is no. . .'

SILVESTRI: 'Then it's not printed. One, two, three, four, five, the sixth bar is *diminuendo*. One, two, three, four. Five is a *crescendo* and the sixth is *diminuendo*.' [Remarks by leader and a woman player inaudible.] 'Nothing. And then *diminuendo molto*. And then the second bar after 17 is a *pianissimo subito* what you made. This is probably printed, yes? The second part of 17 is a *pianissimo subito*. You made this. It is probably printed. Then the sixth bar is a *diminuendo*. (Pause) Can I hear what your hearts say now?

(Clarinet plays.)

'Was first time . . . second time?' (Clarinet again) 'Ah, no, no. This is not *pianissimo* – Ta-ra-dee-da-da-hm.' (Clarinet again). 'There it is. And now you must have been [inaudible] Mr Carpenter, in the fifth bar [inaudible] first, then cor anglais.' (Plays) 'No, no the first beat. . .' [word inaudible before a cough]. (Silvestri sings a passage and the clarinet follows.) 'That's it. Thank you. 17.'

(Trumpet blast.)

'Good trumpet. Very good, Mr Senior, but we don't want, we don't want *you*! You prepared all the things but . . . he (Elgar?) was a big lullaby, huh? 18. Now here is a disaster, (repeats) here is a disaster: the trombones after 19, the four-bar, this *forte*, this is a *shocking* sound.' (He demonstrates with a vehement reverberating ejaculation:) 'Yack! So, a knife cuts something, coming so!'

(And one can imagine the downward-slicing hand.)

APPENDIX 4

DISCOGRAPHY

Since 1990, the following CDs were produced by EMI with works conducted by Silvestri:

BEETHOVEN *Violin Concerto* with Yehudi Menuhin
and the Vienna Philharmonic   EMN CD-EMX 2069 (1990)

TCHAIKOVSKY: *Violin Concerto* with Leonid Kogan
and the Paris Conservatoire   CZS7 67732–2

Violin Concerto with Christian Ferras
and the Philharmonia   EMN CD-EMX2178

ELGAR *In The South* see Appendix 3) Bournemouth
Symphony Orchestra Centenary   CDM 7 64719 2 (1993)

RIMSKY-KORSAKOV *Sheherazade*; MUSSORGSKY *A Night On The
Bare Mountain*; BORODIN *In The Steppes of Central Asia*
Bournemouth Symphony Orchestra   Royal Classics ROY6426

Favourite British Music with the Bournemouth
Symphony Orchestra – Classics for Pleasure   CD-CFP 4611

TCHAIKOVSKY *Manfred Symphony* with the Paris Conservatoire
Orchestra and LISZT *Tasso: lamento e trionfo*
with the Philharmonia   Testament Records SBT 1129

The following LPs were made in the Sixties with Silvestri conducting the:

Philharmonia

TCHAIKOVSKY *Symphony No 4*   ASD 253, G. ALP 1511, Angel S35556,
Stereo Tape: G.SAT 1017

Symphony No 4 coupled with GLINKA *Russlan and Lyudmilla Overture*
SXLP 30066

Symphony No 5   ASD 261, G.ALP 1491, Angel 35566, Stereo Tape
G.SAT 1023

Symphony No 6   ASD 273, G.ALP 1495, Angel 35487

Violin Concerto with Christian Ferras
coupled with MENDELSSOHN: *Concerto*   G.ASD 278, G.ALP 1543,
                                             FALP 514; Angel 35606

HINDEMITH: *Symphony – Mathis der Maler*   ALP 1597

Symphony – Mathis der Maler
coupled with Bartók *Divertimento*   Angel 35643

LISZT: Symphonic poems: *Les Préludes* & *Tasso*   G.ALP 1648, Angel 35636

Piano Concertos 1 & 2 with Samson François   XLP 20028 (mono)

FRANCK *Symphony in D minor*   ASD 408, G.ALP 1831, CFP 40090

STRAVINSKY *Symphony in Three Movements*
and *Song of the Nightingale*   ASD 401, G.ALP 1819

Overtures: HUMPERDINCK *Hansel and Gretel*,
   MENDELSSOHN *A Midsummer Night's Dream*,
   GLINKA *Russlan and Lyudmilla*, RIMSKY-KORSAKOV
   May Night, BORODIN *Prince Igor*   ASD 338, SXLP 30066

London Philharmonic Orchestra

DVORAK *Symphony No 8 (4)*, *Carneval Overture*   ALP1537 (mono)

Royal Philharmonic Orchestra

FRANCK *Symphonic Variations* coupled with
   SCHUMANN *Piano Concerto* with Moura Lympany   G.CLP 1288

Bournemouth Symphony Orchestra

VAUGHAN WILLIAMS: *Fantasia on a Theme of Thomas Tallis*;
   The Wasps coupled with ELGAR: *In The South (Alassio) Overture*;
   Overture The Kingdom Op.50   ASD 2370

TCHAIKOVSKY: *1812 Overture; Caprice Italien;*
   Eugene Onegin-Polonaise   SX 6086, TWO 139

RIMSKY-KORSAKOV *Sheherazade*   TWO 167
                        (First record in EMI's Studio Two Series)

MOUSSORGSKY *Night on the Bare Mountain*, RAVEL *Pavane pour*
   une infante defunte, SAINT-SAËNS *Danse Macabre*, SIBELIUS
   Finlandia, BORODIN *In The Steppes of Central Asia*,
   DUKAS *L'Apprenti Sorcier*   TWO 221

French National Radio Orchestra (ORTF)

DVORAK *Symphony No 9 (5) From the New World* ALP 1550 (mono)

TCHAIKOVSKY *Manfred Symphony, Piano Concerto No 1* with
  Aldo Ciccolini; coupled with LISZT *Mephisto Waltz*   ALP1668

CONSTANTINESCU *Piano Concerto*
  with Valentin Gheorghiu   G.FBLP 1095, Electrecord ECD 46

Paris Conservatoire Orchestra

DUKAS *L'Apprenti Sorcier,*
  SAINT-SAËNS *Danse Macabre,* RAVEL *Bolero,*
  DEBUSSY *Prélude á l'Aprés-midi d'un faune*   ALP 1684 (mono)

  Nocturnes; La Mer   ALP 1689

  Fêtes (from *Nocturnes*), *Jeux de Vagues* (from *La Mer*)   7ERS 166

BERLIOZ *Symphonie Fantastique*   XLP 20036

BEETHOVEN *Violin Concerto*
  with Leonid Kogan   SAX 2386 (stereo), 33CX1738

MENDELSSOHN *Violin Concerto* with Leonid Kogan coupled
  with MOZART *Violin Concerto* No 3 K216   33CX 1744(mono)

BRAHMS *Hungarian Dances Nos 5 & 6* coupled with
  BORODIN *Prince Igor – Polovtsian Dances* and FALLA *El Amor*
  Brujo – Ritual Fire Dance; La Vida Breve – Prelude and Dance
  and DVORAK *Slavonic Dances Nos 1 & 2*   G.ALP 1966, ASD 519

Vienna Philharmonic

SHOSTAKOVICH *Symphony No 5*   G.ALP 1886, ASD 455

BEETHOVEN *Violin Concerto*
  with Yehudi Menuhin   ASD 377, G.ALP 1799

DVORAK *Symphony No 7* (2)   ASD 396, G.ALP 1814

Rhapsodies for Orchestra

LISZT *Hungarian Rhapsody No 4* coupled with ENESCU *Romanian*
  Rhapsody No. 1 and RAVEL *Rapsodie espagnole*   ASD 417, ALP 1842

PROKOFIEV *Love for Three Oranges suite,* KHACHATURIAN
  Gayeneh – Ballet Suite, RIMSKY-KORSAKOV *Capriccio espagnol*
    ASD 400, G.ALP 1818, ASD 417, ANGEL 35677

Before coming to the West, Silvestri had made at least 24 records in East European countries and with the Vienna Philharmonic; and nearly 40 with Western European orchestras, including the Philharmonia, the LPO, the RPO and French orchestras before he came to Bournemouth.

His East European records were, for instance, with: the Bucharest Philharmonic (eg. Beethoven: *Missa Solemnis*); the Romanian Radio Symphony Orchestra and Chorus (eg. Mozart: *Mass in C Minor* K427; *Violin Concerto No 3* with Kogan; and *Le Nozze di Figaro Overture*; Haydn: *Symphony No 27*; Corelli: *Suite for Strings*; Enescu: *Suite No 3; Romanian Rhapsody No. 1*; *Octet for Strings* and *Concertante Overture on Romanian Folk Themes*; Shostakovich: *Symphony No 10*; Alfred Mendelsohn: *The Fall of Doftana Prison*; Paul Constaninescu: *A Stormy Night*; and Constantin Dimitrescu: *Peasant Dance*); the Budapest Philharmonic; the Hungarian State Symphony Orchestra (eg. Falla: *El amor brujo*); the Czech Philharmonic (eg. Ravel *Rapsodie espagnole*; Lalo: *Cello Concerto* with André Navarra; and Enescu: *Two Romanian Rhapsodies*); the Prague Symphony Orchestra (eg. Haydn Symphony No. 27 G Major); and with the USSR State Orchestra (Shostakovich *Symphony No 1*; Britten *Young Persons Guide* and Walter Mihai Klepper: *Four Romanian Dances*.)

This discography was compiled in part from one which accompanied an appreciation of Silvestri by the late Malcolm Rayment in *Music and Musicians* in 1963 and which was produced in collaboration with Silvestri himself. The list of Romanian and Hungarian recordings was not complete.

SOURCES AND ACKNOWLEDGEMENTS

For the facts about Silvestri's forebears, childhood and adolescence I am indebted to his one and only previous biographer, the late Eugen Pricope, for his *Constantin Silvestri: Intre străluciri şi. . . cîntece de pustiu.* (Editura Muzicală, Bucureşti, 1975), which was not translated into English; and to an article by Teodor Bălan simply entitled Constantin Silvestri which was among a considerable amount of valuable material very kindly made accessible by Mme Regina Silvestri in Paris. The article was apparently written in 1974 but unfortunately there is no indication as to the journal in which it was published. Both of these sources have been referred to by name in the body of the book.

Additional useful facts were gleaned from a 23-page typewritten article (also in Romanian), *Constantin Silvestri: Dirijorul şi profesorul*, but with no clue as to the author's identity.

Other sources in Romanian included an interview with Silvestri in *Contemporanul* 25.4.58; transcript of a Radio Bucharest interview by Ada Brumaru entitled *Silvestri on Music and Musicians* 27.3.58; an article by Alfred Hoffman on Silvestri in *România Literară* 1.3.79; another by V. Pop Băleni in *Timpul*, December 1957; one in *Iubiţi Muzica Secolului* 20 by Iosif Sava in 1984 entitled: *Constantin Silvestri: Discipline, Style, Poetry, Technique*; Silvestri's letters in *George Breazul: Scrisori şi Documente* (Editura Muzicală, Bucureşti 1984); *Dirijorul George Georgescu: Mărturii in Contemporaneitate, Ediţie îngrijită de Viorel Cosma* (Editura Muzicală, 1987); a review in *Rampa* 26.1.47 by Cella Delavrancea; and another in February 1947 by Nina Cassian.

I am grateful to Editura Muzicală, Bucharest, for Appendix 2's analysis of Silvestri's works in *Creaţia Muzicală Românească* (Sec. XIX–XX. 1978) and for the references to Pascal Bentoiu's *Capodopere Enesciene* and for the reproduction of the music examples in both works.

I would like to thank Silvestri's archivist in Bournemouth, Raymond Carpenter, for his encouragement and invaluable help from the inception of the book and throughout gestation; for his own lively recollections of Silvestri; and specifically for the tapes of Southern Television's interview with Silvestri when he was appointed principal conductor of the BSO; for another radio interview, in Paris in December 1966; and a third interview, probably broadcast over Radio Free Europe, with Florea Blumen Râmniceanu, in September 1967. I am also indebted to Ray Carpenter for the tape of the *In The South* rehearsal (Appendix 3)

I was particularly fortunate in being given kind permission by the late

Mme Judith Vancea in Bucharest to photocopy and quote from 10 letters in her possession which Silvestri wrote to her husband, the composer Zeno Vancea, between 1934 and 1942.

My sincere gratitude to all those in Bucharest, Târgu Mureş, Paris, London and Bournemouth who so willingly gave their time to be interviewed about a man whom all admired and for whom most had a genuine affection; and to those who gave me their recollections of him on tape or by letter. I am particularly grateful for the invaluable editing and other technical efforts of Jonathan Del Mar, John Beech and Ian Hayter.

Also to Doina Dragomirescu for her valuable aid during my research in the Romanian Academy in Bucharest; to Cristina Mircescu for her prompt and efficient technical assistance; and to those who helped with translations: Nina Pavi and Magdalena Buznea; to Frances Cook, Publications Editor of The London Philharmonic Orchestra and Stephen Pettitt, author of *The Philharmonia*, for researching information for me about Silvestri's concerts and recordings.

I sincerely regret that these acknowledgements of their kind co-operation come too late for some who appear in this book, including Sir Charles Groves, Mircea Cristescu, Judith Vancea, Joan Dickson and Jane Judd. I regret that Gerald Jarvis, the leader of the Bournemouth Symphony Orchestra during much of Silvestri's time, is also no longer with us.

The book could not possibly have been written without the support of my wife, Anda Anastasescu, who, despite her professional commitments, was in turn interpreter, translator, co-researcher, musical adviser and critic.

For references to Dinu Lipatti, I am obliged to Dragoş Tănăsescu and Grigore Bărgăuanu for *Lipatti* edited and translated by Carola Grindea (Kahn and Averill); and to conductors other than Silvestri to: Helena Matheopoulos for *Maestro* (Hutchinson); Norman Lebrecht for *The Maestro Myth: Great Conductors in Pursuit of Power* (Simon and Schuster); Robert C. Bachman for *Karajan: Notes on a Career* (Quartet Books); Martin Bookspan and Ross Yockey for *André Previn, A Biography* (Hamish Hamilton); Solomon Volkov for *Testimony: The Memoirs of Shostakovich* (Hamish Hamilton); Bernard Shore for *The Orchestra Speaks* (Longmans Green); Nancy Phelan for: *Charles Mackerras: A Musician's Musician* (Victor Gollancz); and to Richard Temple Savage for *A Voice From The Pit: Reminiscences of an Orchestral Musician* (David and Charles).

For the section in Chapter VI dealing with the opera, *Oedipus*, Noel Malcolm's *George Enescu: His Life and Music* (Toccata Press) was of particular interest.

Regarding the illustrations, I am grateful to Editura Muzicală, Bucharest, for those on pages 38, 54, 95, 133 and 220; Mme Dorin Speranţia for 92; David Ohanesian for 128, 129, 130, 134 and 137; the Sydney *Sunday Mirror* for 169; Mme Silvestri for 212; the late Malcolm Rayment for 116 and the Bournemouth Symphony Orchestras' archives for the reproduction of photographs in their programmes between 1961 and 1969 as well as pictures of Silvestri and the orchestra.

INDEX